D1042152

WRONG

Also by David H. Freedman

A Perfect Mess: The Hidden Benefits of Disorder—How Crammed Closets, Cluttered Offices, and On-the-Fly Planning Make the World a Better Place (with Eric Abrahamson, 2007)

Corps Business: The 30 Management Principles of the U.S. Marines (2000)

At Large: The Strange Case of the World's Biggest Internet Invasion (with Charles C. Mann, 1998)

Brainmakers: How Scientists Are Moving Beyond Computers to Create a Rival to the Human Brain (1995)

WRONG

Why experts* keep failing us — and how to know when not to trust them

DAVID H. FREEDMAN

*Scientists, finance wizards, doctors, relationship gurus, celebrity CEOs, high-powered consultants, health officials, and more

LITTLE, BROWN AND COMPANY
New York Boston London

Little, Brown and Company
Hachette Book Group
237 Park Avenue, New York, NY 10017
www.hachettebookgroup.com

First Edition: June 2010

Little, Brown and Company is a division of Hachette Book Group, Inc. The Little, Brown name and logo are trademarks of Hachette Book Group, Inc.

Library of Congress Cataloging-in-Publication Data
Freedman, David H.
    Wrong : why experts* keep failing us — and how to know when not to trust them : *scientists, finance wizards, doctors, relationship gurus, celebrity CEOs, high-powered consultants, health officials, and more / David H. Freedman. — 1st ed.
        p. cm.
Includes bibliographical references and index.
HC ISBN 978-0-316-02378-8
Int'l ed. ISBN 978-0-316-09329-3
    1. Expertise—Social aspects.   2. Trust—Social aspects.   3. Reliability.
4. Error.   I. Title.
    BF378.E94F74 2010
    001—dc22   2009051194

10 9 8 7 6 5 4 3 2 1

RRD-IN

Printed in the United States of America

CONTENTS

If he is weak in the knees, let him not call the hill steep.
— HENRY DAVID THOREAU

WRONG

Introduction

*Success consists of going from failure to failure without
loss of enthusiasm.*
— Winston Churchill

I'm sitting in a coffee shop in a pediatric hospital in Boston,
hard by a nine-foot-tall bronze teddy bear, with a man who
is going to perform a surprising trick. I'm thinking of an article
recently published in a prestigious medical journal, an article that
reports the results of a research study, and he will tell me whether
or not the study is likely to turn out to be right or wrong. It's
the sort of study that your doctor might read about, and that you
might learn about from a newspaper, website, or morning TV
news show. It may well be that the results of this study will change
your life—they might convince you to start eating or avoiding
certain foods to lower your risk of heart disease, or to take a certain drug to help you beat cancer, or to learn whether or not you
are carrying a gene linked to vulnerability to a mental illness. But
this man won't need to hear any of the particulars of the study to
perform his feat. All he needs to know is that it was a study published in a top journal.

His prediction: it's wrong. It's a prediction that strikes at the
foundation of expertise and our trust in it.

The man is John Ioannidis, a doctor and researcher whose
specialty is calculating the chances that studies' results are false.

For someone dedicated to spotlighting the inadequacies of his colleagues' lifework, Ioannidis is pleasant, polite, and soft-spoken, even if he discreetly radiates the fidgety energy of someone who habitually packs too much into his day. He looks young for a man heading into his midforties, with a slight build, a wavy mop of fine, dark hair, and a thin mustache. Also a bit surprising about Ioannidis is that he is highly regarded by his peers. Communities usually find ways to marginalize those who expose their flaws, but the world of medical research, in which extraordinary talent and effort are prerequisites for attaining even the lowest rungs of recognition, has kept Ioannidis in demand via the field's standard trappings of success: prestigious appointments, including one at the world-class Tufts–New England Medical Center and another at the University of Ioannina Medical School in his native Greece; frequent citations by colleagues of his work, some of which has been published in the field's top journals; and a stream of invitations to speak at conferences, where he is generally a big draw.

There's no standard career path to becoming a deconstructor of wrongness, and Ioannidis took a roundabout route to it. Born in 1965 in the United States to parents who were both physicians, he was raised in Athens, where he showed unusual aptitude in mathematics and snagged Greece's top student math prize. By the end of college, he seemed on track for a career as a mathematician. But he had come to feel the family pull of medicine and, not wanting to turn his back on math, decided to combine the two and become a medical mathematician. "I didn't know exactly what such a thing might be," he says, "but I felt sure there was some important component of medicine that was mathematical." He graduated first in his class at the University of Athens Medical School, then shipped off to Harvard for his residency in internal medicine, followed by a research and clinical appointment at Tufts in infectious diseases. The math had to this point remained in the background, but in 1993, while at Tufts, he saw his chance to even things up a bit. There was growing interest in the new field of "evidence-based medicine"—that is, trying to equip physicians to do not merely what they had been taught to *assume* would help patients but what had been rigorously *proven* in studies would help patients. "Amazingly, most medical treatment simply isn't backed up by good, quantitative evidence," says Ioannidis—news that would likely come as a surprise to most patients. Distilling this sort of knowledge out of a chaos of patient data often requires more statistical-analysis firepower than clinical researchers bear, providing an opening for Ioannidis to make a mark.

Carrying his new interest to joint appointments at the National Institutes of Health and Johns Hopkins in the mid-1990s, Ioannidis began to look for interesting patterns in those medical-journal studies that explore how patients fare with certain treatments. Such studies are essentially the coin of the realm when it comes to communicating solid evidence of treatment effectiveness to physicians. A good doctor, it is presumed, scans the journals for the results of these studies to see what works and what doesn't on which patients, and how well and with what risks, modifying her practices accordingly. Does it make sense to prescribe an antibiotic to a child with an ear infection? Should middle-aged men with no signs of heart disease be told to take a small, daily dose of aspirin? Do the potential benefits of a particular surgical intervention outweigh the risks? Studies presumably provide the answers. In examining hundreds of these studies, Ioannidis did indeed spot a pattern—a disturbing one. When a study was published, often it was only a matter of months, and at most a few years, before other studies came out to either fully refute the findings or declare that the results were "exaggerated" in the sense that later papers revealed significantly lesser benefits to the treatment under study. Results that held up were outweighed two-to-one by results destined to be labeled "never mind."[1]

What was going on here? The whole point of carrying out a study was to rigorously examine a question using tools and techniques that would yield solid data, allowing a careful and conclusive analysis that would replace the conjecture, assumptions, and sloppy assessments that had preceded it. The data were supposed to be the path to truth. And yet these studies, and most types of studies Ioannidis looked at, were far more often than not driving to wrong answers. They exhibited the sort of wrongness rate you would associate more with fad-diet tips, celebrity gossip, or political punditry than with state-of-the-art medical research.

The two-out-of-three wrongness rate Ioannidis found is worse than it sounds. He had been examining only the less than one-tenth of one percent of published medical research that makes it to the most prestigious medical journals.* In other words, in determining that two-thirds of published medical research is wrong, Ioannidis is offering what can easily be seen as an extremely optimistic assessment. Throw in the presumably less careful work from lesser journals, and take into account the way the results end up being spun and misinterpreted by university and industrial PR departments and by journalists, and it's clear that whatever it was about expert wrongness that Ioannidis had stumbled on in these journals, the wrongness rate would only worsen from there.

Ioannidis felt he was confronting a mystery that spoke to the very foundation of medical wisdom. How can the research community claim to know what it's doing, and to be making significant

---

* Ioannidis did find one group of studies that more often than not remained unrefuted: randomized controlled studies (more on these later) that appeared in top journals and that were cited in other researchers' papers an extraordinary one thousand times or more. Such studies are extremely rare and represent the absolute tip of the tip of the pyramid of medical research. Yet one-fourth of even these studies were later refuted, and that rate might have been much higher were it not for the fact that no one had ever tried to confirm or refute nearly half of the rest.

progress, if it can't bring out studies in its top journals that correctly prove anything, or lead to better patient care? It was as if he had set out to improve the battle effectiveness of a navy and immediately discovered that most of its boats didn't float. Nor did the problems appear to be unique to medicine: looking at other branches of science, including chemistry, physics, and psychology, he found much the same. "The facts suggest that for many, if not the majority, of fields, the majority of published studies are likely to be wrong," he says. Probably, he adds, "the vast majority."

Medical and other scientific expertise aren't exactly the bottom of the barrel when it comes to expert wisdom. Yes, much-heralded drugs get yanked off the market, we get conflicting advice about what to eat, and toxic chemicals make their way into our homes. But you don't have to dig far in pretty much any other field to see similar, or worse, arrays of screwups. I could fill this entire book, and several more, with examples of expertise gone wrong—not only in medicine but in physics, finance, child raising, the government, sports, entertainment, and on and on. (Just for fun, I've stuck a small sampling in Appendix 1.) The fact is, expert wisdom usually turns out to be at best highly contested and ephemeral, and at worst flat-out wrong.

Of course, compiling anecdotes and quoting experts about expertise doesn't prove that experts usually mislead us.* Actually, proving expert wrongness isn't really the point of this book. I've found that most people don't need much convincing that

---

* Why wouldn't John Ioannidis, and the many other experts on expertise I'll be quoting in this book, be just as untrustworthy as other experts? Short answer: experts on expertise may know enough about the traps that experts fall into to avoid falling in as often or as far. But see Appendix 4 for my exploration of that important and interesting question, and of the ways this entire book might be wrong.

experts are usually wrong. How could we not suspect that to be the case? We constantly hear experts contradict one another and even themselves on a vast range of issues, whether they're spouting off on diets, hurricane preparedness, the secrets to being a great manager, the stock market, cholesterol-lowering drugs, getting kids to sleep through the night, the inevitability of presidential candidates, the direction of home values, the key to strong marriages, vitamins, the benefits of alcohol or aspirin or fish, the existence of weapons of mass destruction, and so on. As the world watched its financial institutions and economies teetering and in some cases collapsing in 2008 and 2009, many found it maddening that the great majority of financial experts, from those who advise heads of state to those who advise working stiffs, not only failed to foresee the trouble but in many cases specifically took to the airwaves to counsel that there wasn't much to worry about, and in general failed to have anything consistent and helpful to say about the problems. We can all agree that there is a growing obesity epidemic, but it sometimes seems as if no two experts agree on what works when it comes to losing the excess weight. And those of us who hope to see our children's schools improve can choose between experts who say that the curricula need to be less rigid and test-oriented, and experts who say precisely the opposite. If anything, we live in a time of acute frustration with experts, even as many of us remain dependent on them and continue to heed their advice.

Putting trust in experts who are probably wrong is only part of the problem. The other side of the coin is that many people have all but given up on getting good advice from experts. The total effect of all the contradicting and shifting pronouncements is to make expert conclusions at times sound like so much blather—a background noise of modern life. I think by now most of us have at some point caught ourselves thinking, or at least have heard from people around us, something along these lines: *Experts! One day they say vitamin X / coffee / wine / drug Y / a big mortgage / baby learning videos / Six Sigma / multitasking / clean homes / arguing / investment Z is a good thing, and the next they say it's a bad thing. Why bother paying attention? I might as well just do what I feel like doing.* Do we really want to just give up on expertise in this way? Even if experts usually fail to give us the clear, reliable guidance we need, there are still situations, as we'll see, where failing to follow their advice can be self-defeating and even deadly.

So I'm not going to spend much time trying to convince you that experts are often, and possibly usually, wrong. Instead, this book is about *why* expertise goes wrong and how we may be able to do a better job of seeking out more trustworthy expert advice. To that end, we're going to look at how experts—including scientists, business gurus, and our other highly trusted sources of wisdom—fall prey to a range of measurement errors, how they come to have deep biases that lead them into gamesmanship and even outright dishonesty, and how interactions among them tend to worsen rather than correct for these problems. We're also going to examine the ways in which the media sort through the flow of dubious expert pronouncements and further distort them, as well as how we ourselves are drawn to the worst of this shoddy output, and how we end up being even more misled on the Internet. Finally, we'll try to extract from everything we've discovered a set of rough guidelines that can help to separate the most suspect expert advice from the stuff that has a better chance of holding up.

As I said, most people are quite comfortable with the notion that there's a real problem with experts. But some—mostly experts—do in fact take objection to that claim. Here are the three objections I encountered the most often, along with quick responses.

(1) If experts are so wrong, why are we so much better off now than we were fifty or a hundred years ago? One distinguished professor put it to me this way in an e-mail note: "Our life expectancy has almost doubled in the past seventy-five years, and that's because of experts." Actually, the vast majority of that gain came earlier in the twentieth century from a very few sharp improvements, and especially from the antismoking movement. As for all of the drugs, diagnostic tools, surgical techniques, medical devices, lists of foods to eat and avoid, and impressive breakthrough procedures and technologies that fill medical journals and trickle down into media reports, consider this: between 1978 and 2001, according to one highly regarded study,[2] U.S. life spans increased fewer than three years on average—when the drop in smoking rates slowed around 1990, so did life-expectancy gains. It's hard to claim we're floating on an ocean of marvelously effective advice from a range of experts when we've been skirting the edges of a new depression, the divorce rate is around 50 percent, energy prices occasionally skyrocket, obesity rates are climbing, children's test scores are declining, we're forced to worry about terrorist and even nuclear attacks, 118 million prescriptions for antidepressants[3] are written annually in the United States, chunks of our food supply periodically become tainted, and, well, you get the idea. Perhaps a reasonable model for expert advice is one I might call "punctuated wrongness"—that is, experts usually mislead us, but every once in a while they come up with truly helpful advice.

(2) Sure, experts have been mostly wrong in the past, but now they're on top of things. In mid-2008 experts were standing in line to talk about the extensive, foolproof controls protecting our banks and other financial institutions that weren't in place in the late 1920s—just before those institutions started collapsing.

Cancer experts shake their heads today over the ways in which generations of predecessors wasted decades hunting down the mythical environmental or viral roots of most cancers, before pronouncing as a sure thing the more recent theory of how cancer is caused by mutations in a small number of genes—a theory that, as we'll see, has yielded almost no benefits to patients after two decades. Most everyone missed what was happening to our climate, or even spoke of a global cooling crisis, until we came to today's absolutely certain understanding of global warming and its man-made causes—well, we'll see how that turns out. How could we have been so foolish before? And what sort of fool would question today's experts' beliefs? In any case, the claim that we've come from wrong ideas to right ideas suggests that there's a consensus of experts today on what the right ideas are. But there is often nothing close to such a consensus. When experts' beliefs clash, somebody has to be wrong—hardly a sign of an imminent convergence on truth.

And, finally, **(3) So what if experts are usually wrong? That's the nature of expert knowledge—it progresses slowly as it feels its way through difficult questions.** Well, sure, we live in a complex world without easy answers, so we might well expect to see our experts make plenty of missteps as they steadily chip away at the truth. I'm not saying that experts don't make any progress, or that they ought to have figured it all out long ago. I'm suggesting three things: we ought to be fully aware of how large a percentage of expert advice is flawed; we should find out if there are perhaps much more disconcerting reasons why experts so frequently get off track other than "that's just the nature of the beast"; and we ought to take the trouble to see if we can come up with clues that will help distinguish better expert advice from fishier stuff. And, by the way, if experts are so comfortable with the notion that their efforts ought to be expected to spit out mostly wrong answers, why don't they work a little harder to get this useful piece of information across to us when they're interviewed on morning news shows or in newspaper articles, and not just when they're confronted with their errors?

Given that I've already started throwing the term "expert" around left and right, I suppose I ought to make sure you know what I mean by the word. Academics study "expertise" in pianists, athletes, burglars, birds, infants, computers, trial witnesses, and captains of industry, to name just a few examples. But when I say "expert," I'm mostly thinking of someone whom the mass media might quote as a credible authority on some topic—the sorts of people we're usually referring to when we say things like "According to experts…" These are what I would call "mass" or "public" experts, people in a position to render opinions or findings that a large number of us might hear about and choose to take into account in making decisions that could affect our lives. Scientists are an especially important example, but I'm also interested in, for example, business, parenting, and sports experts who gain some public recognition for their experience and insight. I'll also have some things to say about pop gurus, celebrity advice givers, and media pundits, as well as about what I call "local" experts—everyday practitioners such as non-research-oriented doctors, stockbrokers, and auto mechanics.*

I've heard it said, half kiddingly, that meteorologists are the only people who get paid to be wrong. I would argue that in that sense *most* of our experts are paid to be wrong, and are probably

---

* I'm much less interested in decision makers and leaders—such as corporate executives and political officeholders—who are themselves highly dependent on expert advice. I'm also mostly ignoring engineers and designers, who tend to give us tangible items rather than advice.

wrong a much higher percentage of the time than are meteorologists. I'm going to show that although the process of wringing useful insights and advice from complex subjects may indeed be an inherently slow and erratic one, there are many other, less benign reasons why experts go astray. In fact, we'll see that expert pronouncements are *pushed* toward wrongness so strongly that in the end it's harder, I think, to explain why they're sometimes right. But that doesn't mean we're hopelessly mired in this swamp of bad advice. With a decent compass, we can find our way out. Let's start by exploring some of the muck.

CHAPTER ONE

Some Expert Observations

I got a lot of things wrong.
— INVESTMENT GURU JIM CRAMER

I n early 2008 I happened to catch a television news story mentioning new guidelines for performing cardiopulmonary resuscitation, or CPR, aimed at saving some of the 325,000 lives lost to sudden cardiac arrest every year in the United States alone, not to mention those from trauma, drownings, and shocks. The new guidelines hold that you are no longer supposed to bother with the breathing part of CPR—just keep pumping the victim's chest nonstop, and the oxygen will take care of itself. Having some years ago spent the better part of a day pounding on and blowing air into mannequins to get my CPR certification from the American Red Cross, I did a little digging and discovered that while the change was endorsed by the American Heart Association and the European Resuscitation Council, the Red Cross continues to train the public in the breathing-and-pumping technique. To further complicate the picture, there's a growing call in some circles to switch from chest compressions to abdominal compressions, which may pump more blood and avoid rib damage. So I dropped in on Paul Schwerdt, an interventional cardiologist at Norwood Hospital in Norwood, Massachusetts, who restarts hearts all the time. He told me to forget about CPR, because even trained laypeople almost never do it well enough to make a difference. If you want to save someone with a stopped heart, he said, find an automated external defibrillator, or AED — a highly portable, easy-to-use device that is becoming available in more and more public places, offices, and even many homes. Sure enough, I turned up a 2008 article in the *New York Times* stating that the immediate availability of a defibrillator raises the cardiac arrest–survival rate for those outside hospitals from as low as 1 percent to as high as 80 percent[1] — an astounding difference. Case closed? Well, not quite. Later I came across a study that found home AEDs didn't increase cardiac-arrest survival a whit compared to homes where someone was capable of performing CPR.[2] And the American Heart Association website states that victims whose hearts have gone into fibrillation are up to three times more likely to survive if they receive CPR from a bystander while awaiting defibrillation. I spoke with a second cardiac specialist, an emergency room nurse, and an emergency medical technician and got three additional takes on the issue, all somewhat different. Glad I was able to clear that up.

Expert confusion isn't unique to medical matters. For example, economists weren't exactly lining up in late 2007 and early 2008 to warn us all that national economies, global financial institutions, and real-estate markets were rapidly spiraling toward a black hole of potential collapse. And though plenty of experts did line up to offer advice, many of us ended up wishing they hadn't. For example:

Government officials:

"I don't anticipate any serious problems…among the large internationally active banks that make up a very substantial part of our banking system."
— Ben Bernanke, Federal Reserve chairman, February 28, 2008

Industry insiders:

"Existing-Home Sales to Trend Up in 2008."
—National Association of Realtors press release, December 9, 2007

Financial-rating agencies:

"These errors make us look either incompetent at credit analysis or like we sold our soul to the devil for revenue, or a little bit of both."
—A managing director at Moody's, the most widely heeded rater of financial institutions and instruments

Business gurus:

"It's nineteen twenty-nine all over again."
—Donald Trump, speaking in February 2009, almost a year after the start of the near collapse, as the economy was beginning to stabilize

Your personal broker or real-estate agent:

Well, I have no idea what yours told you, but if she steered you clear of the mess instead of straight into it, then you're in a distinct minority.

In early 2009 I did a search of the past two months' worth of articles in the *New York Times*, the *Chicago Tribune*, and *USA Today*, and turned up twenty-three stories roughly equally scattered between the three papers that included the word "expert" or "experts" in the headline. About half of the approximately fifty people unambiguously presented as experts in the bodies of these stories were scientists or other types of formal researchers. But the list also included consultants, law-enforcement and public-health officials, CEOs, authors, athletic coaches, financial analysts, and the directors of industry trade groups and nonprofit advocacy groups.

Clearly there is a range of titles for those who serve as dispensers of fractured expert conclusions. Though the expert pronouncements of scientists and other researchers tend to have an outsize impact on the public, many less formal sources of wisdom can also serve as occasional "mass experts" whose advice is quoted in newspaper articles and on television. And we also need to consider the role of what I call "local" or "everyday" experts—our doctors, mechanics, tennis instructors, stockbrokers, marriage counselors, lawyers, and so on. These experts don't take on the big questions of the day in the media but rather meet us face-to-face to provide wisdom related to our jobs, pastimes, home lives, immediate health needs, purchasing decisions, or even just our cars or pets. Though the mass media frequently quote such people as "experts," the vast majority never get that sort of exposure. We usually receive their advice only when we walk into their places of business as a client, customer, or patient.

The expert advice we end up with is often a complex blend of the pronouncements of these different types of experts. The scientific conclusions published in research journals, for example, frequently become the operating principles of our local experts. And as communities of local experts debate over or converge on particular ideas and practices, their opinions feed back into what public officials, trade-group leaders, and industrial experts have to say. As all this expert thinking sloshes back and forth between formal, informal, and local experts, much of it inevitably spills onto us, whether we're hit with it person-to-person from local experts, or dig it up on government or organizational websites, or simply settle for the media's take on things. As with CPR or the economic outlook, the result is typically a barrage of conflicting and possibly highly flawed advice.

To understand where expertise goes wrong, we need to pick apart some of these different elements. To that end, we'll be zooming in on all kinds of expert advice and mechanisms, including scientific findings—perhaps our most trusted type of expert advice—as well as the media's handling of expert wisdom, the interactions of expert communities, and even the role we ourselves play in the production and consumption of dubious expert advice, among other topics. But let's start off this chapter by looking at some of the problems that cause less formal and local experts to get off track. In many ways these problems are more obvious and easier to understand than some of the others, and they'll give us a good foundation for examining the additional components of misleading expert advice later on. That, in turn, will give us clues as to how to avoid some of the advice that's likely to turn out to be bogus.

In 1997 the University of Michigan football team decided to give one of its longtime benchwarmers a shot at a little playing time in his junior year. The young quarterback had at one point been ranked behind six other quarterbacks on the team and, discouraged, had been looking into transferring, but he took advantage of the playing opportunity and shined, eventually going on to set Wolverine records for most pass attempts and completions. Outside Ann Arbor, however, his accomplishments didn't seem to count for much. Not only was he utterly ignored when it came time to consider candidates for the Heisman Trophy but he was passed over for virtually every formal recognition in college football, picking up only an honorable mention with a regional all-star squad. The apparent invisibility of his college passing stats persisted through the NFL draft, where he was selected 199th, and only by a team using an extra pick to make up for the loss of a few players during the off-season. He was promptly assigned the familiar role of watching the games from the bench as the team's fourth-ranked quarterback. But a year later a teammate's injury led to this young player once again getting an unexpected shot, at which point it took him only the rest of that season to become widely considered pro football's most devastatingly effective quarterback. He has since led his team to four Super Bowls, winning three of them, and along the way has grabbed two Super Bowl MVP Awards, played in four Pro Bowls, and broken the NFL record for the most touchdown passes in a single season. He also holds the record for the highest single-game completion percentage, the most completions in a single Super Bowl, and the most Super Bowl completions overall. That Wolverine benchwarmer was Tom Brady, now of the New England Patriots, who, while still in the prime of his career, has already nearly assured himself a berth in football's Hall of Fame.

How could the coaches, assistants, scouts, and media sports analysts who pass judgment on player talent and potential have all missed so badly with Brady? You can't dismiss this mass oversight as a wild fluke, not even among the rarefied ranks of current NFL quarterbacks: Super Bowl–winning quarterback Kurt Warner—a player who rivals Brady in the record books, having won two NFL MVP Awards and a Super Bowl MVP, and who has racked up the top three passing-yardage records for individual Super Bowls as well as the third-best passing accuracy in NFL history—garnered so little attention from NFL coaches after college that he was reduced to showing up more or less uninvited at the Green Bay Packers training camp, scrounging only a brief stay with the team before being booted back home to stock grocery shelves for $5.50 an hour. Indeed, in every major sport there have been legions of little-noticed players who have gone on to become superstars, as well as eagerly snatched-up college trophy winners who were washouts in the big leagues. And of course much the same could be pointed out about the hunt for future winners on the parts of literary and Hollywood talent agents, corporate headhunters, political-party kingmakers, military promotion boards, and university tenure committees.

A big part of the problem with sports experts—and with most informal experts, as it turns out—is that they lack good data, or sometimes just ignore it. Sure, everyone's stat crazy in the sports world, and coaches and scouts trying to spot the best players do what they can to gather measurements. Before the NFL draft, college prospects gather for what are known as "Combines," where prospects are tested for speed, jumping ability, weight-lifting capacities, drug use, injury resistance, and even intelligence and personality. Some teams (in baseball in particular) have been moving toward commercially available computer-based systems that gather and parse data on players with a thoroughness, rigor, and zeal that put high-powered medical researchers to shame. Nevertheless, most coaches or scouts wouldn't claim to make their decisions about who ought to play based primarily on the hard numbers. Of course not: the numbers aren't reliable indicators of player desire, maturity, aggressiveness, team orientation, instinct, physical and mental resiliency, the ebb and flow of confidence, and any of a few dozen other characteristics that can be critical to a player's potential contribution. In the end, sports pros do their best to observe and assess these intangibles, mix them in with the hard data, and then come to a conclusion largely based on their gut—they hope they'll know it when they see it. Unfortunately, the way they see it is often just plain wrong. No wonder even Tom Bradys and Kurt Warners slip by right under the noses of talent-hungry scouts. Even when good data are available, coaches don't pay much attention if the information conflicts with their judgment. For example, David Romer of the University of California–Berkeley showed convincingly, via statistical analysis in 2005, that most NFL teams routinely hurt their chances of winning by being overly biased toward kicking on fourth down rather than going for the first down.[3] Coaches are so intuitively averse to the risk of handing over the ball with good field position that Romer hasn't won many converts. But, for what it's worth, the Arkansas high-school football team of Pulaski Academy adopted the approach in 2007 and has rarely lost a game since.

Experts often go through a lot of trouble to make it *look* like they're basing their conclusions on solid information rather than on judgment. In the market for a new car? Perhaps, like millions of people, you consider Consumer Reports to represent the epitome of objective, data-guided expertise when it comes to evaluating products, and thus might go out of your way to choose a car that fares well on its list. But wait—which list? In 2008 the popular subcompact Toyota Yaris came out tops by Consumer Reports' reckoning both in reliability and in low cost of ownership. But the car also made the organization's highly publicized "11 worst cars" list, which dinged the tiny Yaris for unimpressive acceleration and a "vague shifter." According to that second list, you'd be better off with a Chevrolet TrailBlazer, a lumbering SUV that gets fifteen miles to the gallon in city driving. The picture doesn't necessarily become clearer if you look elsewhere for car ratings. Market-research firm J. D. Power's car-quality rankings now get as much attention as those of Consumer Reports, but comparing the two organizations' conclusions will leave you scratching your head. I looked up the car I bought recently, a Nissan Versa, and found that in 2008 J. D. Power gave it a "mediocre" five out of ten in reliability, while Consumer Reports assigned it the third-lowest projected cost of repair and maintenance of all cars sold in America.

Informal experts can have a big impact on our lives through these sorts of rankings, as the media feed us expert lists of everything from where to live to what movie to see. But underlying these often authoritative- and confident-seeming conclusions is a rat's nest of confusion and misdirection largely stemming from one big question: what do you measure? There are usually no obvious or standardized approaches to figuring out which data provide the most useful and reliable insight. The result is that informal experts often simply arbitrarily grab at whatever measurable feature happens to be at hand without much justification for doing so—and they all seem to grab at different ones. What's really going on here is that experts are disguising what is actually highly debatable *judgment* as *fact* through their choice of which data to highlight.

It might sound pretty straightforward, for example, to ask which hospital in a community provides the best care. But hospitals can be rated on any of a bewildering variety of considerations, including inpatient volume, staffing levels, readmission rates, university affiliations, costs of treatment, and specialty practices. Well, we could keep it simple and just look at death rates, as some experts do. Of all the things we'd like to see happen during a hospital stay, avoiding death is usually at the top of the list. But death rates don't simply depend on the quality of treatment rendered by a hospital; they can also depend on how sick or old or poor the population served by the hospital is, the extent to which a hospital takes on more difficult cases, the hospital's ability to administer cutting-edge and higher-risk treatments, and even a hospital's tendency to discharge patients prematurely so that more of them will die elsewhere. The U.S. Centers for Medicare and Medicaid Services attempts to adjust its published hospital death rates for many of these factors, but that doesn't fix the problem—most hospitals simply end up with fairly similar rates, making the list of little use.[4]

You might think experts would at least be able to tell us which cities are the safest, thanks to the fact that the FBI releases crime statistics. The *Congressional Quarterly*, for example, publishes a widely quoted annual "City Crime Rankings" list simply by dividing the number of police-reported crimes in a city by the resident population. Unfortunately, the figures for some cities are thrown off by large pools of commuters, who can be victims or perpetrators of crimes but who don't count as part of the population. When St. Louis's crime rate is adjusted to take into account the surrounding commuter-heavy communities, the city falls from 2nd place on the high-crime list to 120th place.[5] Even if city crime figures weren't distorted, they'd still be just potentially misleading averages that wouldn't tell you much about the sometimes hugely varying crime rates within different neighborhoods of any one city. The FBI itself puts its opinion of city crime rankings this way on its website: "These rough rankings provide no insight into the numerous variables that mold crime in a particular town, city, county, state, or region. Consequently, they lead to simplistic and/or incomplete analyses that often create misleading perceptions adversely affecting communities and their residents."

This sort of measurement mess underlies the advice we get from informal experts in almost any field. Let's face it, if political pollsters keep blowing it—even though you'd think all they have to do is ask one simple question and count the answers—it's a good guess that most other sorts of experts are only likely to do worse. To see how muddled matters can get, consider the closely watched efforts on the parts of experts to tell us which schools our children are best off attending. It's a crowded field. *Newsweek* offers the "Top High Schools," *Forbes* gives us the "Best Cities to Educate Your Child," and *Boston Magazine* is one of the many regional publications that puts out a list of the "Best Schools" in its area. The government is in the school-rating business, too, especially with an eye to flagging those near the bottom of the heap. In New York City, for example, schools are subject to three different government evaluations, each of which can result in a school losing funding or even being shuttered: the federal "No Child Left Behind" law; New York State's "Schools Under Registration Review" list; and New York City's "Report Card" system of grading schools, A through F.[6]

Good luck in trying to make sense of the differences in the results. *Boston Magazine*'s list is based on comparing how students do on standardized state tests to how much money the school system spends per pupil. The *Newsweek* list is based on the average number of Advanced Placement exams taken per senior. The *Forbes* list looks at the average circulation of books at public libraries, among other factors. The criteria for the various federal, state, and local rankings can differ wildly, too; some are based entirely on standardized test scores, while others take attendance and ethnic and racial makeup into account as well. That's why some schools that get a failing grade from New York City meet with New York State's approval, and some of the schools on the state's failure list get a passing grade under the No Child Left Behind law.

Each of the different criteria for judging schools has its expert critics and defenders. For example, enrollment in AP classes is a staple of high-school assessments and rankings. But the fact that a school gets a large number of students to sign up for AP classes doesn't necessarily tell you that a large number of students will heavily benefit from those classes, or even that they'll learn as much as they would have in a non-AP class.* And, of course, the last thing that parents of students who struggle in ordinary courses want is a school system that funnels significant resources into AP classes at the expense of the rest of the curriculum. As for SAT scores, another common measurement underlying school rankings, any number of education experts argue that these scores simply don't reliably reflect students' knowledge or abilities (even when the tests are scored correctly). Robert Sternberg,

---

* A 2007 study at the University of Texas at Austin found that students taking high-school AP courses did better in college than similar students who didn't take AP classes, but a 2006 study conducted by Harvard University and University of Virginia researchers that looked at AP science courses came to the opposite conclusion.

a psychology researcher who is dean of arts and sciences at Tufts University and a past president of the American Psychological Association, described to me a study he conducted at Yale, his former academic home, which indicated that SATs tend to fail to measure "creative" and "practical" abilities that prove critical to performing well in college. Adding in those less easily quantified factors doubled the reliability of predictions of how well students would do in college, Sternberg found, and schools that teach in ways designed to capitalize on these under-recognized skills tend to eke more improvements out of students. But where would that sort of potentially important school competency be reflected on the various school rankings? Not that experts are about to give up on SATs as a convenient yardstick. In late 2008 the real-estate guru Barbara Corcoran even told *Today* show viewers that SAT scores ought to be a major factor in deciding where to live. "If you've got great SAT scores, you've got a great neighborhood," she explained. Who knew that choosing a community could be so easy?

The experts who evaluate colleges in popular books and articles often lazily gravitate to readily quantified money gauges, including how much professors are paid and the size of the school's endowment—though *Washington Monthly*, for one, pointedly heads in the opposite direction with its ranking, assigning significant value to the percentage of alumni who serve in the peace corps.* Many education experts try to cut to the chase by looking at how much graduates of different schools end up earning, pointing out, for example, that people who go to Ivy League schools on average earn more money than graduates of other schools.[7] But it also turns out that Ivy League graduates are more likely than others to pursue

---

* *High Times* magazine, on the other hand, manages to quantify the pot friendliness of college campuses—and it may be on to something, given that even relatively sober college rankers such as the *Fiske Guide to Colleges* now sometimes take the trouble to note marijuana penetration at various higher institutions.

high-paying finance jobs and to come from families with powerful connections, neither of which has anything to do with the effect of an Ivy League education on earning power. The relationship of these sorts of measures to the "excellence" of a college, or its suitability to a wide range of students, is vague and quirky at best.

Any set of criteria used to judge schools is, in the end, likely to be weakly relevant and probably highly misleading. That was certainly the opinion of a group of thirty-eight superintendents of school systems in five different states who formally (and in vain) asked *Newsweek* to keep their schools out of the running for its list, explaining in a joint letter, "It is impossible to know which high schools are 'the best' in the nation. Determining whether different schools do or don't offer a high quality of education requires a look at many different measures, including students' overall academic accomplishments and their subsequent performance in college, and taking into consideration the unique needs of their communities"—a combination of measures that none of the studies can claim to have taken into account.

But accepting some arbitrary factor as a key measurement means not only that experts now have data to hawk but in many cases that they've provided local experts with a means for raising their standings—that is, for gaming the system. Standardized testing in public schools presents a classic example: when a state starts making school funding dependent on standardized test scores, then teachers are likely to end up "teaching to the test"—that is, the curriculum begins to center around making sure the students do well on the exams. The curriculum can even start to take on the measurement-focused nature of testing, as witness the rapidly growing popularity in the United States of the "Accelerated Reader" program, which assigns point values to different books (the teenage-vampire romance novel *Eclipse* is good for twenty-two points; *Hamlet* will get you seven) and then uses computers to test comprehension and award scores. The frequent objection in the education community to teaching to the test, of course, is that while scores are likely to rise, we may well produce less-well-educated students as measured in other, more comprehensive, potentially more important ways. Studies conducted by a researcher at King's College in London, for example, found that while standardized tests in the United Kingdom continue to indicate improving student performance, a study that enlisted a broader measure revealed that by the time today's students enter secondary school, they are two years behind where students of the same grade were in the mid-1970s.[8] In particular, U.K. students have become worse at complex problem solving, the study found, even while improving in their ability to come up with quick responses to more superficial questions—the latter being the sort of skill bred by standardized tests.

Experts frustrated with being low on good data can go through all sorts of contortions to address the gap—but often end up only highlighting how tricky a business measurement is, and especially so when it comes to the complexities and vagaries of human behavior. Advertising is a good example. In researching an article about marketing, I turned myself over to the cutting edge of consumer research, allowing experts to monitor my respiration, sweat, and heart rhythms with a high-tech vest, to read my brain waves through an electrode-studded cap, to probe my opinions via lengthy interviews and surveys, and to track me online, all to help them figure out how to target me and people like me with more effective ads. These testers and trackers were able to determine what sorts of images might quicken my pulse a bit and what sorts of websites I'm most likely to visit, but in the end none of this data seemed to enable anyone to extract insights into what sorts of pitches would most likely get me to think about their clients' products and services. In the end, advertisers are still largely dependent on gut instincts and creative magic. (Though it's certainly possible they're doing a better job with you than they are with me. Been influenced by many ads lately?) Movie-industry executives are similarly stymied by an inability to measure in any reliable way what it is that will make audiences flock to a film—obviously, or they wouldn't be green-lighting movies such as *Surrogates*, a heavily promoted, big-budget, highly commercial picture with a bankable star, which, as of early October 2009, seemed poised to lose tens of millions of dollars for its backers.

Of course, the world isn't much worse off when football, movie, and advertising experts misfire. Unfortunately, experts also operate in painfully data-impaired modes in fields where the stakes are often quite a bit higher. On what do Dr. Phil and Oprah base their widely heeded advice about the way we should lead our lives, other than on experience, intuition, and common sense? And how much useful, reliable data are antiterrorism strategists and tacticians normally able to muster before having to make decisions—conclusions on which the lives of thousands may intimately depend? When medical researchers and other scientists lack data, they're generally out of business. Other sorts of experts are free to—or in some cases are simply forced to—forge bravely forward, shooting from the hip.

Even if they did have good data, informal experts would still get it wrong much of the time. That's because they tend to fall into various traps that we might imagine rarely snag scientists and other highly credentialed experts. Here are some of the biggest.

Bias and Corruption

Most of us think of scientists as being devoted to uncovering truths, not pumping their career prospects. Less formal experts, on the other hand, don't enjoy that sort of halo. To win promotion or even simply keep their jobs, law-enforcement officials have to wrestle with the sometimes vicious politics racking the administrations they serve, and stockbrokers desperately struggle to corral new customers lest they not survive the latest round of pink slips. For such experts, actually being right isn't always the best path to career success compared to, say, making the public *feel* that crime is under control even if it isn't, or getting clients to invest larger sums of money with them. I don't think I'd have to work very hard to convince most people that corruption and fraud are probably significantly higher among most types of informal experts than they are among scientists, and where there are even small levels of fraud and corruption, we're likely to see far higher levels of various types of gaming. There have been endless accounts of doctors ginning up unnecessary or overpriced tests for patients carried out at labs in which the doctors are investors, of government officials who receive favors and kickbacks, of brokers churning accounts to raise commissions, and so forth. Such blatantly inappropriate behavior may not be typical of informal experts, but it doesn't seem to be all that unusual either.

Irrational Thinking

A theory isn't going to be readily acceptable to the scientific community if it blatantly contradicts the data, if it clashes with what has already been reasonably well proven to be true, if it requires bizarre assumptions, or if it just plain doesn't make sense. A scientist who suggests that intelligence in adults is proportional to height, or that dinosaurs still roam in deep underground caves, or that coffee cures cancer, may manage to score a few headlines, but he'd be obliterating his career in science.

Most informal experts, on the other hand, can do quite well advancing exotic, logic-defying, hard-evidence-free ideas.* I'm not thinking here of religion, which is explicitly not based on evidence or logic, nor of cults and conspiracy theories that are plainly off the wall to most of us. Rather, what comes to my mind first is finance. The fact is, there was simply never any rational basis to the notion that banks could withstand loaning more and more money to people of less and less creditworthiness who were buying homes that were becoming more and more expensive relative to income. It all seems pretty obvious to everyone now, and yet the majority of experts of all stripes involved in every aspect of the housing game, from builders to real-estate gurus to financial-industry analysts, couldn't seem to encourage strongly enough throwing more money into the pot.[†,‡]

Or consider stock picking. A wide range of economists and even mathematicians, as well as many nonscientist financial experts, has been demonstrating quite clearly for about a century that no matter what technique you use to pick stocks (short of gathering insider information), you're about as likely to beat the market as you are to win at blackjack—a bit less likely, actually, if you're really good at counting cards. The fact that many of us still put our faith in, not to mention bet our life savings based on, the advice of, say, a screaming, bouncing, bell-ringing

---

* Some physicists grumble that their prominent string-theory-boosting colleagues have accomplished much the same. But the details of that particular brawl are beyond the scope of this book.

† Yes, plenty of economists got in on this, too. But at least some raised the now-obvious objections, and most simply stayed silent on the matter.

‡ Some have observed that a sort of selection bias was operating here, in that those financial whizzes and brokers who saw what was plainly happening and said so were quickly pushed out of the industry due to the simple fact that all the money was being made by those who were only too eager to ride along with and even contribute to the mass delusion.

television personality who claims to have special insight into the movements of stocks is, I think, a sharp illustration of how some experts can ride straight-out irrationality to great personal success.

And then there's the Oprah-endorsed bestseller *The Secret* and its claim that the universe is eager to give everybody exactly what they want, from good health to riches, if only they'd just ask. It would be hard to find better proof that rationality and evidence are not prerequisites for scoring big as a public dispenser of wisdom. But it would also be hard to find more than a short shelf of books that sold more copies.

Pandering to the Audience

Diet gimmick after diet gimmick after diet gimmick has been advanced, published, best-sold, and proven through the experience of millions not to work long-term. Why do doctors, fitness trainers, and nutritionists, not to mention celebrities without any real health or fitness credentials, still keep churning out diet-gimmick books? One reason is that we seem to have an insatiable appetite not just for unhealthy foods but for gimmicks that claim to make it easy to live without such foods or to eat them without gaining weight. In other words, experts sometimes just give us the implausible advice we want, apparently without much regard for whether it will do much good or not. The authors of other sorts of self-help books are often doing much the same.* More on this point a bit later.

---

* Scientists generally don't pander to the public, with some notable exceptions such as those who write diet books. But, as we'll see, pandering is still very much an issue for science.

Ineptitude

Various experts were trotted out by the media during the 2008 Beijing Olympics to talk up the fact that an unprecedented five thousand tests for performance-enhancing drugs turned up a mere six positive results, suggesting a big reduction in the problem compared to the past decade or so. But many observers have pointed out that the tally of forty-three world-record-breaking performances in Beijing, several of them of the shattering variety, ought to raise suspicions. Victor Conte, an infamous sports-nutrition entrepreneur who has served prison time for providing banned substances to top athletes, and who has at times cooperated with authorities in outing users, publicly detailed in 2008 how world-class athletes, including those training for the 2008 Olympics, were generally free to make use of an impressive array of performance-enhancing drugs with little fear of being caught (assuming he didn't turn them in himself). Conte explained that by restricting the most heavily drug-fueled training regimens to the off-season, when testing is infrequent, and skirting random tests via "duck and dodge" techniques that require not answering the phone, disabling voice-mail boxes, and lying about their whereabouts until formally threatened with disqualification, athletes can leave plenty of time for drugs to clear from their bodies before submitting to tests or heading off to competition.[9] If the folks responsible for athlete drug testing know all this, they're doing a good job of pretending they're on top of the game.

Informal experts can't hope to match scientists when it comes to the tricky business of gathering solid evidence for their conclusions. One good place to make a close-to-direct comparison is in government-run forensic labs and studies, where evidence in criminal cases is processed and analyzed. The University of Texas at San Antonio cellular biologist Steven Austad happened to look into how forensic technicians work and was appalled at what he found. "The standards are so far below what you'd find in a university science lab that it's hard to see how anyone could take the results seriously, let alone put people in prison because of it," he told me. The forensic operations of several major cities, most notably Detroit, and even of the FBI have suffered embarrassing revelations about the sorry state of their work, including physical evidence that was lost, contaminated, misanalyzed, and simply lied about.[10]

Law enforcement, like sports, seems in general to be a good source of illustrations for how not-quite-science can run aground. When the state of Texas took 463 children from the Fundamentalist Church of Jesus Christ of Latter-day Saints into protective custody in April 2008, authorities justified the action in part by sharply noting that 9 percent of the children had at some point fractured at least one bone—a measurement that sounds alarming, unless you know that pediatrician estimates of the rates of population-wide bone fractures among all children run as high as 50 percent.[11] (The Texas officials may have been confused by the more widely quoted, and much lower, estimate of *annual* bone-fracture rates among children.) And advocates of the use by police of Taser weapons, which fire a dart trailed by a wire through which a powerful electric jolt is sent, point to numerous studies showing that the weapon, while disabling, isn't dangerous. The result is that Tasers are now sometimes fired by police at people who don't even seem to be posing much of a threat, as a few minutes of browsing Tasering incidents on YouTube can clearly document. But as it turns out, these Taser "studies" are often no more than police or manufacturer demonstrations conducted in quiet rooms with a still, calm volunteer in excellent physical and mental condition. In the field, on the other hand, the very people most likely to draw Taser fire are highly agitated, on drugs or alcohol, in poor physical condition, suffering from a mental disorder, or poised on stairs or in other places where collapsing and thrashing can be dangerous.*

Lack of Oversight

The simple fact is that most informal experts can spew out conclusions without much fear of being intercepted by wiser or more careful parties. Who's filtering the recommendations of investment gurus? What's to stop the FDA from approving a drug that many researchers still have qualms about? Who's going to poke your car mechanic on the shoulder and tell him that he's replacing a perfectly good fuel injector? That's not to say that all informal experts can always get away with major incompetence or serious malfeasance—there are generally higher powers that can eventually intervene in egregious cases, whether it's Congress, a good book editor, or simply the outrage of a chunk of the public. But in the short run, most informal experts can get away with quite a bit, and do all the time.

Automaticity

When you show up at your doctor's office complaining of, say, persistent mild cold symptoms or a slightly sore knee, she probably doesn't call in a team of specialists, order a battery of tests, or sit down at the computer to do a long Internet search. What she probably does is ask you a few questions, perform a quick exam, recommend some

---

* The world of crime also seems to be a source of what one might call tragicomic recursive expert failures: 2009 saw a nationally respected "gang interventionist" arrested on racketeering charges, not long after the kidnapping in Mexico of a prominent kidnapping expert.

sort of mild pain reliever, and suggest you let her know if things don't improve in a week. How does she reckon so quickly that you're not suffering from something that requires immediate and more serious attention? Well, it's because she sees people with your very complaint day in and day out, and thousands of times over a career. She doesn't need to consult anyone, look it up, or gather a bunch of data; she could practically respond to your complaint in her sleep. That's automaticity—the ability, developed with practice, to recognize or do something without having to carefully think it through.

Studies of everyday experts ranging from doctors to pilots to loan officers suggest that it's actually automaticity that tends to separate the highly experienced expert from the novice, rather than the ability to eventually come to the right conclusion. In other words, even hotshot local experts aren't necessarily more capable of making the right decision—they're just more likely to be very quick about it. The downside is obvious: every so often, that lack of close, thoughtful attention leads to a cookie-cutter conclusion that's wrong, sometimes with painful consequences.* According to the well-known physician-author Jerome Groopman, doctors misdiagnose patients about one out of six times, and about half of those misdiagnoses result in "real harm." And an IRS study found that 56 percent of professionally prepared returns showed "significant errors," compared to only 47 percent for self-prepared returns.[†,13]

---

* One U.K. study found an upside to the automaticity of experts: researchers conducted jailhouse interviews with fifty convicted burglars and discovered that the vast majority of them relied on automaticity to determine where to look for the goods in a home. That suggests we can hide our valuables in ways that throw expert burglars off.[12]

† The New America Foundation, a Washington, DC, policy research organization, has made a lot of noise about creating a "financial service corps" that would prod accountants and others to offer financial advice on a volunteer basis to people who couldn't ordinarily afford it. You have to wonder if taxpayers could afford the advice even if it were free.

In taking all these problems into account, perhaps we can now better understand why the sharpest minds in the NFL said "no thanks" 198 times when they were given chance after chance to pick up the player who would soon become one of the winningest quarterbacks in the history of pro football.

CHAPTER TWO

The Trouble with Scientists, Part 1

If we knew what we were doing,
it wouldn't be called research, would it?
— ALBERT EINSTEIN

When you can measure what you are speaking about, and express
it in numbers, you know something about it.
— LORD KELVIN

Philip "P. J." Devereaux, a cardiologist and biostatistics researcher at McMaster University in Ontario, remembers all too well the bolt of excitement that ran through the field of cardiology back in the early 1980s. Cardiologists had already come to recognize that irregular heartbeats were an ominous sign, observing that those who had them within the first twelve days after a heart attack were far more likely to die than those who didn't. Then antiarrhythmic drugs burst onto the scene, and cardiologists seized on them. They gave the medication to heart-attack patients, closely monitored their heart rhythms, and were thrilled to see the heart rhythms smooth out. The fast administration of an antiarrhythmic drug quickly became the standard treatment for heart-attack patients, and remained so through the early 1990s, when the results of a new, large study of these drugs came out. "The trial didn't just show that the drugs weren't saving lives, it showed they actually were killing people," says Devereaux. Yes, the patients' hearts were beating more regularly on the drug, but the patients were on average three times more likely to die. In fact, notes Devereaux, the drugs killed more Americans than the Vietnam War did—roughly an average of forty thousand a year died from the drugs in the United States alone. Where had cardiologists gone wrong?

It would be unusual to make it through a *Good Morning America* broadcast or two, or an issue of the *Boston Globe*, or a day's worth of Yahoo!'s home page, or the like, without being exposed to the considered conclusions of at least one highly degreed scientist or other academic researcher. Not only are the latest medical studies fairly sprayed at us from all directions, but in the course of a week of run-of-the-mill browsing of print, broadcast, and Internet news and other information sources, you're likely to encounter a parade of confident PhDs that might include economists (How long will the recession last?), psychologists (Is your teenager depressed?), sociologists (Is our cell phone obsession ruining society?), zoologists (Can the polar bear be saved?), and more, all obligingly helping to translate their or their field's latest research findings into news you can use. What's more, scientific research studies often underlie the advice we hear from less formal experts, be it the nutrition editor at a women's health magazine, the head of an industry or consumer group, the personal trainer to the stars, the hotshot portfolio manager, the retired general, the author of a book on relationships, the former U.S. vice president, or the celebrated ex-CEO of a successful company. There's a reason that the phrases "experts say," "studies show," and "according to the latest research" all sound like well-worn clichés to us.

Given that much of what we are told about the world is built one way or another on published research, we seem to have a big problem. John Ioannidis's work suggests that wrongness is the rule rather than the exception, and especially in medical research, which has an outsize impact on our lives, gets more than its share of attention in the media, and attracts a stupendous depth of talent and funding—about $95 billion a year, or 6 percent of all money spent on health care, according to a 2005 study.[1] While experts who study research may have become comfortable with the notion that most findings are wrong, it might seem a little hard to swallow for the rest of us. It would help if we had some sense of *why* so much research might be turning out to be wrong.

Scientists and science journalists often dismiss wayward scientific findings as the product of weaker types of studies. But the fact is, it's absolutely typical for studies that have all the markings of high credibility to contradict one another or simply get it wrong. And here's a simple reason: researchers routinely rely on flawed evidence in coming to their conclusions and in working to convince us that those conclusions are right. To put it another way, scientists are often deceptively sloppy in making and analyzing measurements. And that's in spite of the fact that good measurement is at the heart of what separates the respected, high-level expert from the opinionated dilettante, pop guru, manipulative charlatan, blathering pundit, or junk scientist. Let's go on a tour of some of the ways impressive-seeming measurements can and often do go wrong for our most-trusted experts.

Measuring What Doesn't Matter

Can vitamin D supplements help fend off cancer?
No, said a 1999 study.[2]
Yes, said a study in 2006—it cuts risk up to 50 percent.[3]
Yes, said a study in 2007—it cuts risk up to 77 percent.[4]
No, said a 2008 study.[5]

You'd almost have to laugh at these sorts of seesaw, yes-it-is / no-it-isn't findings, if they weren't addressing potentially life-and-death questions. Nearly half of us are going to get cancer at some point in our lives, more than a quarter of us will die from it, and those of us who don't get it will still be deeply affected by it, probably by living in fear of it, almost certainly by losing someone to it. Can't we get a little straight advice here?

An old joke: A police officer finds a drunk man late at night crawling on his hands and knees on a sidewalk under a streetlight. Questioned, the drunk man tells her he's looking for his wallet. When the officer asks if he's sure that he dropped the wallet here, the man replies that he actually dropped it across the street. "Then why are you looking over here?" asks the befuddled officer. "Because the light's better here," explains the drunk man.

It's easy to appreciate the foolishness of choosing to search for something in a way that's relatively convenient rather than in a way that's more likely to be fruitful. But experts do it all the time when it comes to searching for the truth—in fact, in some fields, as we'll see, they almost *always* end up looking under the streetlight. In the case of antiarrhythmic drugs for heart-attack victims, cardiologists knew that what they really wanted to measure was survival. But measuring survival takes long, relatively complex studies. Having observed an apparent link between irregular heartbeats and death, they found it reasonable to jump on irregular beats as a relevant measurement, under the assumption that as the frequency of irregular beats came down, so would death rates. The irregular beats were measured, and doctors saw they were successfully suppressed by the drugs—mission accomplished! But the notion that suppressing irregular heartbeats would keep heart-attack patients alive was simply wrong, and in a particularly deadly way. Or take the 1999 study mentioned previously, which concluded that vitamin D had no effect on the risk of breast cancer. Instead of directly measuring vitamin D, the study, it turned out, had estimated vitamin D levels in the body by relying on what patients reported for diets and on the estimated amounts of sunlight each absorbed as based on geographic location (in that sunlight spurs the body to manufacture vitamin D).

These sorts of indirect measurements are sometimes called "surrogate" or "proxy" measurements, or "markers." Such a measurement is made to stand in for what you really want to measure, typically because it's more accessible in some way—it's more convenient to obtain or can be achieved more cheaply or quickly. Experts often base the bulk of their conclusions on surrogate measurements, and they're especially ubiquitous in medical studies. Instead of having to wait to directly measure cancer survival, researchers have long considered tumor shrinkage to mean that a cancer treatment is effective; lowered blood sugar levels have been considered a sign that the slowly progressing ravages of diabetes are under control; brain scans that show good blood volume are sometimes taken as evidence of the halting of the gradual loss of cognitive function in Alzheimer's; and control of cholesterol levels has stood in for pushing back heart disease and stroke vulnerability. Ioannidis notes, for example, that 21 different studies of asthma he looked at measured a combined 487 different factors in patients in struggling to determine what constitutes genuine improvement; every researcher seemed to have her own idea on the question.

Unfortunately, surrogate measurements tend to lead researchers astray. A number of cancer drugs, including the much-heralded Avastin, have promoted tumor shrinkage without on average adding significant time or any other benefits to cancer patients' lives. (What Avastin did add was blood clots, heart failure, and bowel perforation, among other side effects.)[6] Medications that lower blood sugar have in some cases been shown to sharply *increase* the risk of death for diabetics—the heavily hyped

Avandia raised the average risk of heart attack by 43 percent. The bad cholesterol–lowering drugs Vytorin and Zetia have built up a $5 billion market while continuing to show no evidence of lowering heart-disease or stroke risks on average.[7,8,9] The enormous heart-protection expectations for the "good" cholesterol–raising drug torcetrapib were shattered when it turned out in large trials to raise death rates in general and heart-attack rates in particular. The much-anticipated brain plaque–reducing drug Flurizan consistently failed to show improvement in slowing Alzheimer's before trials were finally halted in 2008,[10] and studies have shown that plaque can be present without dementia.[11]

Researchers really get creative with surrogate measurement when it comes to studying human behavior. For example, given the fact that people and their social behaviors are on full display pretty much everywhere we look, it may seem difficult to imagine what researchers were thinking when, in the following recent studies—all of which received substantial attention in the mass media—they relied on these setups to get at questions about human attraction:

• University of Bristol, U.K., researchers had women rate their relationship interest in twenty-eight men based on silent, animated versions of the men's faces, which were accompanied by a written statement that was either pleasant or antisocial. The researchers concluded that women who are interested in a fling care more about a man's face and less about his social attitudes than do women looking for long-term relationships.[12]

• Harvard researchers measured the vocal pitch of forty-nine men from the Hadza, a tribe of hunter-gatherers in Tanzania, as they said the Swahili word for "hello." By comparing each man's pitch to the number of children he had, the researchers were able to conclude that the deeper a man's voice, the more fertile he is likely to be.[13]

• Researchers at the University of New Mexico compared the tips received by lap dancers on a birth control pill with those amassed by dancers during their fertile periods. The latter tips were larger on average, leading the researchers to conclude that men are more attracted to fertile women.[14]

Or consider a recent, widely publicized study that plunked infants down in front of a sort of crude puppet show in which a wooden block slid up an incline, sometimes "helped" by a block behind it, sometimes "hindered" by a block in front of it. After this performance, the infants were given a chance to grab the blocks, and proved more likely to grab the "helper" block. The study's conclusion: infants are able to judge people's character.[15] Academic researchers, especially in the social sciences, often make use of that pool of easy-to-recruit subjects literally at their doorsteps: their students. For example, a well-publicized 2008 Harvard study that was conducted on students concluded that people are more likely to get others to cooperate by being nice to them rather than by punishing them.[16] But perhaps we ought to be wondering how much a small group of nineteen-or-so-year-old Ivy League students stuck helping out a professor adequately represents the population at large in this matter.

A surrogate measurement that gets an outsize share of science coverage in both journals and the mass media is the claimed insight into thinking and feeling courtesy of "functional magnetic resonance imaging," or fMRI. A souped-up version of the MRI scan routinely used in patient care, fMRI measures the blood flow through regions of the brain in a conscious subject who need wear only a sort of helmet. Functional MRI–based studies have informed us, for example, that psychotherapy has a druglike effect on the brain,[17] daydreams are different in autistic minds than in typical minds,[18] gambling produces feelings of reward similar to those felt with food and drugs,[19] and teenagers who start fights enjoy seeing others suffer,[20] to only slightly paraphrase headlines reporting the results of four out of the hundreds of these studies that have attracted attention in the press in recent years. Economists, too, are flocking to fMRI studies in an effort to feed data to their models about how people make decisions involving judgments about value, probability, and risk. "We're not sure how reliable this data is yet, but it's too potentially valuable to ignore," I was told by the NYU economist Andrew Caplin. But the critical assumption at the heart of most fMRI studies—that there is a close link among activities, feelings, or thoughts that produce similar fMRI brain maps—is highly suspect, says Charles Jennings, an MIT brain scientist and administrator and former *Nature* editor. "Cocaine and gambling may activate the same areas, and that suggests they probably have something in common," he explains, "but that absolutely does not mean the brain treats them the same way." He contends that using fMRIs to draw conclusions about how people think and feel is a bit like trying to infer details about a population's activities by looking at satellite pictures of cities and traffic jams without being able to make out individual cars or buildings, let alone people.

But don't expect such qualms to drive experts away from surrogate measures—they've often pinned their careers to them. "If scientists have been doing it a certain way for years and they've been successful raising money for it, they're not going to change from one day to the other," the University of Missouri biophysicist Gabor Forgacs told me. A particularly striking example of how scientists often hew, sometimes en masse, to a questionable but well-funded measurement tack is the two-decades-long quest to identify the genes of human disease. Genes are a measurement paradise for medical researchers, who are otherwise stuck with trying to decode the actual workings of what may be the most complex machine in the universe: you. Instead of having to wrestle with the nearly infinite ways in which a wide range of molecules interact throughout your body, researchers can in theory just compare the genes of healthy people to those of sick people, and find the one gene or handful of genes that are linked to any given disease. Then a bit of your saliva is all doctors would need in order to know what diseases you're likely to get, and treating the disease would just be a matter of neutralizing those disease genes, or making up for certain missing genes that protect against the disease. You'd think that quest was moving apace, given the fact that for years now practically every time we turn on the TV news or open a newspaper, we hear about the latest discovery of some new gene linked to a disease or trait. Cancer researchers, for example, have since the late 1980s largely focused on finding the specific faulty "oncogenes" believed to be involved in each form of cancer, spawning what could possibly be called the biggest science project in history, one that vacuums up a big share of the $6 billion annually sunk into American cancer research.

Unfortunately, the number of genes labeled as oncogenes has, for almost all forms of cancer, steadily grown far beyond the imagined handful, with no end in sight. A large 2006 multigroup study of the mutant genes in breast and colorectal tumors found that 189 different genes are frequently mutated in these tumors, and that any given tumor cell has an average of 90 mutated genes[21]—far too many to allow accurately predicting cancer risk based on genes. And there are many, many more genes yet to add to the list. "This means that chemotherapy that targets oncogenes is not going to be effective," the University of Washington cancer researcher Lawrence Loeb told me a few years ago. The bottom line: when it comes to treating most adult cancers caught beyond the earliest stages, survival rates for adults grouped by age have barely budged since 1950.

The notion that a small number of genes represents a large component of the risk for a particular disorder has simply turned out to be wrong for almost all major illnesses. While thousands of links have been put forth in journal papers and often duly trumpeted in the mass media, virtually no ills have been conclusively and fully pinned down to genetic roots, nor, except for a precious few instances, has the ever-swelling mountain of genetic data led to cures or even treatments. Our vastly expanded pool of genetic knowledge even fails to tell us much about some of the simplest characteristics of humans. A 2009 study came up with a technique for predicting the height of a person based on looking at the fifty-four genes found to be correlated to height in 5,748 people—and discovered the results were one-tenth as accurate as the 125-year-old technique of averaging the heights of both parents and adjusting for sex.[22] Ioannidis has calculated the average odds of a gene-link study being right at one out of hundreds or worse, depending on the disease. In the case of schizophrenia, for example, his estimates suggest you would have almost as good a chance of identifying some types of genuine gene links by throwing darts at a diagram of the relevant sections of the human genome as you would by reading research journals. The gene most strongly correlated with intelligence accounts for less than half a percent of the observed variation in intelligence, and the top six intelligence genes together predict 1 percent of the variation.[23]

Gene hunters and other scientists can respond that this is how science works—it fumbles its way toward the truth, and there's no shame in slogging through a lot of false leads to get there. But the scientific community could have worked a lot harder to make it clear to the rest of us that the gene hunt hasn't so much been a matter of racing toward a deep understanding of disease as a decades-long fumbling around at the starting gate. That's not to say that scientists shouldn't have bothered with the gene hunt or that they should stop working on it now—it's invaluable basic research that will eventually pay off. But we all have the right to wonder what other insights and potential treatments the billions spent on that research could have bought us.* What's more, when we're led to believe our health problems and risks are due to a small set of genes, we're less likely to pay attention to diet, exercise, and other factors under our control that are turning out on average to have at least as big an impact on our health as the particular genes we happened to have been born with. In any case, scientists are hardly abandoning the search for gene links. Most oncogene hunters, for example, are still at the same game. Jeffrey H. Miller, a UCLA cancer researcher, put it to me this way: "The way science works is, when you end up backing a theory, you can't afford to be wrong or your grant will suffer."

Mismeasuring

In 1914 Albert Einstein and fellow physicist Wander Johannes de Haas calculated just how much an iron bar would twist in a magnetic field, based on a reckoning of an important property of atoms called the "g-factor." Einstein and de Haas figured that the g-factor ought to be precisely 1 for any atom, and they set out to prove it with a highly sensitive version of the twisting-bar setup. It took them about a year of fiddling and fine-tuning, but they were finally able to extract a careful, credible result: an experimentally observed g-factor of 1.02, confirming their theory with remarkable precision.[24]

---

* Ruth Fischbach and John Loike of Columbia University's Center for Bioethics have noted that the George W. Bush administration's 2001 federal funding ban on human embryonic stem-cell research led scientists kicking and screaming into developing alternative cell-transformation approaches—approaches that now show tremendous promise for new treatments.

If only all the experts on whom we depend could regularly achieve the measurement standard set by that Einsteinian achievement! Well, terrific news: they just might. As it turns out, Einstein and de Haas were way off. Three years later, other physicists clearly established, through their own experiments, that the g-factor is actually about twice the value Einstein and de Haas had predicted and experimentally obtained. Einstein was no fraudster, of course, nor was his colleague; but the two of them managed to temporarily mislead their field with flawed research that looked very convincing. They had measured poorly, and in a way that happened to exactly back their flawed theory.*

Let's face it, no matter how smart or careful an expert is, he's probably no Einstein. And it's not unreasonable to imagine that the sorts of problems that trip up first-rate physicists are all the more troublesome elsewhere. These errors can seem small, but they can have big consequences. In 2008 researchers discovered that the record of ocean temperatures on which today's global-warming models intimately rely was thrown off for fifteen years in the mid-twentieth century because ship crews recording the temperatures switched from using the slightly warmed water taken into engine-cooling ports to the slightly cooled water taken from open buckets—it never occurred to scientists until now to check the seemingly basic and critical detail of how these measurements were being made.[26] The difference notably alters the models, even

---

* Nor was Einstein the only physicist of colossal reputation to bungle an important measurement. The physicist Enrico Fermi won a Nobel Prize for transforming uranium nuclei into heavier elements in 1934. But others later realized he had misidentified the elements—he had actually been blowing up the nuclei into lighter ones, thus unknowingly achieving nuclear fission. As the Harvard science historian Peter Galison has pointed out, an accurate measurement could have given the United States the atomic bomb several years earlier—or might have led to a Nazi atomic bomb.[25]

if in this case scientists so far seem to have escaped having to toss out the main conclusions wholesale. In medical studies, technicians can misread blood pressure, height, and heart rhythms, and give subjects the wrong dosages and even the wrong drug.[27,28,29] Studies of the impact of pollution on health have been thrown off by the misrecording of the locations of subjects' homes.[30] How frequent and impactful are these sorts of errors?* No one knows, because relatively few published reports contain enough detail to determine if a measurement technique was sound, let alone whether the actual data are accurate, according to the late, renowned Berkeley statistician David Freedman (no relation; he passed away in late 2008, some months after I met with him), long a critic of weak studies.

Experts can also make the right measurements but on the wrong people — that is, on people who don't adequately represent the population. People in studies may be particularly health-conscious or unusually ill. Many health and drug studies pay people to take part in them, which tends to leave the study group with high percentages of poor people, and sometimes with alcoholics, drug abusers, illegal immigrants, and the homeless.[32] Studies in the 1990s appeared to prove that hormone replacement therapy (HRT) reduced the risk of heart disease by 50 percent; then a large study in 2002 seemed to prove that HRT *increased* the risk of heart disease by 29 percent — as it turns out, the discrepancy was due to the fact that the first study looked at relatively young women, and the second, somewhat older women, leading both to produce misleading results.[33]

---

* The problem is often with poorly managed subordinates. A 2006 study noted that the staff who actually carry out drug studies on a day-to-day basis frequently have little experience and are largely unsupervised; one coordinator of clinical trials confessed to struggling with managing more than twenty trials at once.[31]

Studying the Wrong Mammal

In 2006 the experimental leukemia drug TGN1412 was given to six volunteer human patients. All six quickly fell seriously ill, with multiple organ traumas, some of them critically. You might well wonder, *Don't they safety-test this stuff first?* Well, yes, they do. TGN1412 was heavily tested on animals, and it passed with flying colors. In fact, the drug had shown no harmful effects in animals at doses up to five hundred times higher than what had been given to the volunteers.[34]

It would be hard to exaggerate how dependent health research has become on animals in general, and mice in particular. The disease-treatment breakthroughs, the promising new drugs, and the lifestyle health insights you read about in the paper or see on TV frequently turn out to be based entirely on studies of mice, though that fact isn't always mentioned prominently. But how applicable are the results of mouse and rat studies to humans? As some researchers never tire of pointing out, mice and humans share up to 95 percent of their genes, depending on how strictly we want to define "genes" and "share," and by all accounts the vast majority of human genes associated with disease have rodent counterparts. But three-quarters of the drugs that enter human studies end up, in contradiction to the animal results, failing in either Phase I trials, which look for dangerous side effects, or Phase II trials, which focus more on efficacy.[*,35] Researchers who have tried to get a clearer handle on the relevance of animal studies to human health have come away with sobering conclusions. A *British Medical Journal* study in 2007

---

* The relevance to humans of tests that show compounds to be *harmful* to animals is harder to gauge, since these compounds normally won't go on to human trials. A drug that fails animal tests but that would have worked fine in humans is a drug lost to the world. It is frequently claimed that penicillin might easily have become one of those mistakenly discarded drugs because it sickens rabbits and guinea pigs in large or in oral doses.

took an in-depth look at six treatments for which animal studies had suggested clear benefits or a lack thereof, and which went on to human studies; in half the cases the human studies outright contradicted the animal studies, and the three that agreed did not all agree strongly.[36] In a 2006 *Journal of the American Medical Association* study, two researchers looked at seventy-six of the most highly cited animal studies in which drugs and treatments were found safe and effective, but only one-third of these influential studies were later confirmed in human randomized trials, and only eight resulted in drugs later approved for use on people. Animal studies also tend to be conducted with a great deal less care than are human studies.[37] A 2001 study in the journal *Stroke* looked at twenty studies of a stroke drug and stated without qualification that "the methodological quality of the studies was poor."[38] Not surprisingly, half the studies found the drug helpful, and half didn't.

Yet leading science journals remain brimming with the apparently exciting results of animal studies, and the mass media enthusiastically pass on the news to us as breakthroughs. Thus we've learned from recent headlines, fed by prominent journal articles, that Parkinson's disease has been effectively treated by therapeutic cloning,[39] sickle cell anemia has been cured by skin cells transformed into stem cells,[40] and cancer has been reversed by, variously, injections of cancer-resistant white blood cells,[41] a cocktail of immune-system antibodies,[42] and intense exercise.[43] Never mind that these claims, which were all based on mouse studies, aren't even approaching serious attempts at human confirmation (with the possible exception of exercise as a cancer treatment, though so far it's not clearly supported by human studies) and, if they turn out to be like the vast majority of such reported breakthroughs, will never prove to be successful human treatments.

If we can't find close similarity between mice and people when it comes to physical illness, we certainly shouldn't be surprised by noncorrespondence between rodent and human behavior. One small example: human moms tend to prefer clean rooms, whereas rat moms often eat their young after their cages are cleaned, as one researcher warned in a journal article.[44] And yet mice, rats, and other tiny, scurrying mammals are widely used to inform our understanding of human thought and emotion, and especially for testing psychiatric drugs. Increasingly, much of what we think we know about mental health is coming from rodent studies. In typical antidepressant studies and other depression-related research, for example, a mouse is dropped into a small tank of water and timed as to how long it frantically swims before finally just relaxing and floating; a mouse that doesn't swim very long is judged "depressed."[45] Likewise, a mouse's preference to stay in closed-in spaces rather than explore open areas stands in for human anxiety in drug and other studies. And so on, for a range of human mental states. "When it comes to emotion and cognition, things are manifestly very different in humans than in mice," says Jennings. "You can't be very confident of the results when you use a mouse like that to discover a new drug."

Often the only way to even pretend that mice are experiencing something akin to what a human might experience is to enlist odd setups that have little to do with what normally happens to either mice or people. Does green tea help guard against the ill effects of sleep apnea? Yes, it does, announced one study that got good press—you need only buy into the idea that your sleep apnea is well represented by keeping mice in a container from which the oxygen is periodically purged.[46] Are common skin creams safe? Actually, they cause cancer, said a much-quoted 2009 study—proven by sticking hairless mice under an ultraviolet lamp and then slathering their bodies with cream.[47] Do some of the chemicals in red wine protect against age-related damage? Absolutely, say some highly talked about studies, relying on mice that were plied with chemical doses that had human-body-weight equivalents of as many as a hundred bottles of wine a day.[48] Can the fake butter in microwave popcorn products cause lung disease? Yes, read the 2008 headlines, based on forcing chemical vapors down the throats of mice, even though allowing mice to normally breathe heavy concentrations of the stuff had no effect.[49] Do genetically modified foods create health risks? Yes, according to the 1998 study that kicked off Europe's anti-GM frenzy—a study in which rats' organs were found to be slightly smaller than normal after the animals were kept on a protein-deficient diet of indigestibly raw, genetically modified potatoes.[50] Can schizophrenia be triggered in humans by a parasite? Yes, according to one study, which extrapolated its results from how much time infected rats spent around cat-urine-soaked wood chips.[51] These studies' findings may or may not apply to people in normal situations, but if they do, one would imagine it would be as much a matter of freakish luck as solid evidence.

And how about combining mouse-based research with the gene hunt? Tens of thousands of researchers do nothing but explore genetic links to diseases and traits via mice that are genetically engineered to have symptoms resembling those of human disorders—it's one of the biggest games in all of science. These designer creatures are often the everyday, behind-the-scenes stars of mass-media articles about new health breakthroughs and insights. If the much-publicized 2008 Boston University study declaring that weight lifting can be as good as cardio exercises for burning fat led you to consider swapping the treadmill for dumbbells, bear in mind that the conclusions were based entirely on observation of mice whose bizarrely large muscles came not from intense exercise but from genetic engineering.[52] Headlines have told us recently that Rutgers researchers are on the trail of a treatment for phobias, Harvard researchers have come up with a new

approach for fighting jet lag, and University of Texas researchers have achieved new insights into the chemistry of schizophrenia—based on mice genetically designed to lack, respectively,
fear,[53] internal clocks,[54] and the ability to sniff out buried choco-
late.[55] Likewise, a study warning of a link between eating soy and
sudden cardiac death in men,[56] a study describing a potential cure
for Huntington's disease,[57] and a study announcing a technique
for reversing the progress of multiple sclerosis[58] were all among
the hundreds of stories in recent years that got mass-media attention despite being based entirely on genetically engineered mice.
Never mind that a mouse whose brain accumulates plaque may
well be no more like a human Alzheimer's victim than a mouse in
a tiny tutu is like a human ballerina.

Tossing Out Inconvenient Data

Joseph "J. B." Rhine, the well-known Duke University parapsy-
chology researcher, managed to consistently show in studies of
card-guessing games that ESP is real—thanks to his practice
of simply not including the results of test subjects who guessed
poorly.[59] But the fact of the matter is, highly respected scientists
toss out data all the time. Actually, they pretty much have to. It
would be hard to justify keeping measurements made when a key
piece of equipment is broken, patients in studies are caught cheat-
ing on prescribed regimens, bacterial cultures are contaminated,
or technicians misunderstand instructions.

The problem is that it isn't always clear where to draw the line
between data that is bad and data that the researcher just doesn't
like. Douglas Altman—a statistician who directs the Centre for
Statistics in Medicine at Oxford in the United Kingdom, serves as
an adviser to the *British Medical Journal*, and is one of the world's

foremost experts on how medical studies can go wrong—and a colleague looked at more than one hundred drug studies, comparing raw data with published results. They found that in most of the studies some data were left out—and more often than not these were data that didn't fit the conclusions. In other words, researchers appear to have a tendency to throw out data that might raise uncomfortable questions.*

The ultimate form of data cleansing may be just throwing away a whole study's worth of data by not submitting it for publication, because the results aren't the ones hoped for.† That means when experts try to gather together the data from multiple studies to do a "review study" or "meta-analysis"—considered to be among the more authoritative forms of research—the results are likely distorted by the absence of these studies. A 2008 study revealed that twenty-three out of seventy-four antidepressant drug trials weren't published, and all but one of the unpublished studies had found the drugs to be more or less ineffective compared to a placebo.[60] In contrast, all thirty-seven of the positive studies were published. Researchers who conduct meta-analyses often claim they can adjust for this problem through statistical techniques that estimate the number of unpublished studies, but others are skeptical. "It's a huge problem, and there's no way you can use statistics to make it go away,"

---

* Adding data is a problem, too. Mark Davis, a scientific-fraud researcher at Ohio State University, examined studies and found that researchers often simply filled in missing data with averages or other guesses. But Davis pointed out to me that doing so can disguise the fact that, for example, people are dropping out of the study because they are sick or discouraged—the very sort of thing a study most needs to discover. Such sloppiness isn't likely to be caught: the University of Arizona sociology researcher Erin Leahey studied how research is overseen and published, concluding that "no gatekeeping body oversees middle stages of research where data editing is likely to occur."

† This is the so-called file-drawer problem, which we'll be discussing shortly.

says Kay Dickersin, director of the Center for Clinical Trials at the Johns Hopkins Bloomberg School of Public Health and one of the world's foremost authorities on problems with the publication of research.

Moving the Goalposts

Sheer chance dictates that in just about any medical or psychological study you'll almost always be able to observe *something* change on average for the better in a group of people over time — a slight loss in excess weight, an improvement in mood, an increase in exercise, a little drop in cholesterol levels — and the change needn't have anything to do with what's actually being tested. Thus a researcher conducting a medical study of some treatment or lifestyle change can wait and see what happens to change for the better due to sheer chance, claim it was due to whatever was being tested, and make the case look good by writing up the study as if that change were what was being tested for. "It's rather like throwing darts on a wall and then drawing a dartboard around them," says Altman, the *British Medical Journal* adviser. Or waiting to see where a ball is kicked and then moving the goalposts to retroactively make the kick good. Gerald Koocher, dean of the Health Studies School at Simmons College in Boston and a specialist in researcher misconduct, told me some researchers refer to the technique as using a "retrospectoscope" — in retrospect, you can usually find something that your study "proved." How common is this trick? Altman dug up a number of original study proposals submitted by researchers and compared them to the eventual published findings from those studies. "We found the stated focus of the research was different in more than half the cases," he told me.

Being Confounded

People who get fewer than six hours of sleep are more likely to be obese.[61] People who talk on the phone in bed are more likely to get headaches.[62] We hear about these "people who do this are more likely to be that" studies all the time; they're a staple of mass-media health reports, which are plucked from research journals. But they're among the most frequently misleading of all research studies, and for a simple reason: so many interconnected things are going on in people's lives that it's often nearly impossible to reliably determine that one factor is the main cause of some behavior, condition, or achievement. It may be true that a lack of sleep is linked in some way with obesity, but it's a big jump from there to conclude that if someone starts getting more sleep, they'll lose weight. It may be, for example, that people who sleep less also loosely tend to be people who exercise less, or eat less healthfully, or have a hormone disorder, or are depressed—in which case it could be any of these factors, rather than the sleep levels, that needs to be addressed in order to affect obesity. That would mean the link to sleep is pretty much incidental, mostly useless, and misleading.

When studies try to figure out what is affecting what, there are many possible factors that muddy the picture. These are known as "confounding variables." In a nutshell, the typical problem is that people who have one thing in common probably have other things in common, too, and trying to isolate two of these things to determine if one affects the other can be nearly impossible, especially when such multiple commonalities may all be interacting in complex ways. It's not just lifestyle studies that end up confounded. Researchers trying to pin down the effect on heart disease of medications that control blood sugar levels in diabetics, for example, tear their hair out over the fact that results can depend sharply on factors such as blood pressure, cholesterol levels, episodes of too-low blood sugar levels, and how quickly after disease onset the treatment is started. Ideally researchers would like to keep all these other factors perfectly constant and consistent so that they study only how changing blood sugar levels affect heart disease, but they can't. Or consider how studies seem to have revealed a link between antidepressants and suicide. It has long been known that patients suffering a severe bout of depression are particularly likely to attempt suicide not in the depths of their depression but when they start to emerge from it. That means that in the near term antidepressants might lead to suicidal thoughts because the drugs are *working*—and over the long term would more likely reduce the chances that a patient will attempt suicide. Or it may be that adolescents who end up on antidepressants are more likely to have had suicidal thoughts to begin with than depressed adolescents who don't end up on antidepressants. Or adolescents on antidepressants may be more likely to *confess* to suicidal thinking, or more likely to be asked about it by a doctor, even though they don't experience more of this thinking.[63]

Another confusing recent set of studies centers around findings that people (and rats) who habitually take in artificial sweeteners wind up eating more than those who consume sugar. The University of Texas researchers who conducted one of the studies helpfully calculated that every can of diet soda taken in per day translates to a 36 percent increase in the chances of a person gaining weight.[64] The *ABC News* medical contributor Dr. Marie Savard shared her guess at the roots of the effect: "There's something about diet foods that changes your metabolic limit, your brain chemistry," she said.[65] Well, maybe that's all true. Or maybe, as other researchers have pointed out, people who drink diet soda simply have other traits in common relevant to the picture—such as a tendency to overeat. Indeed, other studies have found that diet soda doesn't affect overall calorie intake differently than soda sweetened with sugar or high-fructose corn syrup.*,66

Here, try one yourself: what are some of the other factors that might be at play when it comes to a link between using phones in bed and headaches?

A related issue to confounding variables is the tendency of some studies to make shaky assumptions about cause versus effect. For example, countless studies have documented the fact that people who exercise more tend to be generally more healthy—but no one has been able to irrefutably determine whether it's the exercise that more often brings on the good health, as the reports usually imply, or the good health that leaves a person feeling up to exercising. Researchers and the media tend to push the former inference, of course, because it suggests we can do something to improve our health, making the study seem more useful.

The mess that confounding variables can and often do make of studies is one reason researchers (and journalists) speak in terms of a hierarchy of study trustworthiness based on study design, and it goes something like this:

> *Observational study:* Interesting but untrustworthy.
> *Epidemiological study:* Somewhat trustworthy if it is large and done well.
> *Meta-analysis* or *review study:* Trustworthy.
> *Randomized controlled trial:* Very trustworthy if large—the gold standard of evidence.

---

* Researchers often claim in their findings to have "controlled" for a confounding variable by comparing subgroups of people who are alike—for example, comparing smokers only with other smokers. But the subgroups can become so small that flukes start to dominate, and if you create enough subgroups it becomes a form of moving the goalposts. And some confounders are hard to control for because they're hard to measure, such as the level of a person's suicidal thoughts prior to treatment.

Observational studies, a staple of many research journals, consist of researchers observing how a small group of subjects fare—typically physicians observing patients, but it could be a behavioral study or an animal study—when given a drug or subjected to some treatment or condition. Findings from these studies tend to be highly suspect, because chance and confounding variables can play a large role and because the researchers might be biased.

An epidemiological study (some types of which are called "case control" or "cohort" studies) usually involves following a large group of people—as many as tens of thousands—over months, years, or even decades in an effort to spot associations between various behaviors (diet, exercise, attitudes, etc.), physical characteristics (height, weight, genes, etc.), demographic characteristics (age, gender, race, location, and so forth), and disease and longevity, often via health markers such as cholesterol levels. But these studies, too, fall prey to confounding variables, as well as to questions about cause and effect. What's more, the links these studies turn up tend to be based on small differences between large groups of people, so that even if the result is right it often involves only trivial changes in disease risk. According to multiple studies of the link between depression and cancer, for example, an undepressed person with a 3 percent chance of developing cancer over a certain period of time would see that risk rise by an average of less than half a percent with depression—and one study found the risk would very slightly drop.[67] The Penn State biological anthropologist Kenneth Weiss and his colleagues have compiled a long list of widely publicized epidemiological links that have failed to hold up, ranging from baby aspirin's effect on heart-disease prevention to the effect of sunlight on cancer risk, and they note that epidemiological studies appear to leave the medical community helpless to take a consistent position on what would seem to be some of the most basic and heavily studied healthy-lifestyle questions. "It is not encouraging," they write, "that we do not yet know whether it is better to eat butter or margarine, or whether it is excessive cleanliness or pollution that causes asthma." But these claimed links *sound* impressive and important, especially when we hear they are multiyear efforts involving many thousands of subjects.

The meta-analysis, or review study, in which the data from many previous studies are combined and reanalyzed, is often held up as a much more reliable type of study. But these studies can be distorted by researchers' failure to publish many studies (more on this later). What's more, Ioannidis has shown mathematically that meta-analyses based on data from studies that weren't terribly reliable in the first place, while more likely to be reliable than the individual studies, are still more likely to be wrong than right. That's why different meta-analyses examining the same question sometimes end up coming to different conclusions, according to a 2003 meta-analysis of meta-analyses in the *Journal of the Royal Society of Medicine*.[68]

Occasionally a scientist or science journalist will make a point of loudly decrying epidemiological and observational studies as unreliable, encouraging us to conclude that these are the "bad" studies in a field of otherwise "good" studies. Randomized controlled trials, or RCTs, are the especially "good" studies in this worldview. "Controlled" means that there are at least two groups in the study, typically one of which gets the treatment under study while the other gets a placebo (though there are many variations). "Randomized" means patients are randomly assigned to one group or the other, to avoid confounding variables, and usually neither the patients nor the people who conduct the study know who is in which group until all the data are gathered, making it a so-called double-blind study, to avoid bias. It has become almost reflexive among researchers (and science journalists) to refer to RCTs as research's "gold standard."

But besides being notoriously complex, expensive, and time-consuming, RCTs often end up wrong, too. "Randomized controlled studies can go off the rails," Freedman told me. "No matter how you do it, it can be a disaster." Vioxx was backed by large randomized studies, as was hormone replacement therapy for menopausal women—but the studies' published conclusions were wrong in a deadly way, as has turned out to be the case for many widely prescribed drugs. In 1999 a large, prominent RCT conducted at multiple prestigious institutions "proved" that heart surgery patients are more likely to survive if someone they've never met secretly prays for them; a later RCT found that secret prayer was slightly likely to *reduce* a patient's survival chances.[69, 70] In considering a stream of refutations of highly regarded, influential randomized studies, the *British Medical Journal* noted in a 2002 editorial that "randomized trials have strengths over observational studies, but they are hardly the last word."

RCTs can go wrong in any number of ways. For one thing, randomization of large pools of people does little to protect against most of the other problems with studies we've looked at, including shaky surrogate measurements, mismeasurement, unreliable self-reporting, moving the goalposts, tossing out data, and bad statistical analysis. As with epidemiological studies, large RCTs often traffic in exceedingly small effects.[71] What's more, RCT findings are usually just averages for results that often vary wildly among different individuals, so that the findings don't really get at what's likely to happen to you. For example, drug RCTs often report that the drug is of modest benefit and poses a small risk of harmful side effects—but the typical reality for such drugs is that a small percentage of patients is likely to safely do quite well with the drug, a small percentage of other patients is likely to suffer harm without benefit, and most patients won't experience much of anything. Even established, major drugs don't work on

40 percent to 75 percent of people, according to a 2005 review paper in the *New England Journal of Medicine*,[72] and the variation in effectiveness and risk of side effects tends to be much greater for newer, less proven drugs.

The widely held notion that the largest randomized studies, or "megatrials," are the most trustworthy is nonsense, according to Bruce Charlton, a researcher with the Centre for Public Health Policy and Health Services Research at the University of East London. Charlton writes that "this aggrandizement of megatrials to a position of superiority is an error," wonders "how it was that such a transparently ludicrous idea has gained such wide currency," and criticizes "some of the fundamental deficiencies of the megatrial methodology which mean that—in most cases—megatrials are highly prone to mislead."

Researchers can respond to these sorts of criticisms by insisting that randomized studies, as imperfect as they may be, are still the best tools for assessing the effectiveness of treatments—but they may be wrong to say so. After evaluating the quality of many types of studies of treatments for chronic pain, the George Mason University statistician Daniel Carr concluded that randomized studies "did not necessarily carry greater strength and consistency than higher quality studies of less rigorous design."[73] Given that we're constantly being told by researchers and the mass media to place special trust in randomized studies, it may be that randomized studies are ultimately the most misleading of all.

Juggling the Numbers

"Computers are useless," Picasso once said. "They can only give you answers." He could have been referring to how researchers analyze the raw data they gather in their studies—namely, by running them through "statistical analysis" software on a computer. These programs have been designed essentially to do mathematically whatever it takes to find a useful pattern, including ignoring "outliers," or data that just don't seem to fit. The researchers don't have to understand anything about the slick mathematical gymnastics or dubious data-massaging the program is enlisting to produce its conclusions, and may not even bother to note the details. When the data don't seem to be yielding positive, interesting results, Freedman explained to me, researchers sometimes simply keep reanalyzing data using different statistical models until they get a match.* He added that researchers rarely bother to mention in their reports exactly which analysis methods they employed, and even when they confess to using exotic techniques in order to reach a positive finding, journals typically welcome the news as a sign of cutting-edge research.

It isn't just fancy analytical footwork that distorts study conclusions—sometimes it's more like slipping on a banana peel. Researchers at Spain's University of Girona went back over the data from forty-four papers from the *British Medical Journal* and *Nature*, and found statistical errors in a quarter of the *British Medical Journal* papers and in 38 percent of the *Nature* papers. Even experts whose sole function is to analyze test data sometimes slip up on this straightforward task in impactful ways. For example, in 2006 the College Board admitted that it had misscored the SATs of some four thousand students and had failed to adequately check the scores of another sixteen hundred tests.[74] How rare could we expect it to be that experts mess up who have to reckon far less

---

* For example, a 1997 study compared two widely used analysis methods for deciding if patient complaints are due to a drug's side effects. The methods agreed only 41 percent of the time. In other words, catching side effects usually wasn't a matter of who got sick but rather of which analysis technique was used.

constrained, far more complex, and far less closely watched measurements?

Being Paid to Get It Wrong

I spoke with an industrial researcher who argued passionately that it is utterly unfair for researchers or anyone else to assume that just because a study was conducted by someone attached to a company, it means the study's findings are less trustworthy. I was sympathetic to that notion; my father was an industrial scientist, and of the many industrial researchers I've met over the years, some have simply seemed models of brilliance and integrity. But there's just no getting around it: statistically speaking, being on the payroll of a company cranks up the risk of gamed study results. In fact, the corrupting effect of industry funding on drug research has been documented so strongly by researchers themselves that I hesitate to lay out the sordid details, fearing that it may distract from the fact that virtually *all* research is highly troubled. To point out that nonindustrial research is more trustworthy than the industrial version isn't really saying much at all. What's more, most of us already have the good sense to be at least a bit suspicious of industry-driven research, to the extent that we're capable of identifying when research is industry funded. But I'll offer one tidbit: a 2003 *Journal of the American Medical Association* review of conflict-of-interest meta-studies involving some 67 conflict-of-interest studies and 398 other research reports confirmed a strong correlation between industry sponsorship and positive findings.[75] And the problem may be worse than it looks, because companies often disguise that they are behind certain findings by paying university researchers to put their names on studies actually conducted and written up by the companies themselves—so-called ghost authorship.[76]

You might hope that the vast majority of researchers knows to steer clear of this sort of ugliness, but consider a few factoids:

- Lower estimate of percentage of published medical researchers who, according to one study, had been in a potential conflict-of-interest situation: 30.[77]
- Lower estimate of percentage of these researchers who, according to the same study, fully disclosed potential conflicts of interest: 2.[78]
- Percentage of published industry-backed drug trials in which the true authorship of the study was obscured by ghost authorship, according to a 2007 study conducted by Altman and his colleagues: 75.[79]
- Percentage of the 170 psychiatric experts contributing to the fourth edition of the *Diagnostic and Statistical Manual of Mental Disorders (DSM IV)*—universally used at least in the United States to diagnose psychiatric disorders—who have had financial ties to manufacturers of psychiatric drugs: 100.[80]
- Percentage of respondents to a 2007 survey conducted by the employment section of the journal *Nature* who said they want to pursue an advanced degree in business: 53.[81]

This chapter has identified quite a lot of opportunity for error and distortion in research findings. But pointing out that scientists and other highly credentialed people engage in these sorts of misleading and sloppy measurement games raises two important questions: First, why aren't they more careful to avoid these problems, or at least to be forthcoming about it when they can't? And second, why, given science's celebrated dedication to maintaining the highest standards of truth-seeking through rigorous self-policing, is all this flawed stuff making it into journals and thence to the media and public consumption?

I'm going to answer those questions. But first we need to lay a little groundwork in the next two chapters by looking at the ways in which the human mind can be attracted to wrongness and how expert communities tend not only to fail to improve the output of individual experts but to actually make it worse.

CHAPTER THREE

The Certainty Principle

There is always a well-known solution to every human problem — neat, plausible, and wrong.
— H. L. MENCKEN

If a man will begin with certainties, he shall end in doubts. . . .
— FRANCIS BACON

I magine you've developed chronic back pain, and you decide to get opinions from two orthopedic specialists. The first one examines you, looks at some MRI images, and tells you the following: "I've seen many, many cases just like yours, and it's usually very hard to say exactly what's wrong. Different treatments work to varying degrees for different people with this sort of problem, it's very hard to predict which will work for any person, and most of the time none of the treatments is all that successful. I really can't predict what, if anything, is likely to work for you. I suggest we try treatment A, which usually doesn't work but which at least tends to work slightly more often on patients like you than do any of the other treatments. Come back in a month, and if it's working we'll continue it, and if it isn't we'll try something else." The second doctor examines you, looks at some MRI images, and tells you the following: "I've seen many, many cases just like yours, and I can tell exactly what's wrong with your back. Most patients with this problem respond very well to treatment B, and I'm pretty sure you will, too. Come in once a month for the treatment, and that should do the trick."

Which doctor do you go with? When I ask people this question, almost all of them say they'd go with the second doctor. At which point I ask them another question: if you were told one of these doctors had recently been named Wisest Orthopedist of the Year by the state orthopedic society while the other was known to his colleagues behind his back as Bozo the Orthopedist, which would you guess is which? Almost everyone guesses without hesitation that the second doctor is the one who gets no respect. But why would we prefer the advice of someone whose wisdom we're so quick to question? Apparently we *like* the second doctor's advice so much that we're willing to take a chance on it, in spite of whatever qualms we might have about its reliability.

We've seen that even experts who may be more than capable of closing in on the truth end up providing us with findings that are wrong. But it also appears that part of the problem lies with us, in that we don't merely fail to distinguish good expertise from bad expertise—we actually sometimes *seek out* the lesser stuff. What's going on in the minds of experts and in the minds of those of us who listen to them?

Not long ago I made my way to the auditorium of a local elementary school to see Richard Ferber, the Harvard child-sleep specialist, speak to a crowd of a few hundred people, mostly in their late twenties and thirties, many with bag-rimmed eyes and other telltale signs of the sleep-deprived. They hung on his every word, and I could see why. Ferber presents as a mixture of the kindly and the authoritative, half pediatrician at the bedside with homilies and anecdotes, half professor at the podium with graphs and tables.

Ferber is famously an advocate of a disciplined consistency in getting children into bed and keeping them there through the night with a minimum of intervention, even if it requires waiting out a certain amount of wailing. A key to success, he emphasized to the audience, is to make sure that if the child wakes up at night, it will be to the same environment as the one in which he fell asleep—don't rock the child to sleep in a well-lit den and expect him to react well to waking up three hours later alone in the dark, he explained. Imagine, Ferber said, what it might feel like to fall asleep in our beds and wake up on the floor in a strange room. What could be more distressing? Smiles and nods in the audience—*So* that's *why kids cry at night!* Moving on to the subject of nightly sleep cycles and how they can get out of whack, Ferber explained the counterintuitive notion that a child who is consistently having trouble falling asleep when put to bed can usually be righted via a later bedtime and fewer hours of sleep—the late hour leaves the child unusually tired, so she'll fall asleep more easily, and because she'll be sleep-deprived the next day, she'll fall asleep at earlier and earlier times night by night until she's on a normal schedule. In a long question-and-answer session during which at-wit's-end parents peppered him with richly varying tales of their insatiable feeders, nonstop babblers, grim screamers, escape artists, and many more incarnations of the young and the restless, Ferber repeatedly played the later-bedtime card, and everyone seemed pleased with and grateful for the advice.

I'm a fan of Ferber's ideas, and in fact my own kids were more or less successfully "Ferberized" into sleeping through the night. I enjoyed his talk and found him utterly convincing as I listened. But in the time it took to get from my seat to the auditorium door after his presentation, I started to have second thoughts. Yes, I would find it highly disturbing to wake up in a place other than where I fell asleep. But my children, and those of every parent I've known, routinely fell asleep in a bewildering variety of environments, including cars, strollers, backpacks, friends' homes, and more, only to wake up in their own cribs or beds without complaint. As much as Ferber's hypothetical analogy hit home, it seemed on reflection to say nothing about how children sleep. And putting children to bed later? I think most parents experiment with that trick, whether they intend to or not, when evening events conspire to prevent sticking to the bedtime schedule. The results are not always pretty—children put to bed late can become overtired and nearly sleep-proof for hours, as well as out of sorts and hard to keep awake the next day. I'm sure it works with some kids, but I couldn't imagine it being the sort of panacea it seemed to be during Ferber's talk.

It wasn't the first time I've been struck by how nuggets of mass experts' advice that feel nearly epiphanic when you hear them can fall apart on even slightly closer inspection. In my research on the get-organized industry a few years ago, I found that organizing gurus are able to keep audiences of normally sharp and skeptical business executives enthralled with advice that can be seen with just a moment's careful thought to make almost no sense whatsoever—for example, setting aside an hour a day for dealing with all phone calls (as if you can control when other people are available to talk), avoiding desk clutter by immediately acting on every piece of paper that crosses your desk (as if you can afford to deal with expense reports when you're up against an urgent deadline), or never checking e-mail in the morning (as if the world will wait for you to get around to whatever crises might be pulsing radioactively in your in-box). And some expert dieting rules, though almost certainly more likely to cause problems than promote long-term weight loss, can reverberate in the public for months or even years, be it drinking large quantities of water, eating enormous breakfasts, or cutting out fruit. What is it that draws us to this sort of advice, even when our personal experience, common sense, or a few minutes of research into actual evidence ought to be enough to warn us that the advice is probably flawed?

Sometimes it's the expert himself that we're sold on. An expert's reputation, credentials, and style can all play a role in the reception we give the advice. Ferber was so well thought of by the audience when I saw him, and he carried such a confident, pleasant, wise demeanor, that I think he could have urged us to wear fright wigs when going to a crying child and most of us would have considered it. We aren't all won over by the *same* experts, of course. Expert appeal can split to a certain extent among political, cultural, and philosophical lines, for example. Liberals in the United States and Europe tend to be especially impressed with scientists and other academics, while an anti-intellectual streak runs through some conservative circles, leaving a chunk of these parts of the world suspicious of what most academics have to say. (Or, as Richard Nixon once grumbled within range of an Oval Office tape recorder, "The professors are the enemy, professors are the enemy.") Many conservatives, to continue these gross generalizations, perhaps tend to pay at least a bit more attention to the advice of less highly credentialed popular gurus, media pundits, and religious figures than do liberals—though there's a sizable, new-agey core of support among liberals for alternative medicine and for positive-thinking movements such as *The Secret*. In a 2000 survey of the British public sponsored by the United Kingdom's Office of Science and Technology and the Wellcome Trust, 56 percent of respondents agreed that "we depend too much on science and not enough on faith."[1] Still, the poll showed broad respect for what scientists do, with 75 percent of respondents stating they're "amazed" by scientists' achievements. Apparently, though, people are left to form their opinions of scientists based on what they can learn about them through the mass media or word of mouth, given that a 2005 U.S. poll conducted by the nonprofit health care–advocacy group Research!America found that 82 percent of respondents said they didn't personally know any scientists.[2]

In any case, most of us seem willing to put our faith in *some* form of mass expert. Well, of course we are. How could we avoid it? We're brought up under the spell of what we might call the "*Wizard of Oz* effect"—starting with our parents, and then on to teachers, and then to the authoritative voices our teachers introduce us to in textbooks, and then to the mass experts whose words we see our parents hanging on in the newspapers and on TV, we're progressively steeped throughout our upbringing in the notion that there are people in the world who know much, much more than we do, and that we ought to take their word for whatever it is they say is so. Evolution may well have primed our brains for trusting experts. The advantage to recognizing that some people have more experience and insight than others seems obvious, and (as I detail in Appendix 2) it's hard to find evidence of societies anywhere at any point in history that didn't make room for the ascendance of and dependence on mass experts. What's more, there's a hint of genetic influence on our faith in experts: neuroscientists have isolated a chemical found in the human brain called oxytocin that seems to affect our willingness to trust others—it was squirted like a nasal decongestant up the noses of people in game-playing studies, and those people were quicker than nonsquirters to turn small sums of money over to other game players to invest on their behalf.[3] (Perhaps Bernard Madoff and his representatives slathered it on before meeting with potential clients.)

We're not all equally trusting of experts. For example, Paul Slovic, a psychology researcher at the University of Oregon, found in studies that the percentage of white males who endorse bowing to the viewpoints of the authoritative few is higher than that of women or that of nonwhite males. "Those people thought we should leave decisions to experts and let them run things," he told me. But placing *some* level of trust in *some* form of expertise is fairly ubiquitous. Even experts themselves turn around and put their faith in überexperts, when they ought to know better. In 2000 the Japanese archaeologist Shinichi Fujimura revealed the secret technique that had led him to an astounding string of ancient stoneware finds for which he had become legendary in the field and even in the Japanese public: he was caught burying stoneware that he planned to later "find." Numerous archaeologists later confessed to having long considered the appearance of many of Fujimura's finds spectacularly inconsistent with their supposed ages but couldn't see challenging an expert who was so much more prestigious than themselves.

We may all invest different levels of trust in different sorts of experts. But given two similar sorts of experts with differing advice, why might any one of us prefer the advice of one expert over the other? In other words, what makes certain advice appealing in and of itself?

There are consultants for everything, I suppose. I know, for instance, that there are consultants who specialize in getting magazines to sell well on the newsstand, because I sat in on a talk one gave some years back. Dreaming up magazine covers that will entice people into a purchase is a bit of a black art, and it's a skill more highly prized than you might think in an age where overall physical magazine readership is being steadily whittled down by the Internet, and newsstand sales of most magazines are dwarfed by subscription sales—only about a tenth of *Time* magazine's circulation comes from the newsstand, for example. But newsstand sales are regarded as an important surrogate measurement of a magazine's health, because they serve as an issue-to-issue signal to advertisers of where the buzz is, and magazines make their profits by selling advertising, not by selling copies.

The magazine-cover expert I heard wasted no time in disabusing the journalists in the room of the quaint notion that newsstand sales have much to do with brilliant turns of phrase, the tackling of bold topics, or the promise of rich storytelling or clever analysis. There are only two sure bets when it comes to getting magazines off the shelves and into people's hands, he explained: photos of young, attractive celebrities or models, and headlines placed high on the cover that follow this template—"The [number between six and thirteen] tips [or secrets, rules, etc.] for [aspect of the world the reader would like to master]." This advice isn't just for celebrity gossip, lifestyle, and trade magazines. Here are some headlines I found in just a few minutes of online browsing:

American Lawyer: "Four Essential Elements of a Strong Law
   Firm Culture"
Fast Company: "The 6 Myths of Creativity"
Scientific American: "Seven Paths to Regulating Privacy"

It's not going out on a limb to say we love advice that seems simple. I have trouble thinking of any expert advice that's gotten any sort of traction in any segment of the public anywhere that could be put in the form "the 138 things you might have to do to have some chance of partly achieving your goal, depending on which of these 29 conditions best describe you and your situation." Instead, we look for the twelve steps, the seven habits, and, of course, the secret—that one-step recipe that enables any person to achieve any type of success under any conditions. We want our expert advice boiled down to ABC's, essentials, executive summaries, and guides for idiots and dummies. To be sure, if we could handle all the complications, we wouldn't *need* experts. But if there's a happy medium, most of us don't appear interested in it.

Here are some other characteristics we seem to look for in expert advice:

Clear-cut: Most of us would prefer to be told what the right answer is, without confusing ifs, ands, or buts. Qualifications that require matching different answers to different conditions, or that may render the advice entirely inappropriate to some situations, are an unwelcome complication and make the advice seem less fundamental. An expert who hedges his bets, after all, must not really be on top of the matter. It's more reassuring to be told which medical·treatment is best, for example, rather than having to wrestle with long lists of pros and cons that have to be carefully weighed and may not clearly favor a particular choice.

Doubt-free: We can be turned off by experts who don't transmit full confidence in their advice. Why listen to an expert who's not sure if she's right? I remember being struck by the confident tone of the resident real-estate expert trotted out in early 2008 by one of the major network morning news shows to assure prospective buyers that housing prices had just about bottomed out and that it was a swell time to run out and grab a home. For sure!

Universal: How confusing and bothersome to have to sort through a forest of choices in order to select one that's specific to our personality, experience, age, ethnicity, symptoms, finances, life goals, and so on. To accept that only bespoke advice works is to accept that most advice out there simply doesn't apply. One-size-fits-all advice, on the other hand, not only is easier to apply but has the ring of important truth. Researchers and gurus hawking diet books rarely take the trouble to suggest that their favored strategies are likely to work well with mere fractions of the population.

Upbeat: Most of us would prefer not to hear that we simply can't fix something troublesome in our lives or, if there are solutions, that they are elusive, murky long shots, or difficult compromises, or unpleasant to implement. Psychologists have long known that most people drift toward positive points of view, even to the point of being irrational, and gloomy advice can clash with this "optimism bias," as it's called. In 1952 the link between cigarette smoking and lung cancer was nailed down beyond any reasonable doubt and splashed across headlines, and after that the evidence and publicity just kept building. How did the public deal with the solidly supported finding that a popular, highly enjoyable habit was a good way to invite a gruesome form of premature death? In large part by refusing to accept it. A Gallup poll in 1958 indicated that only 44 percent of the U.S. public believed in the smoking-cancer link, and as late as 1968 nearly 30 percent of the country still thought the link was baloney.[4]

Actionable: What good are expert findings that merely explain things? People usually want to be told what to *do* to improve their situation. As Woody Allen once put it, "You want to feel you can control things to some degree, because if you can't, life is scarier." Dale Carnegie's *How to Win Friends and Influence People*, seventy-third on the all-time global list of bestselling books in any language, triumphed by laying out a simple formula (smile; listen) that is supposed to allow anyone to accomplish what must surely be one of the least-formulizable tasks in all of existence: being likable. The book still sells well—it was roosting in Amazon's top 100 as of early 2009—though it faces competition from efforts more closely tailored to our impatient times, such as *How to Make People Like You in 90 Seconds or Less.*

Palatable: Most of us are loaded with biases, beliefs, and prejudices. It's asking a lot to try to get people to swallow advice that challenges these ingrained ideas, no matter how grounded the advice may be. Thus many conservatives continue to put their faith in abstinence programs and virginity pledges as a way of limiting sex, pregnancy, and sexually transmitted diseases among teens, even though experts continue to pile up evidence that these approaches don't reduce the rate of sex among adolescents and lead to higher rates of pregnancy and STDs.[5] Many liberals, on the other hand, seem constitutionally incapable of giving fair consideration to, or in some cases even acknowledging, expert evidence and arguments (even if in the minority) that question whether we are really in the midst of a man-made global climate crisis. Animal research, marijuana usage, stem-cell research—experts who weigh in on these and many more hot-button topics win mindshare only to the extent that their conclusions validate what people already believe.

Putting together these characteristics of appealing advice gives us what we might call the "certainty principle": we're heavily biased to advice that is simple, clear-cut, actionable, universal, and palatable. If an expert can explain how any of us is sure to make things better via a few simple, pleasant steps, then plenty of people are going to listen. No wonder we like that second doctor.

And there are other ways experts can make their advice connect with us. Here are some of the most important:

Dramatic claims: Expert advice and findings are far more likely to capture our attention and get us rooting for them if they promise to make big, positive changes in our life. Cures for cancer and other major diseases, new forms of energy, techniques for significant, permanent weight loss, opportunities for large returns on an investment—these kinds of claims take over headlines and conversations, and raise our hopes.

Stories: Sometimes expert advice doesn't hit home until we hear it placed in the context of someone's experience or in a compelling narrative. We love to learn about the patient who was cured, the woman who lost 110 pounds, the couple who made a million dollars. When Ferber asked us to think about what it would feel like to wake up somewhere else, he was pulling our thinking down from the abstract to the visceral, and it scored points. When we can relate at a personal level, we find the information easier to believe. For that reason, political campaigns today are almost entirely woven around simple stories and narratives that obscure the more subtle and complex realities—Barack Obama "pals around with terrorists," and John McCain is "out of touch." And sometimes science is more about stories than facts, too. When, in 1930, a young amateur astronomer named Clyde Tombaugh at the Lowell Observatory somehow picked out a dim object shifting position against a field of stars, the observatory churned out press releases noting that the object had been found close to where the observatory's deceased founder, Percival Lowell, had loudly predicted a giant "Planet X" was lurking, based on tiny wiggles observed in the orbits of Uranus and Neptune suggesting that a large object was tugging on them. (Lowell had even more loudly claimed that long scars vaguely visible on the surface of Mars were canals built by Martians.) The discovery of what was apparently a ninth planet electrified the world, and the newcomer was named Pluto—symbolized by "PL," Lowell's initials—to honor Lowell's brilliant prediction. It all made for a wonderful story, but the truth was a bit different: Lowell's calculations had been flawed, the wiggles he had based them on never existed, Tombaugh hadn't focused his search on that predicted location, and the new object's dimness was consistent not so much with that of a giant planet as with that of a comet. Other comets in similar orbits were found in the 1990s, making it clear that Pluto was just one of the larger members of a belt of these small rock-and-ice balls, and Pluto's planetary status was officially revoked in 2006. But the excellent story of Planet X had kept Pluto in planethood for three-quarters of a century.[6]

Numbers: Numbers add a sense of precision and authority to an observation, even if entirely illusory. Anyone can insist that one pain reliever works better than another, but surely only a well-informed expert would be in a position to claim that a pain reliever reduced patient discomfort by 73 percent, compared to 46 percent for another medication. In fact, people are almost three times more likely to believe an expert finding when it's presented in terms of numbers. (Just kidding.)

Retroactive fixes: We all understand the problem with locking the barn door after the horse has wandered off, but most of us are eager to see experts do it anyway. Whenever something traumatic happens, we pay special attention to advice aimed at preventing it from happening again, even if there's little chance it will happen, or at least happen in the same way. No one paid much attention to experts who warned of what a freakishly powerful hurricane might do until Katrina struck New Orleans, after which time we couldn't get enough of their wisdom, though no hurricane since has come close to warranting it. Warnings about the risks of terrorists converting jetliners into flying suicide bombs had been circulating for years in law-enforcement, aviation, and security circles but weren't acted on until after 9/11, at which point preventing such attacks became a focus of Homeland Security, even though other types of threats are now considered more likely.

When advice fits the certainty principle and gets dressed up along the lines just mentioned, we end up with advice that's highly *resonant*. It's advice that gets our attention and strikes the right notes with us; it's easy to like it. Whether or not it's advice that's especially likely to be right doesn't necessarily enter the equation.

Why do we get so many conflicting opinions about obesity from medical researchers and diet gurus? Ioannidis offers one explanation:

there are as many as three thousand different factors that can come into play when trying to understand the causes and consequences of obesity, he estimates, and individual experts tend to focus on just one or two of them, with different experts zeroing in on different factors. In other words, they try to force various simple answers onto a complex question—no wonder we just end up being misled.

We happen to be complex creatures living in a complex world, so why would we expect answers to *any* interesting questions to be simple? In particular, the problems that lead us to turn to experts—how can we become healthy, wealthy, and fulfilled; how can we get our businesses and nation to flourish—tend to be bound up in extraordinarily high levels of complexity. Experts operate at the very boundary of the unanalyzable, and that's as it should be; were there simple truths to be had, we would have come across them long ago and might not even need experts. And that gives us a clue to recognizing advice that's likely to be right, or at least on the right track: it will be complex, it will come with many qualifications, and it will be highly dependent on conditions. Because of all the ifs, ands, or buts, it will be difficult to act on. Because our beliefs tend to be simplistic and optimistic, it will probably be incompatible with them. In other words, good expert advice will be at odds with every aspect of the sort of advice that draws us to it.

But that clash between resonant advice and advice that's likely to be good apparently doesn't stop experts from offering what at least sounds like the straightforward, complete, one-size-fits-all answers we're looking for. That's especially true of informal and pop experts—the less credentialed, nonacademic experts whose careers are tied to prominence in the mass media and on lecture circuits, be it an alternative-health guru, a fitness trainer, or a mediagenic business tycoon. These experts can't thrive if their advice doesn't resonate with us; their careers are dependent on connecting with the public. Who would buy their books, read articles about them, or watch them on television if they offered advice that had no appeal to us, no matter how right it sounded? And if the masses aren't paying attention to them, then they're not mass experts. For informal experts, simplistic, universal, doubt-free advice—often whipped up without the benefit of evidence other than personal experience, anecdotes, and intuition—is a key to success. Here's a small sample of advice offered up by celebrity experts, taken from their own published pronouncements:

Donald Trump:
> Love what you do.
> Never give up.
> Stay focused.
> Think positively.

Mega-church pastor and life coach Joel Osteen, author of the bestseller *Become a Better You:*
> Keep pressing forward.
> Develop better relationships.
> Form better habits.
> Stay passionate about life.

Radio relationship counselor "Dr. Laura" Schlessinger:
> Never say no to a husband who wants sex.
> Never force a man to wash dishes.
> Stay together for the sake of the children.

There's no evidence that this sort of highly resonant advice is likely to gain much for the majority of people who attempt to follow it, though it might invite a placebo effect—that is, the advice itself might do little, but the advice follower's belief that it will work might create at least the perception of success, or even inspire real success. (Many would argue that that's good enough—I disagree, but you can decide for yourself.) Even if it doesn't help many people, highly resonant advice is usually harmless—assuming it doesn't keep followers from better advice that might be at hand. In the case of advice that, like Schlessinger's views on sex and housework, some of us would find eccentric, if not objectionable, it's hard to imagine anyone taking it seriously if he weren't already predisposed to thinking along those lines. More generic advice such as Trump's and Osteen's—often just riffs on the classic, endlessly recycled positive-thinking and "give it your best shot" themes—also tends to merely emphasize the sort of attitudes most of us recognize as desirable in the first place. In other words, highly resonant advice often simply echoes what we've believed or suspected all along.

Highly resonant advice isn't always benign, though, particularly when serious health issues and large financial investments may be involved. When the television financial guru Jim Cramer makes enthusiastic but wildly erratic market predictions, people can lose their life savings. And when the actress Jenny McCarthy describes in a bestselling book, on the talk-show circuit, and on the Internet how her child "recovered" from autism through diet and alternative medical treatments, she is inflicting highly dubious advice on vulnerable parents, with the possible result that children may be deprived of urgently needed effective therapies.

Academic, medical, and other well-credentialed, formal experts usually aren't as quick to lapse into resonant advice. But it's not always easy to tell the research laureates from the gurus. Some well-credentialed scientists do indeed whip up at least semiresonant advice—backed by research, to be sure—and take it to the public, usually via popular books, à la Ferber. Gimmicky diets are a perennial favorite of researcher-gurus, with dozens of science-backed diet books lining the shelves at any time. Among some of the recent approaches you can choose from are a "waist management" strategy (Michael Roizen and Mehmet Oz of the Cleveland Clinic and Columbia University, respectively), a "volumetrics" strategy (Barbara Rolls, Penn State), a "food instinct" strategy (Susan Roberts, Tufts), or the "Shangri-La Diet" (Seth Roberts, Berkeley, who is refreshingly open about the fact that his research mostly consisted of trying his olive oil–swigging diet out on himself—it worked!). The Harvard researchers Jorge Chavarro and Walter Willett managed to hit two advice sweet spots with one book: *The Fertility Diet*. And why shouldn't academic and medical researchers get in on the guru game? Though it may not be saying much, I'd certainly agree their advice is likely to be less wrong and more useful, on average, than that of celebrity gurus. But given what we've seen about the unreliability of the evidence researchers assemble, I wouldn't recommend putting much faith in their advice, either.

One important difference between researchers and gurus is that while gurus often traffic in exotic, dramatic claims, researchers tend to avoid making extreme claims in much the same way that pilots think twice before reporting UFOs—doing so is a good way to be branded a flake by colleagues. Thus, while Deepak Chopra became wildly popular hawking techniques he insisted could dramatically slow the aging process, antiaging claims have been a reputational minefield for several academic researchers—including the Harvard Medical School near-celebrity researcher David Sinclair, who was publicly chastised in 2008 for allowing his name to be attached to unproven claims for a commercial version of resveratrol, the red-wine ingredient he and his colleagues found to apparently slow signs of aging in mice, at least in massive doses.

But credentialed experts may be pushed in the direction of the certainty principle in other ways. For example, they often fail to properly express doubts about their own and, in some cases, others' findings. That's partly out of fear that doing so might erode the public's trust in their work and perhaps in all of science, ruffle colleagues' feathers, or endanger funding. The retired industrial and academic toxicology researcher Iain Purchase told me that though his colleagues fretted over the public picking up on their uncertainty, he himself found that laypeople were likely to be *less* distrustful of scientists when the scientists confessed to uncertainties. But experts' tendency to stay mum about doubt may also be due in part to the fact that they can remain surprisingly ignorant about what it is they ought to be doubting. Studies have shown that experts asked to determine the uncertainty in their findings tend to underestimate it—and continue to do so even after the problem is pointed out to them.[7]

In many ways, formal experts may actually do a *worse* job than gurus. Tufts' Sternberg has studied some of the problems with expertise and contends that because being a high-level expert requires years of developing and polishing a very deep but narrow knowledge base, experts often have more trouble adapting to new ideas, data, techniques, and opportunities than generalists do. "If you think you've been successful at something for a long time, it's very hard to change," he told me. Overspecialization can also lead to a lack of perspective, leaving some experts emphasizing the small piece of a problem they happen to be single-mindedly chipping away at, drawing attention from bigger questions and more promising avenues of exploration—as when, for example, economists continue to bicker over the best way to prevent a 1 percent rise in inflation when the economy is actually on the brink of a tailspin. And highly credentialed experts are typically far outshined by gurus when it comes to communicating clearly with the public. Surprisingly, the problem isn't always that experts are overly technical—an equally big problem, according to one study, is that experts often *under*estimate the public's knowledge and end up pushing their ideas out in such simple terms that they fail to communicate much of anything.[8] What's more, there's the issue that formal experts tend to want to present themselves as thinking in terms of hard evidence untainted by opinion, emotions, or drama, while much of the public relates better to stories and exciting ideas and has relatively little means for or interest in evaluating hard evidence. In that sense, when formal experts try to communicate their work to the public, it's a bit like a person with Asperger's syndrome trying to advise a schizophrenic.

Of course, just because *many* or even *most* experts fall prey to such problems doesn't mean the problems won't be attenuated before they do much damage. That's because experts, like most of us, don't operate entirely independently. Rather, they tend to work in communities of experts. And, as we all know, communities are great at smoothing out the wrinkles that wayward individuals might introduce. Aren't they?

CHAPTER FOUR

The Idiocy of Crowds

Even when the experts all agree, they may well be mistaken.
— BERTRAND RUSSELL

I n the late eighteenth century, the Frenchman Marie-Jean-Antoine-Nicolas de Caritat, alias Marquis de Condorcet, took to mulling over the question of whether juries are more likely to render correct verdicts than are individuals. Condorcet started with the assumption that people on average have at least a slightly better than even chance of rendering the right verdict—after all, what sort of jury pool would be composed mostly of people who would probably come to the wrong conclusion? He then whipped up a bit of clever math to suggest that the answer is yes, juries are more likely than individuals to get it right. To understand why, you need to imagine that a coin is subtly weighted so that it comes up heads 51 percent of the time. If the coin is flipped once, or even a few times, that 1 percent advantage for heads won't matter much—the coin is, for all practical purposes, as likely to favor tails. But if the coin is flipped a thousand times, that 1 percent difference will assert itself, so that it's much more likely that heads will outnumber tails. In the same way, as the number of decision makers who on average have just a slightly better than even chance of being right increases, the chances that the group's majority vote will be right approaches certainty. In other words, the "Condorcet jury theorem," as that insight came to be known, offers a mathematical argument that while a single individual with borderline good judgment may be about as likely to blow a decision as nail one, combining many such individuals into a group drives toward an assurance of a correct decision.

And that result dovetails nicely with how most of us see the world—namely, we expect the group to do better than individuals. Of course, we know some individuals are blessed with exceptional talent and judgment that groups can't match, and occasionally group behavior degenerates to mob rule, mass delusion, or fealty to Hitlers and McCarthys. But we're brought up on the notion that, generally speaking, two heads are better than one, team spirit trumps the self-involved, and the more power to the people, the better. The primacy of groups and teamwork is so ingrained that we seldom stop to think about it. In an age of instant messaging, wikis, social-networking sites such as Facebook and MySpace, and videoconferencing on cell phones, collaboration and consensus are gaining yet more currency. We can, and often do, literally get almost *everyone* to weigh in, all the time, whether it's by phone, e-mail, website click, or text message. There will always be fools and miscreants and people who are just plain wrong, but when we mix enough of us together, we get, as James Surowiecki nicely phrases it in the title of his bestselling book, "the wisdom of crowds."

All this would seem to bode well for expertise, given that most experts don't operate as lone wolves. They set up shop in universities, medical centers, consultancies, corporations, and government agencies; they're attached to societies, trade groups, management staffs, and advisory boards; they work directly with colleagues, students, employees, bosses, funders, and journal editors. Not only do they join or lead teams but their teams collaborate with other teams, sometimes forming vast networks of experts—the first several pages of the physics paper reporting the discovery of the top quark in 1997 consisted entirely of the names of the more than one thousand physicists connected to the project. And whatever putative wisdom experts produce is subject to the up-or-down thumbs of consensus, be it of fellow experts, clients, journals, the mass media, or simply the public.

Perhaps, then, I've been misleading you by calling attention to the foibles of experts as individuals. So what if many, perhaps even most, experts are biased, and prone to err and distort, if not simply cheat? Surely the sea of collaborators, overseers, assistants, advice disseminators, and advice consumers in which these less trustworthy experts operate is healthily seeded with sharp, objective, honest, and meticulous folk. And that being the case, the wisdom of the crowd must be poised to save the day. In the end, the best expert findings and opinions will be brought to the fore while the junk is filtered out, all courtesy of the magic of community.

Just one problem: the general effectiveness of groups, teamwork, collaboration, and consensus is largely a myth. Crowds, far from being reliably wise, turn out to be at least as good at discouraging and suppressing the production and dissemination of excellent work as highlighting it, and tend to bring some of the worst work to the top. Not only do group effects usually fail to protect us from flawed expertise but they introduce entirely new kinds of defects above and beyond what experts inflict on us. Crowds aren't the solution to bad expert advice; they're a big part of the problem.

It's harder than you might think to find someone who knows much about the Condorcet jury theorem, given that it has been knocking around for more than two centuries. But I had to only listen for a few minutes to Christian List at the London School of Economics, as he explained to me his work on the theorem, to understand why most experts steer clear of it, even though it has much to suggest about how group size affects whether or not a decision is likely to be right—an important consideration not only in the legal arena but also in business and especially in politics.

The problem is that while the marquis's original proposition is simple enough for an astute seventh grader to master, any attempt to even slightly broaden the theorem to make it applicable to a wider range of situations reveals it to be the intellectual equivalent of an exploding cigar—one second you're puffing contentedly on some elementary probability calculations, and the next you're staring down the end of your nose at a jagged, smoldering clod of advanced mathematics. Since most mathematicians don't set foot in political problems, and political scientists don't often embrace serious mathematics, Condorcet's explorations end up the territory of a few unusually multidisciplinarian experts such as List, who happens to be a mathematical political scientist.

A youngish- and austere-looking man who works out of an equally austere-looking office, List seems to take on more color as he describes the ways he and his colleagues have tried to stretch, squeeze, and clarify the dynamic of Condorcet's deceptively uncomplicated theorem. Among their probings: Are large groups more likely to render *fair* decisions—that is, decisions that best represent the judgment of the various individuals—or *correct* decisions? What happens to group decisions when individuals can influence one another? Can Condorcet's theorem assure a *best* group decision when there are many choices and no one right answer? Far from straightforward, the answers to these questions depend on a bewildering collection of variables, conditions, and assumptions—and even then, different scholars who have wrestled with the knotty mathematical logic come to different conclusions. I won't try to do justice to the debates here, but List assured me that one point is clear and indisputable: Condorcet jury theorem is not the unqualified plug for group wisdom that it seems at first glance. Far from it.

Actually, Condorcet himself noted that his theorem can be as quick to ensure a wrong group decision as a right one. The hitch lies with the assumption that the individuals in the group are on average at least a bit more likely than not to come up with the right answer on their own. It sounds reasonable enough, at least with regard to juries. In a trial there are usually just two choices—innocent or guilty—so you're starting off with a 50 percent chance of being right before any lawyers or witnesses open their mouths. If there's even merely a smidgen of good guidance in the evidence, it should be enough to tip judgment into the more-likely-to-be-right category. Many other types of judgments, on the other hand, require sifting through only murky and even outright misleading evidence to decide between two possible conclusions. Indeed, the sorts of questions that experts tackle not only tend to depend on some of the most confusing evidence but are often characterized by having far more possible wrong answers than right answers. Which vitamins and foods are likely to fend off cancer? What marketing scheme will return the biggest sales boost? What would destabilizing North Korea accomplish? How do I get my child to sleep through the night? What's the best way to safely invest money and still get a decent return? For many of these highly challenging questions, the chance of an individual expert coming up with the right answer is most likely less than 50 percent—maybe a lot less.

The Condorcet jury theorem doesn't claim that pooling the judgment of the individuals enhances their decision-making abilities or corrects for their deficiencies. It merely points out that having a lot of decision makers cuts down the odds that a fluke will tilt the ultimate decision. The effect of the group is essentially to amplify, or lock in, whatever proclivity toward rightness or wrongness exists on average in the individuals. But Condorcet recognized that if the individuals in the group are on average even slightly more likely to seize on a wrong answer than a right one, that tendency becomes *far* more likely in the group. While some of the individuals in this group may be smart enough, or intuitive enough, or hardworking enough, or lucky enough, to have an excellent shot at reaching the right conclusion, the Condorcet jury theorem virtually ensures that the pooled opinion of the group will still be wrong. This isn't good news for expertise, given all the ways we've seen that individual experts can go wrong.

On the other hand, the Condorcet jury theorem, at least in its simplest form, relies on a blatantly unrealistic model of how most groups make decisions. Specifically, it ignores interactions within the group—for example, ways in which those who are right may convince those who are wrong to change their minds. Many of us have been on juries where the stances of several or even most of the jurors were flipped by a particularly strong or reasoned voice who helped others to see the light (or have seen the movie *Twelve Angry Men*). This sort of interaction is often the very purpose of a group—not merely to tally the individual judgments but to craft a combined judgment through a process of give-and-take, and persuasion. Condorcet jury theorem notwithstanding, it may not really matter if individual experts are on average more likely than not to be wrong. In interacting with less flawed colleagues, they may be set right, or at least prevented from spoiling a good group decision.

A proclivity for putting our heads together to figure things out is hardwired into our brains, or so studies have found.[1] In fact, chimps work together to solve problems, and so does at least one type of bird—the rook.[2] Experts are no exception. Few question that science, for example, is a collaborative affair; sociologists have been particularly emphatic on this score, some even suggesting that science is about collaboration and not much else.* But putting that more controversial view aside, collaboration is usually regarded by scientists themselves as an important element of what they do. In fact, to judge by what ends up in journals, scientists would appear to have acquired an unbridled devotion to collaboration. As the University of Puget Sound scientist and historian Mott Greene has noted, the average number of authors per contribution to *Nature* has quadrupled since 1950. Today no one raises an eyebrow at 100 plus–author papers, and lone authors, once the rule in science, have become something of a rarity. That may not, however, be entirely because scientists are convinced that collaboration results in better science. It's well known in academic circles that collaboration is a great way to jack up your recognition in the community—why slave away on your own work and get cited for only one paper, when for the same time commitment you can collaborate to get your name on several?

Our instinct is to applaud people for teaming up. And yet it's not hard to show there are problems with collaboration. For starters, there is the question of simple efficiency. Research in the 1990s by the Purdue psychologist Kip Williams and his colleagues documented the phenomenon of "social loafing"—that is, the ways in which people in groups tend simply not to try as hard as individuals working on their own. Or consider that paragon of group magic, the brainstorming session. Bernard Nijstad, an organizational psychologist at the University of Amsterdam who studies collaboration, explains that if you take a group of twelve people, and have half brainstorm together on a topic while the

---

* The French sociologist Bruno Latour, for example, who spent two years in the 1970s as an embedded observer in a Salk Institute lab, has portrayed scientific findings in part as a sort of group storytelling ritual. Some scientists still grit their teeth at the mention of his name.

other six go it alone, all twelve will usually agree that the group experience was the more productive one—even though the people working alone almost always end up with more good ideas. Why? Nijstad believes it's because people in groups spend most of their time listening to others rather than thinking on their own, while lone brainstormers are forced to stew in productive but unpleasant silence. Thinking back on the experience, the group brainstormers remember a constant flow of ideas, while the loners remember the agony of brain freeze. "When you're alone, it's painfully clear when you're not producing, but in a group you can just sit there and not notice you're not contributing," Nijstad told me. No wonder we love to work in groups.

Various researchers in different fields have studied the ability of committees and groups to get useful work accomplished and meet important goals, and most end up concluding that the larger the group, the less that gets done. Some decades ago the British historian Cyril Northcote Parkinson examined the question at length and concluded, only partly waggishly, that increasing group size can be characterized by a "coefficient of inefficiency." In 2008 three physicists at the Medical University of Vienna updated this work by gathering data on government cabinets in 197 countries—they found that larger cabinets were roughly correlated with decreasing health, wealth, and education in a nation and with the likelihood of a cabinet being deadlocked in disagreement.[3]

Not all research indicates that groups always degrade performance. Looking at students presented with a logic puzzle, researchers found that groups of three did in fact solve the puzzle more efficiently than did three individuals working separately, though groups of four or five students weren't able to do better than the groups of three—suggesting that in some well-defined situations, at least, a group can be effective as long as it's kept extremely small.[4] But, in general, the notion that individuals tend to outthink, outdecide, and outperform groups is so well established that it isn't even studied much anymore. "The average person certainly believes teamwork trumps individual work, but the evidence says otherwise," says Natalie Allen, an organizational psychologist at the University of Western Ontario who has studied what she calls the "romance of teams." "We've been trying to find out what seduces us into thinking teams are so wonderful."

If the biggest problem with groups was simply a lack of efficiency, we wouldn't be so bad off. No one's complaining that experts aren't churning out *enough* advice.

Unfortunately, things usually get worse when the output of a group or community is judged not by its quantity but by its quality. Nearly four decades of research have exquisitely detailed the ineffectiveness of groups. The problems with collaborative and community thinking have been repeatedly highlighted by a stream of studies, starting with the Yale psychology researcher Irving Janis's classic examination of "groupthink" back in 1972, which showed how groups could reach terrible decisions that none of the individuals in the group ever would have made on his own. As Janis and many others have shown—and as most of us know all too well—groups are frequently dominated not by people who are most likely to be right but rather by people who are belligerent, persuasive, persistent, manipulative, or forceful. Those who are even mildly adept at getting people to go along with them can quickly form small alliances of viewpoint that may in turn convince others to join in, eventually swaying even those with doubts—most of us don't want to be the odd man out. (Some of us may recall the old *Candid Camera* segment in which an unsuspecting victim steps onto an elevator filled with several in-on-the-joke riders who turn to face the back of the elevator, leading the victim, clearly against her better judgment, to do the same.)

As Colin Camerer, a decision-science researcher at the California Institute of Technology, told me, "Groups distribute responsibility for being wrong, so that individuals drop their guard against errors and bad judgment." Researchers have noted that the larger the number of people who contribute to a research project, the greater the chances that at least one of them will fabricate, misanalyze, or otherwise distort data, and the harder it will be to track down the culprit.[5,6]

Once a majority opinion is formed, even highly competent, confident people are reluctant to voice opinions that go against it, thanks to the notion, drilled into our heads from elementary school up through the workplace, that forging cooperation and agreement is critical. "There's a cultural norm of how we're supposed to behave as professionals, and part of it is that we're overly trained in consensus," says Daniel Eisenstadt, the director of the Philadelphia-based private-equity firm CMS. Eisenstadt, a Harvard Business School graduate, points out that students at graduate schools are expected to quickly adapt themselves to a culture that favors building on others' opinions rather than challenging them while also absorbing the opinions of their instructors wholesale. And the pressure to achieve consensus doesn't apply to only genteel and abstract debate: of the ten deadliest plane crashes in history, cockpit tapes reveal that six of them — killing a total of some 2,400 people — took place with at least one crew member being fully aware of the mistake that was about to bring the plane down but staying mostly quiet because the rest of the crew thought differently. The fear of dissenting too strongly with fellow or senior experts only becomes magnified in a website, e-mail, or instant-messaging exchange, Eisenstadt notes, because participants know their comments can be saved and widely distributed. Instead of briefly offending six people at a meeting, you have the chance to enrage hundreds of people for years to come with your independent thinking.

Academic, financial, and clinical researchers submit to a pack mentality at least as easily as most sorts of groups or communities. "They go off together in the wrong direction, following one another like any collection of humans," says Peter Sheridan Dodds, a University of Vermont mathematician who also does work in sociology and biology, among other fields. Herd thinking can keep the community trudging along in one direction for years, resistant to all kinds of contrary evidence — and then quickly send it thundering off in a different direction. Christopher Gillberg, a child psychiatrist at Gothenburg University in Sweden and one of the world's leading experts on autism, has been studying the disorder for three decades, during which time he has seen the psychiatric community shift nearly in toto from insisting that autism is a narrowly defined and rare disorder associated with bad parenting to insisting that it is a brain flaw manifesting as almost any odd behavior, personality glitch, or communication problem in a very young child. The result is that autism has gone from being grossly underdiagnosed to heavily overdiagnosed, says Gillberg, whose own extensive studies over the years have indicated that the rate of autism in the population has remained steady at 0.7 percent. "There's a tendency for people in the field to believe in things if they've been told this is how it is, and they'll see it that way even if the reality is different," he told me. The pack mentality can also shift dramatically not just with time but with location: Laurence Robel, a child psychiatrist and autism researcher at the highly regarded Necker Children's Hospital in Paris, told me that most French autism experts look askance at the notion of providing autistic children with behavioral therapy, a reward-for-appropriate-behavior approach they regard as akin to animal training, and instead focus on psychotherapy to treat autism; experts in the United States and United Kingdom, on the other hand, are fairly unanimous and at least as adamant in taking precisely the opposite stance. Both sides, of course, have research backing them up.*

The phenomenon of groups clinging to the party line wouldn't be so bad if we could believe that the opinions that hold sway among groups tend to be the right ones. But Robert MacCoun, a University of California–Berkeley decision-making researcher who studies the various biases that can cloud expert judgment, pointed out to me that a wealth of sociological and psychological research, including his own, indicates that though there are many reasons certain ideas rather than others might survive the interactions in a group and therefore achieve consensus, being correct is not one of them. "Groups amplify bias, squash minority points of view, and can even overcome the correct point of view when it's the majority view," he told me. "In most situations, truth doesn't win out in groups."

The long U.S. housing bubble that burst toward the end of 2007, nearly wrecking the world's economies and leading to the worst recession since the 1930s, is a striking example of how expert communities can nurture and maintain utterly wrong and even near-delusional thinking. Yes, there were voices that warned housing was dangerously overpriced and that the inevitable crash would cause trouble for homeowners in hock up to their eyeballs and for the financial institutions that would be holding a lot of suddenly bad loans. But these voices of caution couldn't say exactly *when* the bust would occur, and some, including economists Robert Shiller and Nouriel Roubini, and researcher-author Nassim Nicholas Taleb, had been saying it for years. Meanwhile, everyone appeared to be doing so well heeding the many, many other voices that insisted the system was solid—too many, surely, to take

---

* Worldwide the tide has strongly turned toward behavioral therapy, for which the evidence is broader and far more solid.

seriously the notion that they were all dead wrong—that it would have seemed almost foolish to pay attention to the few doomsayers who appeared to be getting it wrong year after year.

Now, of course, in keeping with our bias toward retroactive fixes, the public and the media have anointed as sages experts such as Taleb for having "called" the bust. In a way they did, but in general we need to be careful about picking out certain experts as heroes after the fact, lest we fall into a potential crowd-related trap I call the "Hitchcock effect," after an episode of the old television show *Alfred Hitchcock Presents*. That story revolved around a man who receives a series of mailed predictions that all prove correct, at which point he is ready to trust this infallible predictor with his money—but as it turns out, the predictor had started off mailing various predictions to a large number of people, then focused each subsequent mailing on the increasingly smaller subset of people who had received only the predictions that happened to prove correct, until he had one victim who had by pure chance received all the winning predictions. It sounds like a far-fetched scheme, but in fact we often pick our leading experts this way—that is, we look back to see which expert among a field of many happened to call it right and then hold up that expert as having special insight. But we need to remember that if there are many experts predicting many things, some of those predictions will have to prove right, though it may be entirely a matter of luck or even *bad* judgment.* Many of us put enormous faith in, for example, those stock pickers and fund managers who, yes, can point to a long record of successful

---

* There are also non-crowd-related variations on this theme. Any one expert may be able to sort through her long history of various predictions and find the few that proved correct, holding these up to our attention while glossing over the others. Or an expert can make somewhat vague predictions, fortune-teller-style, and then sharpen them after the fact to make the predictions seem highly accurate.

calls—but such records almost invariably turn out to have been nothing more than a lucky streak, or a streak built on risky positions that were bound to end badly.* Thus the mutual funds given a top, five-star rating by fund-tracking firm Morningstar, based on a history of good returns, fell on average in 2008 about as much as the rest of the stock market did, and some fell farther. The hedge funds run by Citadel Investment Group, long celebrated for brilliant management leading to outstanding returns, lost more than half their value in 2008, compared to the 18 percent lost by the average hedge fund.

None of this is to say that Surowiecki and other boosters of crowd wisdom are entirely wrong. They just tend to cherry-pick the few sorts of situations where groups can in fact work pretty well. In groups in which individuals tend to deviate from the truth more or less randomly, the crowd can average things out in a useful way. Thus a crowd does a remarkably good job of estimating the temperature, and a group of investors will often outperform a single expert. In these cases, the bad opinions in the crowd tend to cancel out, so that the average is "wise." Google can tap a sea of websites to provide useful answers, and crowds have done a great job developing Linux and other "open source" software (programs created by scattered, informal groups that anyone can join)—but that's because, in these cases, useful contributions from the crowd can be readily leveraged, while noncontributors stay harmlessly out of the way.

Forming groups and tapping the masses make sense in certain well-defined circumstances. In some cases, it's more important to achieve buy-in to a decision than it is to get the best possible decision—for example, letting collaborators determine who will take on which tasks in a project, or allowing a community of experts

---

* Or naked fraud, as in the case of Bernard Madoff.

to vote on new ethics guidelines. Crowd participation is also useful when what's needed is to get as many ideas on the table as possible, without regard for how many of them are terrible—as, for example, when NASA solicited ideas from the public in 2006 for a new lunar-landing vehicle, hoping to end up with some interesting, lower-cost concepts among the likely ocean of duds (as well as to stir up excitement for the agency's planned return to the moon). Group successes, according to research, tend to depend on certain conditions: that a group is highly diverse, for example, and that there is little or no interaction between its members on the subject at hand. Unfortunately, these conditions rarely apply to expert crowds.*

So what does determine which expert ideas come to the front of the crowd? One way of answering that is to consider a twist on the Condorcet theorem. Suppose we have a group of twenty experts who separately produce findings, and let's be extremely generous and suppose that for each individual expert, the average chance of being right is 95 percent. What are the chances that at least one of the experts will be wrong? A straightforward calculation† shows it's pretty good, actually—about two out of three. The marquis might have put it this way: even if there is only a very small chance that any one individual in a group will be wrong, there is still a very good chance that the wrong answer

---

* Expert crowds might do better if there were a way to give the wisest, most honest, most diligent, experts more influence than others. Economists have come up with schemes for how the opinions of individuals in the group could be "weighted" in favor of the best and brightest, but even if the schemes proved reliable, it's hard to picture any expert fields putting up with them.

† The chances that one will be right are 95 percent, or 95 out of 100, or 0.95 out of one; that two will be right are (0.95 × 0.95) out of one; that three will be right are (0.95 × 0.95 × 0.95) out of one; and so on. Multiplying 0.95 by itself twenty times, which comes to about 0.36, gives the chances out of one that all twenty experts are right, which means the chances that not every one of the twenty is right are (1 − 0.36) out of one, or 0.64 out of one, or 64 out of one hundred, or about two out of three.

will be produced by at least one individual anyway. On the other hand, it's hardly damning of groups of experts to suggest that a relatively small number of individuals among them is likely to be wrong. What we'd expect, of course, is that the bad work of this small minority would be drowned out by the better thinking of the majority. It's not as if the correct opinion of the great majority in a group is simply discarded, leaving the entire group to be represented by the wrong opinion of the small minority.

Well, actually, that's sometimes *exactly* what happens in expert communities. How that works depends on what sorts of experts we're talking about. Who makes up the "crowd," for example, that brings the work of certain pop gurus and other informal experts to the fore? It's us, of course — the masses, voting with our eyeballs and wallets as we turn to certain television channels, click on certain websites, and buy certain books. And as we saw in the last chapter, informal experts win us over simply by virtue of providing the sort of advice that resonates with us because it is simple, actionable, entertaining, or universal. And that's the kind of advice that is most likely to be wrong, of course. Thus the stock picker Jim Cramer, with his sometimes reckless but forcefully presented advice, is a media star, while, say, David Swensen, the highly successful manager of Yale's investments and a fellow much admired by industry insiders, is not. Swensen's 2005 book *Unconventional Success*, though aimed at the individual investor, suffers from the mass acclaim–killing handicap of offering sound and (in spite of the book's title) mostly conventional advice, namely, to spread out investments among a variety of assets and to focus on stock-market index funds with low overhead costs. Nobody is going to put Swensen on TV five mornings a week with that sort of good, boring advice — not to mention the fact that experts of Swensen's levelheaded demeanor aren't likely to chase that sort of gig.

As for how scientific findings might be distorted by the

scientific crowd, let's hold that thought for just a bit. Because now we're ready to tackle those two remaining mysteries about the ways in which scientists get off track—namely, that scientists don't seem nearly as careful as we might expect in avoiding and confessing to the serious measurement problems we've looked at, and that the resulting wrongness appears to slip through scientists' much-admired mechanisms for policing their own work.

CHAPTER FIVE

The Trouble with Scientists, Part 2

Good men are still liable to mistakes, and are sometimes warmly engaged in errors, which they take for divine truths, shining in their minds with the clearest light.
— JOHN LOCKE

Reality is that which, when you stop believing in it, doesn't go away.
— PHILIP K. DICK

S cientists Hail Human Stem-Cell Breakthrough," trumpeted the *Times* of London in 2004, echoing the worldwide headlines made by the South Korean biomedical researcher Woo Suk Hwang after *Science* magazine published details of his lab's stunning success in cloning human embryonic stem cells—cells believed to be critical to developing new types of treatments for a range of diseases. In 2005 Hwang was back in international headlines again, this time for being indicted on charges of having fabricated the cloning-research data (the *Times:* "'I Faked My Cell Research,' Admits Cloning Pioneer"). Hwang was later kicked out of his position at Seoul National University and barred from conducting human-cloning research.

He was hardly unique in his deception. Some of the most towering figures in the history of science, including Ptolemy, Galileo, and Newton, have been fingered as likely cheats, in that some of their observations don't quite jibe with the real world. They apparently modified parts of their data, or "cleaned it up" by simply tossing out the data that didn't support their theories. Also likely fudged or neatened were two of the most iconic experiments in all of science: Gregor Mendel's breeding of peas in the 1860s to determine the rules by which inheritable characteristics are passed down through generations, providing the foundation for our understanding of genes; and Robert Millikan's 1913 measurement of the electron's mass via oil drops suspended in an electric field, an experiment that high-school students around the world repeat today.[1] A few examples from the extensive, more recent history of scientific fraud: the prominent cancer researcher William Summerlin was lauded in 1974 for developing a major breakthrough in tissue transplantation by facilitating skin grafts on genetically incompatible black and white mice at the prestigious Memorial Sloan-Kettering Cancer Center—and soon confessed to having used a marking pen to blacken patches of fur on white mice to fake the transplant results. And John Darsee, a leading cardiac researcher in a celebrated Harvard lab, published more than one hundred papers in the 1970s and early 1980s, many of them appearing in top journals and judged to be dazzling works of science, before his long-standing and wholesale fabrication of data came to light. Today's researchers seem to be maintaining the endless stream of impressive discoveries that turn out to be naked fraud, ranging from a stunning series of top-journal papers from Bell Labs' Jan Hendrik Schön describing electrical components made out of individual molecules (and outed as baloney in 2002) to the Frankfurt University anthropologist Reiner Protsch von Zieten's three-decade run of human-fossil dating on which some thirty millennia's worth of human history was based (and outed as phony in 2005).

I've included a sampling of several other relatively recent

scientific frauds in Appendix 3—a sampling especially notable for the fact that it mostly involves leading researchers, or prestigious institutions, or highly acclaimed work in top journals, and in some cases all three, and also includes one Nobel laureate. It would be reasonable to suspect that if there's fraud among the best and brightest, there's probably more of it among research's hoi polloi, even if the world is far less likely to catch it or even care. Of course, this sort of anecdotal evidence doesn't tell us much of anything about the rate of fabrication in research, other than that it is apparently nonzero. A 2007 editorial in *Nature* that followed on the heels of the Hwang cloning debacle stated, "There is broad agreement within the community on two main points regarding outright scientific fraud: it is rare, and it is serious."[2] But is it really rare? Is it really taken seriously? To claim, based on highly publicized cases, that this is so is a bit like taking the occasion of the incarceration of a Charles Manson to announce that there's no crime problem—after all, Charles Mansons are rare and are taken seriously, and the system has proven itself capable of handling them.

Well, we could just go out and ask scientists how dishonest they and their colleagues are. Of course, it would be reasonable to expect this survey to reflect a dishonesty rate quite a bit lower than the real one, since we can hardly assume a community will be honest about its dishonesty. But let's hope that that's not so, because when asked privately, scientists say there's quite a lot of dishonesty in their midst. Or so found Brian Martinson, a senior research investigator with HealthPartners Research Foundation in Minneapolis, who has been funded in part by the U.S. government's Monty Python–esquely named Office of Research Integrity's Research on Research Integrity Program. In an anonymous survey conducted by Martinson and his colleagues and published in *Nature* in 2005,[3] and responded to by some 3,200 researchers who had received funding from the National Institutes of Health, about one-third of participants admitted to at least one act of misconduct with regard to designing, conducting, interpreting, and reporting the results of studies within the previous three years. Most of this confessed misconduct was less serious than the outright fabrication of data—it more often involved "massaging" data—but for all we know that could be because admitting to making up data can lead to prison time, as Eric Poehlman, a prominent University of Vermont obesity expert, found out the hard way.

Nicholas Steneck, a science historian at the University of Michigan who moonlights as a researcher for the U.S. National Institutes of Health's Office of Research Integrity (ORI), is another of the many observers who are highly skeptical of the claimed rarity of research fraud, and he notes there's plenty of reason to feel that way. In a 2000 survey of biostatisticians, half said they personally knew of research studies that involved fraud, and of that group, about half went on to say that the fraud involved the fabrication or falsification of data.[4] Just under a third of all respondents admitted to having personally been involved in a project in which there had been some form of research misconduct. In a 2001 survey of hospital medical consultants, 56 percent said they had observed research misconduct, 6 percent admitted to having committed it themselves, and 18 percent said they thought they would commit it in the future.[5] A 2005 survey of the authors of clinical drug trials reported that 17 percent of the respondents personally knew of fabrication in a research study within the past ten years, with 5 percent having been directly involved in a study in which there had been fabrication.[6] In a study by the American Physical Society, 13 percent of young physicists said they had observed other physicists intentionally misreporting research.[7] It's worth bearing in mind that most of these misconduct figures are self-reported and may well represent a significantly low assessment.* Altman and colleagues examined a total of 190 published randomized drug trials and found that 65 percent of the findings associated with harm caused by a drug were not fully reported in the published results—a sobering thought for those taking any medication—but only 14 percent of the authors of these trials admitted to underreporting.[8,9,10] Taking an extremely conservative estimate that one in ten thousand studies involves some form of fabrication—the surveys seem to suggest that the rate is at least well over ten times higher, and perhaps several hundred times higher—Steneck calculates that there are fifteen hundred cases of research fabrication every year in the United States alone, of which about twenty are actually identified and reported.

Most of us don't think of scientists and other academic researchers as cheaters. I certainly don't. What could motivate such surprisingly nontrivial apparent levels of dishonesty? The answer turns out to be pretty simple: researchers need to publish impressive findings to keep their careers alive, and some seem unable to come up with those findings via honest work. Bear in mind that researchers who don't publish well-regarded work typically don't get tenure and are forced out of their institutions. It's an oppressive system and one that's becoming more so, contends Tomaso Poggio, a tenured computer-science researcher at MIT. "There's much more competition for tenure in academia now than there was twenty years ago," he says. "It's almost a little sick."

Then again, many of the most-publicized scientific fraud cases were perpetrated by professors who were safely tenured. Martinson, the HealthPartners researcher who conducted the

---

* An extremely rough rule of thumb in the social sciences: you should consider a specified percentage of self-reported misbehavior as representing half or less of the true percentage.

self-reported misconduct survey for the Office of Research Integrity, suggested to me one reason could be that the viciousness of the tenure process "may lead to bringing into the research communities the most competitive, most driven, perhaps most avaricious and warriorlike personalities." One of his surveys revealed that 79 percent of early-career researchers, as well as 75 percent of those in midcareer, "agreed" or "strongly agreed" with the statement "The top people in my field are successful because they are more effective at 'working the system' than others." Nearly half of both early- and mid-career researchers reported that in the past three years they had "observed or had other direct evidence of a colleague using [his or her] position to exploit or manipulate others."[11]

Perhaps more important, tenured researchers still have to bring in research funding, and the pressure to do so often considerably increases with tenure, since senior researchers sometimes have to take most of the responsibility for getting entire labs funded. Snagging research funding has always been hard in the vast majority of fields, and it's getting harder. The National Institutes of Health approved funding for 20 percent of the applications it received in 1999, but that had dropped to 9 percent by 2005.[12] Scientists know that winning one of those precious grants tends to be dependent on previously published work, according to a survey Martinson conducted of scientists in 2006.[13] "The main thing that advances your career as an academic is academic publication, for sure," says Tufts' Robert Sternberg. (He told me this while sitting in his office in front of a wall of books that I eventually realized were mostly authored or edited by him. He has published some twelve hundred books and articles.)

Actually, it isn't as hard as you might think to get published. There are well over fifty thousand scientific journals, and most of them aren't very picky. But tenure review committees and funding boards take into account not just the number of articles published but also their "impact"—that is, the prestige of the publishing journals and how often other researchers cite the work in their own articles. And that's what makes the publishing game so ferociously competitive. *Science* and *Nature*, generally considered the top scientific journals, have rejection rates of well over 90 percent. And less than half a percent of all published research articles reach the milestone of two hundred citations, while as much as half of all published research articles are never cited at all.[14]

Why would a paper fail to make the cut with a prestigious publication? Most often it's because the results just aren't considered interesting or important enough. *Nature*'s editors, for example, reject out of hand 60 percent of the articles submitted to them, mostly for that reason. "There are many factors that influence publication, but the number one factor is the interest in the study topic," I was told by Altman. What makes a study's results important or otherwise interesting? There are no hard-and-fast rules, but editors and researchers tend to speak of results that break new ground, or that might have an impact on what other researchers study, or that have important real-world applications such as drugs for major illnesses.

It's also widely understood in the research community that, all things being equal, journals much prefer to publish "positive" findings—that is, studies whose results back the study's hypothesis. If a researcher proves that eating blueberries improves eyesight—that's exciting. Proving that they don't—who cares? After all, we wouldn't want to have to sit there and listen to a friend tell us about all the interesting people he didn't run into yesterday; we want to hear about the intriguing possibilities that panned out. This leaning toward studies with

positive results is known as "publication bias,"* and researchers are so resigned to it that they typically don't even bother to
submit for publication studies with negative results, leading to
what's widely known as the "file-drawer problem," in reference
to where negative studies end up languishing. One group of
studies analyzed by Kay Dickersin, the publication-bias expert
at Johns Hopkins, and her colleagues found that for every negative study rejected by a journal, there was an average of about
ten negative studies that weren't submitted for publication.
The pressure to produce positive results is intense and ubiquitous throughout a researcher's career, says Martinson, who
confesses that he himself can't help feeling it keenly in his own
work, which as of early 2008 was focused on putting together
an NIH-funded study to look at whether motivating older people to exercise more will improve their health. "As I get further
into it, I think about the fact that if it doesn't succeed, what am
I going to do next?" he told me.

So researchers are pressured to come up with study results
that are both interesting and positive. But Ioannidis, among
many others, is quick to note a problem: the more surprising,
novel, and exciting an idea, the less likely it is to be right.[†] An
idea that seems highly likely to be true, that is utterly plausible,
is probably not going to seem exciting—it's the implausibility
that often provides most of the novelty and enthusiasm. Would
it seem exciting to hear that eating healthy foods, exercising, and

---

* The NASA researcher Jeffrey Scargle pointed out to me that the earliest-
known reference to publication bias has been attributed to the Greek sage
Diagoras of Melos in 500 BC, who, when shown a temple ringed with portraits
of sailors who narrowly escaped drowning as proof that the gods protect the
faithful, replied, "Yea, but...where are they painted that are drowned?"

[†] That large percentage of scientists and others who proclaim themselves to
be "Bayesian"—that is, fans of "Bayesian analysis," a branch of probability
theory—are often essentially expressing this straightforward notion.

keeping up with your medical checkups added an average of two months to your life? How about hearing that drinking two cans of ginger ale a day would add five years to your life? For this simple reason, we ought to be most skeptical of the most interesting, exciting ideas—the very ones that journals are eager to publish. "We have a culture of praising those who come up with the most significant claims, which turn out to be the most extravagant as well," Ioannidis says. In other words, researchers are essentially highly incentivized to test exciting ideas that are likely to be wrong—and far more likely to be published. Back in 1989 economists at Harvard and the National Bureau of Economic Research estimated that virtually all published economic papers are wrong, attributing this astoundingly dismal assessment to the effects of publication bias.*,[15]

And therein lies the motivation to fudge research. If a study's results don't clearly support an interesting hypothesis, a researcher is free to stick it in a file drawer and possibly kiss his career or funding good-bye—or, alternatively, he can imagine salvaging the situation by fabricating data, or by doctoring the way the study is conducted in order to produce more attractive data, or by manipulating the analysis of the data, in order to come out with a dubious positive result.† As Einstein once put it: "If the facts don't fit the theory, change the facts." Einstein wasn't actually encouraging research fraud, of

---

* The researchers pointed out that if at least some of a pool of papers were right, then at least a small minority of them should be backed by very strong evidence—but the researchers found that none of the many papers they looked at was backed by such evidence. Only a pool of all-wrong papers would fail to produce any strong evidence, they reckoned. All this was backed up by some fairly high-powered statistical analysis.

† For example, China has been quite explicit in demanding that researchers consistently produce important, positive findings in order to retain funding. The apparently direct result has been a strikingly long string of fraudulent research scandals; thirteen scientists were singled out for fraud in one month alone in 2007. [16,17,18]

course, but in virtually all cases of known fraud, that's exactly what happens, and in surveys, this is what respondents say happens far, far more often than is ever reported. The system seems almost designed to corrupt straight shooters.

So is all the wrongness we see in published research due to outright fraud? Of course not. There's much more fraud than we might have expected, but no one claims it accounts for a big portion of the skewed findings. It doesn't have to. With the ready availability of all those mismeasurement problems we looked at earlier on, most researchers can get highly publishable and utterly wrong findings simply as a matter of carelessness or oversight, perhaps goosed by a little bit of subtle gamesmanship, even if unconsciously. If fraudsters can occasionally get away with blatant manipulation of data, imagine how easy it would be for a legion of gamers and goof-ups to operate with impunity.

It may seem strange to say it, but experts are rarely interested in getting at the truth, whatever it may be. What they want to do is prove that *certain things* are true. Which things? Well, whatever they happen to believe is true, for whatever reasons, or whatever will benefit their careers or status or funding the most. Hawkers of diet plans need their gimmicks to help people lose weight, golf pros need their tips to take strokes off their clients' games, relationship gurus need their insights to strengthen marriages—if there's evidence that their advice *doesn't* in fact pay off, don't expect to learn it from them.* But I think most of us already suspect that what gurus and local experts conclude can be partly about what's in it for them—do I really need that costly brake job, or yet another expensive test for that aching knee, or more boxes of diet-expert-branded low-carb snacks?

---

* Am I playing the same game in this book? I remind you again that I explore this and related questions in Appendix 4.

It's a cornerstone of science, on the other hand, that researchers aren't supposed to favor particular outcomes in their studies. And yet Penn State's Kenneth Weiss and his colleagues have noted that the beliefs of researchers are shaped by "all of the vanities, vested interests, hunches, experiences, politics, careerism, grantsmanship tactics, competing cadres of collaborators, imperfections, and backgrounds of the scientists investigating problems at any time."[19] If a scientist *wants* to or *expects* to end up with certain results, he will likely achieve them, often through some form of fudging, whether conscious or not—bias exerts a sort of gravity over error, pulling the glitches in one direction, so that the errors tend to add up rather than cancel out. Francis Bacon noted in the late sixteenth century that preconceived ideas shape observation, causing people, for example, to take special notice of phenomena and measurements that confirm a belief while ignoring those that contradict it. Thomas Kuhn, the MIT science historian who famously gave the world the phrase "paradigm shift," argued in the early 1960s that what scientists choose to measure, how they measure it, which measurements they keep, and what they conclude from them are all shaped by their own and their colleagues' ideas and beliefs. And Berkeley's Robert MacCoun told me that once an expert jumps to a dubious conclusion, she'll simply tend to ignore or explain away conflicting evidence.

In fact, given all the biases we see in experts and the many ways that bias can lead them to be wrong, I find it far harder to explain how some minorities of scientists and other high-powered experts manage to be *right* on a fairly consistent basis. And yet the rolls of Nobel Prize winners are filled with such researchers, and in every expert community there are standouts who seem to be able to hit the nail on the head again and again. How do these exceptional scientists and other experts resist succumbing to the biases that seem so critical to publication and career advancement but that are so toxic to the rightness of conclusions?

Jack Cuzick, a prominent researcher at Cancer Research UK, the U.K. counterpart of the American Cancer Society, supplied me with one possible explanation. "Some people have a good nose for sniffing out right answers," he said, "and some people don't." In other words, some minorities of experts end up with interesting, positive, and right results not because they avoid biases but because they somehow manage to repeatedly adopt the *right* biases. These experts are able to correctly intuit which interesting, groundbreaking ideas are likely to hold up, even though these ideas are the very sorts that are, statistically speaking, the least likely to be right.

I asked Cuzick how we can spot the experts whose noses will prove trustworthy. "I don't have an answer for that," he said.

Robert Crease, a science historian who studies expertise and who chairs the Philosophy Department at Stony Brook University, agrees that "good" and "bad" biases tend to look alike. "You find out eighty years later who was right," he told me.

But can that majority of scientists with less beneficial biases really expect to get away with the sorts of shenanigans we've looked at? After all, we know that researchers closely vet one another's work, religiously guarding the integrity of science—and we know this because scientists and science journalists keep reminding us of it. For example, it seems reasonable to assume that the people who toil in the lab alongside fraudulent or gaming scientists, or who are charged with reviewing said scientists' work for journals, are in an excellent position to point the finger. And researchers do in fact sometimes come forward to raise questions about colleagues. The best-known example is the so-called Baltimore case, which began in 1986 when a postdoctoral biomedical researcher named Margot O'Toole stumbled on what seemed to be discrepancies between the data in a prominently published paper by her boss, the rising-star researcher Thereza Imanishi-Kari, and what she found in Imanishi-Kari's lab notebooks. The work, which had important implications for the treatment of AIDS, happened to list as a coauthor the celebrated Nobel laureate David Baltimore, raising the stakes, though as is often the case with high-powered researchers, Baltimore apparently had little to do with the work. Research big shots at MIT and Tufts, where Imanishi-Kari worked, opened inquiries and immediately dismissed more or less out of hand all of O'Toole's accusations, essentially telling her to keep her big mouth shut. Two separate federal investigations were undertaken, and both found that fraud had indeed been committed. But in 1996 an appeals board overturned those findings. Baltimore would later publicly apologize to O'Toole for the way she was treated, but she lost her job at MIT. The message sent to young researchers everywhere was clear: the science community isn't a lot friendlier to whistleblowers than are police departments and tobacco companies.

There's plenty of evidence that O'Toole's experience accurately reflects the research culture. In a 1993 study, 53 percent of graduate students said they would expect reprisals for reporting a faculty member's misconduct, and 26 percent of faculty members said they "probably or definitely" would expect retaliation for reporting a colleague—where retaliation can include blocking promotion or sending unflattering reviews of research to journals and funding committees.[20] Only 18 percent of assistant professors stated they "definitely" could report conduct and not expect retaliation.* Gerald Koocher, the Simmons College dean who studies research misconduct, has gathered online more than two

---

* The retaliation isn't always sub rosa: In one odd case in 2007 at the University of Colorado at Boulder, a researcher who was found to have engaged in misconduct after a lengthy investigation by other professors turned around and formally accused his investigators of research misconduct for having inappropriately found him guilty of misconduct.

thousand anonymous accounts of research misconduct that wasn't otherwise reported. "I wasn't surprised when I got a lot of people saying, 'I was afraid my boss would fire me if I blew the whistle on what he was doing,'" he says. "I was more surprised to get people saying, 'I caught my research assistant fabricating data, so we fired them or moved them out of the lab, but we didn't report it because we were afraid our grant wouldn't get renewed.' The whole notion that the vigilance of colleagues is a defense against bad science is based on the underlying premise that people wouldn't cheat if they knew their colleagues wouldn't let them get away with it, but there *is* a culture of letting them get away with it." He then told me the story, from his graduate-school days, of a prominent professor in his department who had devised a technique for treating people with an intense fear of snakes—and who cooked the results by sticking a well-fed snake in the refrigerator for five minutes before showing the now-lethargized creature to subjects who had received the treatment under study, while exposing the control group to a hungry, warm, and thus relatively squirmy snake. "All us graduate students knew about it, but we were depending on him in our doctoral committees," Koocher explained, noting that the professor was never outed. "The pressures to not speak up in these situations can be enormous." Nicholas Steneck, the ORI researcher, confirms the plentiful evidence showing the reluctance to report misconduct. "Almost every time I speak to a group, at least one or two students or young researchers will come up to me afterward and say, 'This is what's going on. What should I do?'" he told me. "Or they'll say, 'I'm not going to do anything about it until after I leave the lab'—but why would they report it after they've left? It's almost signing your own career death warrant to blow the whistle."

The failure of senior researchers to report the inappropriate behavior of the junior researchers and graduate students who work directly under them may often stem not from a clear intention to hide misconduct or incompetence but from a failure to have any idea whatsoever of what their people are up to. The ORI found in a 2003 survey that a quarter of all lab heads fell short when it came to taking their supervisory responsibilities seriously, and another study found that 40 percent of misconduct cases were marked by inadequate record keeping.[21] A 2006 survey of thirty-nine misconduct cases involving clinical drug trials determined that a little more than half the cases were characterized by "overwhelming workload, sloppy management, unclear or unwritten procedures, and lack of availability of essential records."[22]

The fellow researchers of exposed scientific fraudsters, and the journal editors who publish them, are often quick to bleat that they shouldn't be raked over the coals for having unwittingly gone along for the ride, because fraud is so hard to detect. That may often, or perhaps even usually, be true, but Steneck points out there's reason to believe that the entire scientific community at times seems incapable of, or unwilling to, call out potential fraud even when it should be glaringly obvious that something is amiss. He notes, for example, that there were several flashing-neon-sign clues to Woo Suk Hwang's stem-cell research fabrications, including the fact that the time frames he reported for some of his achievements were markedly shorter than could reasonably be expected; Hwang also reported having collected eggs from two hundred volunteer donors, when researchers routinely struggle to get a half dozen volunteer donors. In 2005 the Norwegian researcher Jon Sudbø prominently published an oral-cancer study, based on largely faked data that were simply repeated for padding, a fact that could have been picked up by even a casual, untrained eye engaged in a cursory check. Jan Hendrik Schön's molecular-switch studies and Eric Poehlman's nutritional studies were coauthored by researchers who, like Baltimore, quickly confessed to having had little idea of how the data had been produced. Journal editors, meanwhile, thrilled at having a chance to publish an article that could make headlines in the mass media, may cast a soft eye over the work. "The journal itself is not an investigative body," the *Science* editor in chief Donald Kennedy said in a published statement after the Hwang scandal broke. The *British Medical Journal* took more than a decade to go public with its doubts about a widely quoted 1992 study it had published reporting how a low-fat, high-fiber diet cut in half the risk of death from all causes—an extraordinary claim that is so far out of line with every credible study ever performed on diets, not to mention with everyday observation, that suspicions were rightly high from the start.

Jennings, the MIT neuroscientist and former editor at *Nature*, insisted to me that he and fellow editors never knowingly subordinated customary caution when looking at potentially groundbreaking research, though he concedes they may not always have gotten the balance between skepticism and enthusiasm quite right. "We really never lowered our scientific standards to make a splash," he said. "We made mistakes, and sometimes with exciting papers, but it certainly wasn't deliberate policy." Some outside observers have taken a more skeptical view, though. After the Schön scandal, *Nature* quoted the Princeton professor, Nobel laureate, and former Bell Labs researcher Philip Anderson as saying, "*Nature's* editorial and refereeing policy seems to be influenced by the newsworthiness of the work, not necessarily its quality. And *Science* seems to be caught up in a similar syndrome."

Universities set up their own offices, committees, and procedures for rooting out and addressing fraud among their researchers, but it's hard to find researchers who consider these to be highly effective safeguards. The ORI, frustrated with the poor level of misconduct self-policing at research institutions, tried in 2001 to force institutions to establish more stringent standards under the threat of loss of federal research funding, but the hue and cry from universities at being told how to do things led the ORI to back down. "The scientific community reacts to outside policing the way my Roosevelt-hating mother reacts to any new taxes," says Steneck.

Thank goodness for peer review, the 350-year-old research-journal tradition of sending candidate articles out to knowledgeable researchers for vetting and comments. It's peer review that, more than anything else, is supposed to separate the genuine, reliable science served up in research journals from the apparently frequently junky stuff we get in the mass media. Unfortunately, anecdotal evidence that the peer-review process is an effective way of picking out lousy and even fraudulent work is not encouraging. A panel of researchers and editors assembled to advise *Science* magazine after the Hwang scandal issued a statement noting that reviewers don't even *look* for fraud.[23] Perhaps they don't look for gross experimental error either: peer reviewers didn't raise red flags with the bizarre, world-headline-grabbing finding of a 2002 Johns Hopkins study published in *Science* claiming that the widely used recreational drug MDMA, or "ecstasy," readily caused serious brain damage and even death in primates; it soon came to light that most of the animals in the study had been accidentally pumped full of far more dangerous methamphetamines instead of MDMA. When, as a test, 221 of the *British Medical Journal*'s frequent referees were sent an article purposely tainted with eight presumably detectable problems, the reviewers managed to catch an average of two.[24] More than half the time, peer reviewers don't even agree on publication worthiness, according to one study of a range of journals; reviewers for the *New England Journal of Medicine*, for example, see eye to eye only one-fourth of the time.[25]

In fact, it is typically science journalists and other outside observers who imagine peer review to be an assurance of study reliability, and less so scientists. "Scientists understand that peer review per se provides only a minimal assurance of quality, and that the public conception of peer review as a stamp of authentication is far from the truth," Jennings has written. Martinson found in a survey that half of midcareer scientists had "direct evidence" of a colleague providing an "inappropriate or careless review of papers or proposals" within the past three years. And researchers sometimes line up to grouse that peer review offers preferential treatment to the work of scientists who already have some weight in their fields, in part because heavy-hitting scientists often abuse their own peer-review duties by arbitrarily dinging anyone who challenges them. "Prestigious investigators may suppress via the peer-review process the appearance and dissemination of findings that refute their findings, thus condemning their field to perpetuate false dogma," states Ioannidis. Robert Sternberg, the Tufts dean, told me that while reviewers often make good points, a reviewer's scathing comments are as likely as not to stem from the fact that she "had a bad day at work, or is an angry person, or doesn't like you, or doesn't like what you represent, or is competing with you."

Okay, so lousy research can slip past peer review into journals. But surely as soon as other researchers put the published results to the test, the truth will out, right? Possibly—except that the vast majority of published research is never replicated or validated, or if it is, there is no record of it in research journals. All but the most prominent research tends to enter the records and forever persist as apparently legitimate by default. Martinson estimates that more than 95 percent of medical research findings aren't replicated. No wonder: replication is more or less unfundable, and if someone does it on his own nickel, the results probably won't come to light. Even a study that fails to replicate a published result, stated *Nature* in an editorial, "is unlikely ever to be published, or even submitted for publication." In 2006 *Nature* reporter Jim

Giles dug up the fact that two out of the four stories plastered on the cover of a 2002 issue of the journal—that is, half of the biggest stories in the world of science that week—had failed replication, without all that much notice being taken of it.[26]

Even when research errors are outed, the original claims often manage to persist for years and even decades. A study by the computer scientist Murat Çokol and his colleagues at Columbia University found that a good deal less than one-hundredth of 1 percent of all journal articles published between 1950 and 2004 were formally acknowledged as seriously flawed, a percentage that Çokol's computer model suggested should be as much as 200 times larger.[*,28] Ioannidis, too, found evidence of the persistence of bad findings. He looked at studies reporting the cardiovascular benefits of vitamin E, anticancer benefits of beta-carotene, and anti-Alzheimer's benefits of estrogen—important studies that were published in 1993, 1981, and 1996, respectively, and that were each convincingly and prominently refuted in one or more larger studies around 1999, 1994, and 2004, respectively. In 2005, the most recent year Ioannidis checked, half of the researchers who cited the original study of vitamin E did so in the context of accepting the original results, and through 2006 a little more than 60 percent cited the original beta-carotene and estrogen studies, though the results had been solidly refuted—thirteen years earlier in the case of beta-carotene.[29]

Does the scientific community do *anything* effective to single out lousy research? Actually, yes—it makes sure that some of the worst

---

* That study was controversial, but many scientists echo the claim that retraction rates are dramatically lower than what might reasonably be expected. According to a study by the Emory University public-health researcher Benjamin Druss and his colleagues, the most prestigious journals have retraction rates that, while still suspiciously low, are substantially higher than average retraction rates in the journals in which the vast majority of research is published, suggesting that most flaws simply go unnoticed in the majority of published research because of a general lack of scrutiny.[27]

research gets the most acclaim. But that happens in a slightly convoluted way, so please bear with me as we walk through it. To begin, consider the fact that study results usually aren't publishable unless they are statistically "significant." Though reporters and experts often speak as if a "significant" or "statistically valid" finding is a "true" finding, all "significant" usually means is that there's a nineteen-out-of-twenty chance the finding isn't due to a statistical fluke. Sounds impressive, until you realize it also means that 5 percent of studies with "significant" findings *have* been thrown off by a statistical fluke. Now let's imagine there's interest among twenty teams of scientists in testing a novel scientific theory, bearing in mind that, as we've discussed, most novel theories are likely to be wrong. If they all end up with "significant" findings, then we can reasonably propose that nineteen of them will have failed to confirm the theory, quite correctly, and one team will suffer a data fluke that will have led it to mistakenly conclude its work has confirmed the theory. Guess whose study is most likely to be published? Research by Dickersin and others suggests that on average positive studies are at least ten times more likely than negative studies to be submitted and accepted for publication. That might well mean that if the one mistakenly positive study is published, on average only two of the nineteen studies that correctly ended up with negative results will be published. The seventeen others will probably go into a file drawer, so to speak, or if they're submitted for publication they'll probably be rejected for having ended up with negative results that simply confirmed what everyone suspected was true anyway. That means we're not talking about one in twenty positive studies that you read about in journals being wrong—we're talking about *one out of three* being wrong.

But statistical flukes aren't the only problem with research. "Significance" doesn't tell you if the equipment used in the testing was working right. It doesn't tell you if the people conducting the study were well trained. It doesn't tell you if the subjects of the study had reason to lie or exaggerate. It doesn't tell you if the very design of the experiment was deeply flawed. It doesn't say anything about whether the researchers were deeply biased, threw out contradictory data, "moved the goalposts," ignored confounding variables, or relied on shaky surrogate measures. By the time all these other problems are taken into account, we'd expect far more than one in twenty studies to wrongly end up with positive findings. Let's very, very conservatively estimate that an additional one out of five studies—that is, another four out of twenty—succumbs to any of the array of problems we've considered and comes to the wrong conclusion. So now we have a total of five out of twenty studies that are wrongly positive, and fifteen that came to the right, negative conclusion. If all five of the wrongly positive studies get published, and one-tenth of the fifteen correctly negative studies get published (1.5, but let's be conservative again and call it two), then on this question the portion of published articles that are wrong will be five out of seven. In other words, if you accept all of my admittedly rough and debatable assumptions, you'd expect that, in published studies that test a new, incorrect theory, more than two out of three would mistakenly conclude the theory is correct—a wrongness rate that's in keeping with what Ioannidis has observed in top journals.*

I truly don't mean to convince people that they should hold science in low regard, particularly compared to other types of expertise. I think scientists *are* our most trustworthy experts, and the basic methods of science are exactly the right way to approach the problems and mysteries that face us in the world. In short, when it comes to experts, scientists ought to be seen as perching at the top of the heap. But that doesn't mean we shouldn't have a good understanding of how modest a compliment it may be to say so.

---

* I didn't adjust any of these numbers to make things come out in this neat way, in case you feel like taking my word for it.

Chapter Six

Experts and Organizations

Buy the truth and sell it not.
— Proverbs 23:23

I t isn't often that a piece of fruit makes headlines, but a banana in Scotland pulled it off in January 2007. The produce in question was allegedly perched on the desk of an employee of Her Majesty's Revenue and Customs service—roughly the U.K. version of the United States' Internal Revenue Service—when a visiting consultant demanded to know if the fruit was "active." Most of us would find that question as impenetrable as "What's the frequency, Kenneth?" but HMRC workers were by this time teeth grindingly familiar with what such queries were about. It seems the government had squirted $10 million at a consulting firm that promises to help organizations join the Toyota-inspired "lean" revolution, in which employees get rid of whatever processes and things that aren't contributing to the company's goals—the "inactive"—so that said employees can focus attention and time on the "active," becoming in theory more productive. An inactive banana, in this worldview, would be one not firmly slotted for imminent consumption and thus wouldn't belong in the ranks of keyboards and staplers and those very few other items that merit a patch of valuable desktop real estate. Nothing cries "We're no Toyota" so much as work spaces cluttered with inactive snacks.

HMRC employees apparently were unenamored of the initiative, to the extent that some of them directed complaints to a union of government workers, who in turn passed the fruit story on to the press, and the $10 million banana-suppression effort temporarily became a giddy symbol of the sort of waste that one would think "lean" efforts would be targeting. (Or would if the efforts were aimed at senior management and high-priced consultants rather than the rank and file.) Much of the criticism of the inactive-fruit affair, oddly enough, cropped up on some of the many websites run by ardent supporters of lean initiatives, who rushed to pronounce the incident a classic example of why so many lean projects fail—between 50 percent and 75 percent, according to the field's own literature, depending on how you define "lean" and "failure."* Among the reasons routinely ticked off by lean defenders for these poor showings: management doesn't fully understand what lean is all about, the program is unleashed in a heavy-handed way, the message isn't properly communicated to employees, the company doesn't make a solid enough commitment, and so forth. In fact, there are so many ways for companies to prove unworthy of true leanhood that the notion of success seems rooted in Spanish-Inquisitional logic: throw the suspected heretic on the bonfire, and if he burns, well, he must not have been a true believer.

In the face of all these disappointments, the excitement over lean initiatives may be starting to fade. That was inevitable, really; lean leanings took hold a few years back, around the same time as a waning of enthusiasm hit the world of Six Sigma, a quality-improvement approach that sought to tap the wisdom of the once

---

* Only 2 percent of the 884 U.S. companies responding to a survey by *IndustryWeek* magazine claimed to have achieved "World Class" status, a designation often used in the lean world to denote those who have fully made the grade.[1]

highly successful Motorola, and which itself came on the heels of the decline in interest in "total quality management" programs based on Japanese manufacturing principles that were themselves based on earlier U.S. manufacturing principles, and which came into popularity in the United States and Europe following the rise and fall of the "business process reengineering" movement. Each of these approaches surfed to prominence on transient swells of acclaim from business-school academics and management consultancies, some of which were specifically formed to help usher organizations into the latest revitalizing paradigm. (HMRC's $10 million in lean aspiration went to the Unipart Group, a $1.5 billion, nine-thousand-employee company that proclaims itself to be a "pioneer of lean thinking"—likely shelf life not always being a prime consideration in consultancy slogans.)

In mentioning this handful of major movements, I'm not coming close to doing justice to the impressive volume of expert-inspired paradigms, styles, and solutions that have paraded in and out of management mindshare in just the past few decades, many of them midwifed by bestselling books from business academics, management consultants, the occasional business journalist, or some combination thereof. These books usually fit one of two templates. One involves the authors placing a number of winning companies or CEOs under a microscope, distilling what management principles these role models follow that losers don't. The archetype is 1982's massive blockbuster *In Search of Excellence*, written by Thomas Peters and Robert Waterman, both of whom had been with the fabled consultancy McKinsey. A few examples from the uninterrupted stream of roughly similar books since then: *Good to Great*, in which the consultant Jim Collins tells us *Why Some Companies Make the Leap . . . and Others Don't*; *First, Break All the Rules*, in which the consultants and motivational speakers Marcus Buckingham and Curt Coffman detail *What the World's Greatest Managers Do Differently; The Breakthrough Company*, in which the Harvard business professor Keith McFarland explains *How Everyday Companies Become Extraordinary Performers;* and *Talent Is Overrated*, in which the journalist Geoff Colvin points out *What* Really *Separates World-Class Performers from Everybody Else.* The other template relies on the authors having observed or derived a new strategy, trend, or management technique that will determine which businesses will succeed in the coming years, showing how winning companies are already taking advantage of the new thinking. Examples: *Competing on Analytics: The New Science of Winning*, by the consultant and Babson College business professor Thomas Davenport and the Accenture researcher Jeanne G. Harris, who tell us that future winners will be those who do a better job wringing insight from data; *The World Is Flat: A Brief History of the Twenty-first Century*, by the journalist Thomas Friedman, who insists that winners will be those who most effectively globalize; *Wikinomics: How Mass Collaboration Changes Everything*, by the consultants Don Tapscott and Anthony D. Williams, who reveal that winning is tied to the wisdom of crowds; and *The Future of Management*, by the London Business School professor and consultant Gary Hamel and the journalist Bill Breen, who explain that winners will shed conventional management hierarchy.

That's just a tiny smattering of popular business wisdom, of course—I could have listed hundreds of books. Unfortunately, as with weight loss and politics, there is a vast sea of ideas pointing in all sorts of different directions for solutions to the same basic problems. They can't all be right, and even if they could, how can you tell which advice best applies to your company? For one thing, no one with a day job could read a substantial fraction of the field. That must be a concern weighing on a lot of managers, since as a result a subgenre has sprung up within business publishing specifically aimed at gathering, filtering, and compacting the daunting flood of published management wisdom. Thus there's the *Guide to Management Ideas and Gurus*, a book that doesn't claim to offer any new ideas of its own but rather helps harried executives quickly get up to speed on "active inertia," "triple bottom line," and "the long tail," among many other trendy concepts. Likewise, the book *Entrepreneurial Excellence* spells out ways to *Profit from the Best Ideas of the Experts*. Meanwhile, BizBriefings.com offers to send subscribers an eight-page summary of a business book every week. (From BizBriefing's summary of *Group Genius: The Creative Power of Collaboration:* "Successful innovations are always a combination of many good ideas—with aspects emerging at different times and put forward by different people. Synergy often results when many ideas come together." I confess gratitude at not having to read a multipage version of that argument, though of course I may not know what I'm missing.)

But even the business literature–summarizing industry may have an increasingly difficult time keeping up with the onslaught of new books, due to another growing business-publishing sub-industry—one that seeks to convert ever more academics, executives, consultants, and other professionals into business-advice authors. Turning out a book has never been easier, thanks to this "vanity press" industry, which charges authors as little as a few hundred dollars for the privilege of publication, along with related editing and marketing services. Author Solutions, Inc., for example, claims to have published nineteen thousand titles in 2008, noting in its pitch to business professionals that "when it comes to business and establishing yourself as an expert in a specific area, nothing provides more credibility than a book." Well, Harvard professors and McKinsey consultants might argue that point, but having a tome to thump obviously can't hurt.

Other than a possibly stimulating read, what do the consumers of bestselling business-advice books stand to get out of the deal? They stand to be misled, says Jerker Denrell, a professor at Stanford's business school who specializes in studying how business wisdom goes astray. Like many academics, Denrell maintains an impressive wall of books, with the overflow cairned throughout his office, but his collection is the first I've ever seen to be used as a prop. He repeatedly sprang from his chair as we spoke to grab one business book after another, reading mockingly from the front or back cover, sometimes literally squeaking with laughter. "Every year there are, like, five hundred books published that claim to have the ultimate answer to becoming a fantastically highly profitable firm," he told me. "It's absurd. It's ridiculous. As if a book you buy at the airport could finally solve the business problems that no one has been able to solve until now."

For one thing, notes Denrell, most of the authors seem to imply that any companies that follow their books' advice can become winners—which he deems as unlikely a proposition as that of a swimming coach who claims that any swimmer taking her suggestions will win swim meets. "You might be able to get companies to improve, but that doesn't mean they'll do better than their competitors, and that's what's important," he explained. "*Good to Great* isn't a good book, because most companies don't even do simple things well, like accounting. A better book would be *Incompetent to Okay*. But if you're in academia, you won't seem very interesting saying that sort of thing, and if you're a consultant, you can't make money off it."

Denrell isn't a lone voice of objection to the high-profile business-advice-book industry. There is, in fact, a rich literature essentially debunking the notion that much if any of this stuff can be considered reliable. The skepticism goes back almost to the beginning of formal management theory, generally pegged to the stunning ascendancy of Frederick Taylor after the turn of the twentieth century. An engineering manager at a Pittsburgh steel plant, Taylor watched laborers lugging steel bars around and became convinced he could make them more efficient by measuring and analyzing their motions, designing a new set of movements that eliminated the "awkward, inefficient, or ill-directed" ones (the inactive actions, some might say today), and then forcing all the laborers to precisely adhere to the same new routine. The results led Taylor to write a book, *The Principles of Scientific Management*, which ignited a virtual mania for management-guided efficiency at U.S. companies, with some 69,000 people turning up for a Tayloristic "efficiency exposition" in New York's Grand Central Palace in 1914, just three years after the book's publication. The work had an enormous influence on Henry Ford, thus playing a large role in the birth of the factory assembly line, and an army of Taylorite consultants drove a devotion to stopwatch-measured efficiency into organizations around the world. (And even into homes, as anyone who has read the nonfictional *Cheaper by the Dozen* or seen the original 1950 movie can attest.)

Taylor also managed to get some Harvard professors interested in his assertion that, as he put it in his book, "the best management is a true science, resting upon clearly defined laws, rules, and principles, as a foundation," and he prodded the university into setting up the United States' first graduate school of business. And so was born both management academia and a thriving management consulting industry. But one of the first things some of the new researchers and consultants noticed was that Taylor had never bothered to amass good data backing up his assertions; they were mostly based on small demonstrations that seemed in retrospect to be highly rigged to make his improvements look good. Even worse, companies that had sworn they had seen improvements from Taylor's methods usually discovered that the benefits proved temporary; indeed, after only two years, Taylor and his programs had been booted out of the steel mill where he had originated his ideas. Taylorism was finally put to rest as far as most management experts were concerned in the late 1920s by a series of studies conducted at Western Electric's Hawthorne Works factory in Illinois. Researchers there concluded that almost any change introduced by management—even something as meaningless as slightly lowering or increasing the lighting—tended to invite at least a brief improvement in the output of workers involved in the study. Management experts and psychologists would later evoke the so-called Hawthorne effect to explain away the improved performance of people who know they're being observed, though the Hawthorne study was itself eventually recognized to be a highly flawed one—its results can't be trusted to apply to the real world, leaving the Hawthorne effect a victim of, well, the Hawthorne effect. In any case, Taylor's ideas were discarded by the fields he had founded, leaving management academics and consultants to move on to new solutions that would catch fire and then themselves end up debunked and replaced, establishing a pattern that would continue to the present day.

Any number of management academics and other observers have decried the business world's addiction to "management fads," sometimes disparagingly referred to as "TLAs" (for "three-letter acronyms," because somewhere along the line business experts picked up on the fact that their ideas were more likely to catch on if anointed with a three-word name; hence MBO [management by objectives], BPR [business process reengineering], BSC [balanced scorecards], JIT [just-in-time], TQM [total quality management], and many others that temporarily held special cachet with anyone packing an MBA). Management theories that turn into fads, not surprisingly, tend to meet all the usual requirements for resonant expert advice. A 2002 *Harvard Business Review* study that looked at forty years' worth of management fads—defined as ideas that went from "sudden prominence to obscurity"—noted that they tended to be "simple," "prescriptive," "falsely encouraging," "one-size-fits-all," "in tune with the zeitgeist," and "novel but not radical."[2]

That's not to say management fads are entirely bad or useless, even if they don't deliver the benefits they promise. Some observers have suggested that embracing even a nonsensical fad can act as a shot of espresso for the organizational metabolism, engendering new enthusiasm and higher levels of activity that, when they inevitably fade, can be renewed simply by latching on to the next fad.[3] Others have argued that just because a management idea explodes onto the scene only to disappear doesn't mean it hasn't left a longer-lasting mark on management practice. In much the way that dieters who try and then abandon extreme low-carb approaches may continue to take it easier on sugar than they did before, so managers at a company might emerge from a fling with, say, Six Sigma with an enhanced appreciation for quality improvement without demanding that the organization be obsessed by a specific approach to it. As a 2005 article in the *Quality Management Journal* noted, "Even when management fads don't work out as planned, they still benefit by adding to the firm's collective knowledge."[4]

But there are real downsides to the faddish nature of management advice. The conga line of Dilbertian corporate initiatives thrust on wary, weary employees—who correctly sense that they and probably the company stand to gain little in the long run from the attendant retraining and meetings and paperwork and supervision and consultant meddling required to get with the program of the day—can be oppressive and counterproductive. Eric Abrahamson, a professor at Columbia University's business school who has studied management fads (and who was my co-author for a previous book, not of the business-advice ilk), has argued that strings of repeated management initiatives have led to an epidemic of "change burnout" at businesses — an outbreak that saps morale and makes it difficult for companies to achieve more meaningful transformations when their industries genuinely demand it.[5]

The effect of faddish, bestselling business advice on people who actually run companies can be equally perverse, insists Eric Goldman, who directs Santa Clara University's High Tech Law Institute. "These ideas make big claims that push entrepreneurs to swing for the fences," he told me. "But it leads to cutting corners on all the other things you have to do to build a company that's going to be successful in the long run. The short-term payoff that can accrue from following this advice can blind a company to the fact that eventually it will be punished for it." Goldman's skepticism led me to recall a talk I sat in on a few years ago given by the *World Is Flat* author Thomas Friedman to a group of a few hundred highly successful CEOs of small and midsize firms. These entrepreneurs seemed transfixed by Friedman's exhortations to restructure their businesses along global lines, as the Internet broke down all the barriers to overseas partnerships and markets. Afterward I asked some of the attendees how the apparent rush to globalization was affecting them, and every one of them said that while they were currently doing little or nothing in terms of overseas business, they were feeling fired up by Friedman into taking international initiative. I hope for their sakes that they were judicious about it, because that was just about the time a backlash against globalization hype started to build. The Harvard Business School's Pankaj Ghemawat, for example, pointed out in a 2007 article in *Foreign Policy* that what had really mushroomed over the past decade wasn't so much the globalization of business — 90 percent of fixed investment worldwide is still domestic, and the United States actually has a slightly larger share of global-manufacturing output than it did in 1980—but rather the popularity of books that push globalization, of which four thousand appeared between 2000 and 2004, at a rate that was doubling every eighteen months.[6] And that was before the deep recession of 2008 took an especially large toll on exports worldwide and led to a rush to reestablish many trade barriers. Wouldn't you know it? Time for books about how the world is curved again.

In 1942 a fighter with the Czech resistance jumped up from a roadside hiding place as the open Mercedes convertible carrying the German SS leader and mass murderer Reinhard "Blond Beast" Heydrich slowed for a tight turn outside Prague. Drawing a bead on the nonplussed Nazi, the commando pulled the trigger of his submachine gun, only to hear it click desultorily. Fortunately there was a plan B, and a second commando lobbed a bomb at the car, fatally emplacing shrapnel in Heydrich's spleen.

It's no coincidence that there was a backup plan. The gun carried by the first commando was a Sten, aka the "plumber's abortion," a wildly inaccurate British weapon hastily cobbled together for World War II and so unreliable that the only thing troops counted on from it was a jam at the worst possible moment. And yet the Sten was one of the hit products of the mid-twentieth century, with a run of some 4.5 million—a number that has placed it among the all-time bestsellers in the world of weaponry. In contrast, the U.S.-made Thompson M1 submachine gun and its variants, standard-issue weapons for U.S. troops in World War II and praised for accuracy and reliability, saw runs of only 1.7 million in their half-century lifetimes. How could a gun as lousy as the Sten sell so well? One big reason: it was easy to copy. The Sten's blueprint was widely circulated, and the gun was purposely designed to be manufacturable by anyone with modest metalworking skills and tools, making it the darling of resource-strapped

Allied underground units. Even the Germans grudgingly copied it. Though none of these Sten-alikes produced royalties for the Sten's originator and maker of record, London's Royal Small Arms Factory, the Sten's sheer familiarity became such that, after the war, Britain and other countries around the world ordered it from the factory by the truckload well into the 1960s, turning the Sten into a gold mine for the RSAF.

The Sten makes for an interesting case study, but what lesson should businesses draw from it? That they should make crummy products that are easy to copy? The fact is, the Sten was simply the right solution for a particular set of conditions, and whether by luck or design the RSAF hit on it and was able to capitalize for two decades. I think the real lesson of the Sten is that a company's success normally can't be attributed to a few clear principles that most companies can apply to most situations. In other words, learning how one company won probably won't much help another company to win. That would raise some serious questions about expert business advice, of course, in that the lessons of winning companies tend to form the very foundation of that advice. Basing advice on successful companies certainly at first glance appears to be a reasonable approach. After all, unlike the case with health, parenting, national affairs, or relationships, there would seem to be readily measurable bottom lines—sales and profits—that enable a clear definition of success in business and a way to distinguish the winners from the losers. But relying on corporate winners to shine a light on the secrets to success tends to cause more problems than it solves. That's because the nature of winning and losing in business is actually far more convoluted and contestable than you might suppose, with the result that lessons from seemingly successful organizations are as apt to point the way down as up, if they point anywhere at all.

Naturally, to illustrate the notion that case studies don't

necessarily illustrate much, I'm going to turn to a case study: Toyota, the global corporate darling of the past few decades.* Toyota has been loudly admired in any number of business books and articles, and it's not hard to see why the company gets tapped so frequently for its guiding principles. In 2007 Toyota surpassed GM in unit sales to become the world's largest car company, and in that year Toyota recorded $17 billion in profits, while GM lost $39 billion and started circling the drain. As of 2009, in the United States, Toyota's Camry is the bestselling car, and its Lexus lineup outsells all other luxury brands. The Toyota Prius is widely seen as the most innovative and environmentally friendly popular car on the market.

But is it really inarguably clear that Toyota's business approach is that much more worthy of emulation than, say, GM's? It's well known that Toyota isn't saddled with the staggering pension and health-care costs that helped bleed GM. It's also widely accepted that Toyota's ascent as a low-cost, high-quality manufacturer was largely fueled by its access in Japan to a lower-cost, fanatically loyal pool of workers, engineers, and managers; to a semicaptive home market that used to reflexively shun foreign products; and to the far more nurturing relationship that the Japanese government had with its largest companies—advantages of the sort that enabled a number of Japanese megacorporations, including Honda and Sony, to come from nowhere and overtake competition around the world in the 1970s and 1980s. Toyota seems far smarter than GM for having focused on its small and midsize cars while GM bet big on SUVs and trucks—but both companies were simply giving their core markets the vehicles they were asking for. For perhaps fifteen years, GM's bet

---

* Some might award that distinction to Google, or even to Apple, but actually most—though not all—experts have had the good sense to hold off on declaring the successes of those two oddball companies as widely emulatable. Then again, check back next year.

appeared to be exactly the right one in the United States, with some of its trucks consistently outselling all of Toyota's vehicles, including the Camry, even into early 2008, until gas prices sky-rocketed. GM also turned a bigger per-unit profit on its trucks and SUVs than Toyota did on its Camry. In fact, until recently Toyota had been desperately—and not particularly success-fully—trying to move into the truck and SUV markets. Now that late start and ongoing failure appear to have been lucky breaks that many observers mistake for genius. Toyota's vaunted quality advantage? GM all but closed the gap some years back, according to many automotive-industry experts—in 2009 J. D. Power ranked Buick above Lexus in its closely watched if de-batably reliable dependability rankings—and Toyota has been hit with more and bigger recalls than GM in recent years. The notion that Toyota's executives are smarter and utilize more ef-fective operational techniques than GM's is highly suspect, given that both companies, along with other Japanese and U.S. car manufacturers, have been swapping executives and openly shar-ing virtually all their management and production techniques for many years. Is Toyota more innovative? In 2002 I spent a few days talking to GM's senior management and top engineers and touring its research facilities, and learned of the extensive work the company was putting into developing futuristic ultralight ve-hicles that could run on electricity or hydrogen and that could even have their engine, transmission, and suspension character-istics upgraded at a stoplight via a wireless Internet connection. Toyota's Prius made it to the market far sooner because it was far *less* innovative than the sort of car GM wanted to build.

Any number of companies held up as corporate idols have in retrospect been iffy role models at best. General Electric is a dynamo of steady, impressive profits that can only be attributed to its brilliant and unique management techniques, we've been told, given that its success is shared by its many divisions scattered across multiple industries—until 2009, when, as GE threatened to implode, experts suddenly noticed that about half of the company's profits had long been coming from its financial services division, which appeared to have depended to some extent on some of the same risky strategies that inflated and then devastated earnings at banks, hedge funds, and brokerages. Dell had cracked the code on selling PCs at a profit, we were told, by outsourcing the manufacturing of virtually all of its components and of its base laptops, ignoring marketing channels other than online direct sales, growing its business internally rather than through acquisitions, and retaining a strict focus on selling PCs—all strategies that lowered costs to levels competitors couldn't hope to match. Until 2006, when Hewlett-Packard, by doing pretty much the opposite of everything for which Dell had been praised, started a PC sales run that would eventually leave Dell behind and force it to follow suit. Home Depot, Starbucks, Nokia—the list of organizations that have gone from business-expert hero to goat is a long one. Not that the experts are necessarily forced to hang their heads in shame when one of their superstars tanks—they just transition from explaining why the company's management techniques ensured success to why they ensured failure, as happened with GM in the 1980s, for example, and IBM in the 1990s. In fact, at least to the extent that expert pronouncements about business winners and losers are reflected in the business press, one of the more reliable ways of determining who is really best positioned for success and who for failure is by simply reversing what the experts say. So concluded a 2007 study in the *Financial Analysts Journal* that looked at twenty years' worth of feature-story headlines in *BusinessWeek*, *Fortune*, and *Forbes*, finding that stories praising companies or declaring trends tended to appear when things were about to go south.[7]

Why do we keep swallowing experts' assertions that they

can explain why certain businesses succeed, even in the face of so much evidence that today's big winners are often tomorrow's losers? Part of the reason, says the Pomona economics researcher Gary Smith, is a well-established cognitive bias known as the "hot hand" phenomenon, which basically holds that we tend to believe a recent run of unusually good performance will continue into the future. "If people see a company's profits have been way up for a few quarters, they think the profits will stay up," Smith told me. But isn't it often the case that "hot" performers really are more likely than not to keep up the exceptional work? Nope, it's just a bias, insists Smith. To prove it, he tested the theory in the realm of sports, where it's most often applied. Trying to figure out whether an athlete's hot streak is likely to continue isn't as easy as you might think, because a player's performance can be affected by confounding variables, including how teammates are playing, differences between competitors, and changes in playing environments. To minimize such variations, Smith hit on bowling, where every single roll of the ball is undertaken under pretty much identical circumstances—it's just the player against the pins at the end of the lane. And, sure enough, Smith found there was very little change on average in how likely any particular bowler was to throw a strike, no matter how many strikes in a row the bowler had thrown in previous frames.

Other academics have observed that the process by which experts come up with business role models is often marked by circular or "short-circuited" logic: experts look at winning companies, describe their successes in similar terms (the companies come up with innovative products, they have good relationships with customers, they globalize, and so forth), and then make the unwarranted leap to declaring that other companies will become successful if they do these same things. Phil Rosenzweig, a professor at the International Institute for Management Development in Switzerland, sees that sort of sloppy thinking as having its roots in another well-known cognitive bias, the "halo effect" (also the title of a book he wrote on the subject). The halo effect involves mistakenly ascribing certain characteristics to something based on that thing's other characteristics—for example, some of us might inappropriately assume that if someone is good-looking, he's also likely to be smart and friendly. In the context of business advice, contends Rosenzweig, experts proclaim that because some group of companies is profitable, those companies must also be...well, different experts hold up as the North Star different principles and management techniques. In the case of Toyota, for example, there are business books ascribing the company's success to, variously, its production system, its culture, its people development, its product development, its leaders, and its innovation. Among all of these books, there's nothing *not* pointed to in Toyota as the secret to its success.

Though Rosenzweig and many other academics argue that it's usually a cognitive bias or statistical anomaly underlying what appears to be a company's prolonged, brilliant success, Stanford's Denrell points out there can be other reasons why some companies outperform others for a while. Unfortunately, the specifics are not encouraging for business-book readers. For example, imagine a race between two competitors based on twenty-five coin flips—heads advances one competitor, tails the other. Which is more likely: that the lead will swap back and forth equally between the two contestants, or that one contestant will immediately take the lead and go on to win the race? Surprisingly, probability says it's the latter, and for a very simple reason: someone has to take the lead with the first flip, and the rest of the flips will on average be divided equally—which means the winner of the initial flip will have an edge, if a slight one. In business, says Denrell, a company's small initial lead over competitors, even if acquired by dumb luck, can more strongly tilt the playing field in that firm's favor, because that early, slight lead can bestow certain benefits: customers may not want to be bothered to switch to a competitor with a newer, slightly better product, talented prospective managers might be more interested in signing with the lead player in the field, suppliers may be willing to give that player more attractive deals, the press may pay more attention to the front-runner. In other words, an initial, all-but-meaningless lead can in a way become a self-fulfilling prophecy—and as that tiny lead becomes a bigger one, the advantages can become further amplified. "The most expected outcome is that there will be huge sustained profitability differences between firms," Denrell told me. "But there are no impressive management lessons to be had from the companies that have that high performance." Toyota can again serve as an example: even though by most measures its vehicles no longer hold any significant quality advantage over GM's, the company's early lead has left the public with a strong perception that it continues to dominate GM in quality.

Experts can hardly expect to hit bestseller lists by pointing out that the way to succeed in business is to, well, succeed, any more than a financial-advice book can score by focusing on the fact that the rich often get richer. Besides, adds Denrell, even though initial success can somewhat mechanically lead to extended success, it usually doesn't lead to *long-term* success—big winners are regularly taken down due to missteps, the emergence of new technologies, and changes in market needs. It's widely known that some of the companies highlighted by *In Search of Excellence* were already starting to tank by the time the book hit store shelves, and some researchers have concluded that a better-performing group of companies would have resulted from picking firms that enlisted exactly the opposite management principles of the ones espoused by the book.

But to say that studying big winners won't reveal useful

strategies for winning big isn't to say that there's no such thing as a strategy for winning big. In fact, notes Denrell, there is one, and almost any company can employ it: take big risks. Unfortunately, the catch is that big risk taking is the same strategy for losing big. "If you take a lot of risk, you're probably going to get either great results or terrible results, and terrible results are more likely," Denrell explained to me. "But if in a book you're only pointing out the companies that are succeeding, risky strategies look great." That's how the geniuses running Enron ended up lionized in dozens of business books, in studies, and on the covers of business magazines, even as the company was about to go up in flames. And then there were the many banks and investment firms that in the early to mid-2000s just couldn't get enough of mortgage-backed securities, or of derivatives that counted on a rising stock market. Those companies did *great* for quite a while. And now, with the constant emergence of waves of new, exciting, high-concept Internet companies that quickly capture the attention of millions of people (pay no attention to that anemic or nonexistent revenue stream—profits are in the works!), experts have gained a reliable source of innovative winners to point at, even if the experts have to keep swapping them out, as when Facebook replaced MySpace as the online hero of the hour, only to have Twitter steal the spotlight.

But though journalists, consultants, and business gurus may mislead us by focusing on supposedly winning companies of dubious distinction, don't most business academics know better? If so, they can do a pretty good job of hiding it, says Denrell. Business studies published in journals sometimes play the same game of claiming to prove that a management technique works by looking at a group of profitable companies and showing that most of them enlisted the technique. But that's highly flawed reasoning, notes Denrell, because it doesn't rule out the possibility that those companies were doing something else besides the technique in question to succeed, it doesn't establish that the technique was the cause of the profitability rather than an effect of it, and it doesn't offer evidence that these companies will continue to be profitable. What's more, the fact that most profitable companies do things a certain way doesn't really suggest that their technique confers a strong advantage unless we're sure that unsuccessful companies aren't also relying on the technique. For example, Denrell and his colleagues looked at a study that proclaimed successful companies tend to focus on a single core business rather than diversifying into a range of products and services; the study backed up that assertion by determining that 78 percent of companies meeting certain profitability criteria were focusers. "But that's not what we want to know," Denrell told me. "We want to know what percentage of *all* companies that focus on their cores will be successful." Denrell's recalculation provided the answer: a mere 35 percent. That is, 65 percent of focusers didn't end up making the grade, hardly proving core focus to be a dependable strategy.

The reliability of such studies further erodes, notes Denrell, when you realize that many and probably most studies that try to pump up a particular strategy or management technique fail to account for a critical set of companies: those that went out of business, or never even got off the ground. Information on defunct business ventures can be difficult or even nearly impossible to track down when tallying up companies and their performance—but those missing firms may have enlisted the same, supposedly wonderful management approaches that did so much for the winners. In fact, that's exactly what you'd expect if the technique is a highly risky one—it may be the secret to the spectacular success of many companies, but it will also have been the secret to the catastrophic failure of a larger number of firms ignored by studies. "It's completely misleading to only look at firms that survive," says Denrell. "But if we eliminated all the business studies that made these sorts of errors, there wouldn't be any studies left."

And don't count on the problems being brought to light when other academics try to repeat the studies. The Wharton School's Scott Armstrong examined the replication rate among marketing studies and found that it was just over 1 percent. David Sleeth-Keppler, who was directing the Behavioral Lab at Stanford's business school when I met with him and who is now a senior consultant with Strategic Business Insights, says that the low figure is in keeping with the fact that business studies tend to suffer from any number of credibility problems, many of them related to researcher bias. "The same authors come to the same findings over and over again," he told me. "They end up building their careers around them. But there isn't enough basis to conclude that any of the findings are real."

But what if experts somehow *could* figure out and agree on a way to meaningfully and accurately determine which businesses really deserve to be labeled successful role models? We'd still end up being misled, says Denrell. "There's too much randomness involved in business success," he told me. "Even if you identify the right companies and study them closely, you can't figure out how to be like them. It's not like billiards, where the laws of physics determine the absolutely correct, predictable way to play the game. In business, there's too much to take into account."

A sobering thought, considering how small a percentage of billiards players ever get really good at the game—even if they follow the advice of people who are expert at it.

Chapter Seven

Experts and the Media

One of the best ways of getting publicity is for a doctor to make some startling claim relative to people's health regardless of whether such statement is based on fact or theory.
— Edward Darr, former president of R. J. Reynolds

Mundus vult decipi, ergo decipiatur.

Let me shock the world and admit it: I want ratings. I want the largest possible audience so I can charge advertisers higher rates, so I can get more money.
— Rush Limbaugh

I n April 2005, BBC News posted a story on its website that began this way:

"Infomania" Worse than Marijuana

Workers distracted by email and phone calls suffer a fall in IQ more than twice that found in marijuana smokers, new research has claimed....

The study, carried out at the Institute of Psychiatry, found excessive use of technology reduced workers' intelligence.

Those distracted by incoming email and phone calls saw a 10-point fall in their IQ—more than twice that found in studies of the impact of smoking marijuana, said researchers.

The *San Francisco Chronicle* also covered the "infomania" story, noting: "The study, conducted in Britain earlier this year, involved 80 volunteers who took part in clinical trials and interviews with 1,100 subjects." CNN added these details: "In 80 clinical trials, Dr. Glenn Wilson, a psychiatrist at King's College London University, monitored the IQ of workers throughout the day." Similar articles were run by the *Times* of London, the *New Scientist*, and many other established, respected members of the mainstream media. The story was of course picked up by hundreds of websites and blogs, and for a few weeks at least it seemed difficult to avoid the tale of the mind-altering perils of electronic distraction. No wonder: many of us can't make it two minutes without shifting our attention to an e-mail, text message, or phone interaction, and scientific proof that our new social network–centric lifestyles are impairing us cognitively is surely news we need to hear. And a series of clinical trials tracking the shifting IQ of workers throughout the day certainly sounded like pretty good evidence.

I decided to look up Wilson, the man named in the news accounts as the author of the research. Though he was indeed affiliated with the Institute of Psychiatry at the prestigious King's College London, it turns out Wilson is more or less retired, and I met him at his modest London home, where the affably donnish fellow regaled me with enthusiastic accounts of a long, active career's worth of colorful and highly cited, peer-reviewed research. Wilson's specialty had been artfully exploring surrogate measures of various human mental states and tendencies. He had done a fair amount of research, for example, into the correlation between homosexuality and the relative lengths of a man's ring and index fingers. (This isn't as silly as it may sound—it's well established that fetal testosterone levels affect relative finger length.) He had also achieved some popular and even a bit of commercial success with a readily computerizable design for questionnaires that gauge the compatibility of prospective couples—that is, a matchmaking program—based on theories he had developed about what attracts people to each other. "There's only so much you can do with a series of questions," he told me, "but it wasn't bad for a first pass."

But when I asked him about the infomania study, Wilson's enthusiasm temporarily abandoned him. "Oh, that damned thing," he mumbled, shaking his head. He explained that the entire affair had been the bright idea of a marketing executive at the PC manufacturer Hewlett-Packard. The executive had called Wilson out of the blue and asked him if he would be willing to conduct a bit of paid research into the effects of multitasking. This sort of research-for-hire, or "consulting," is common and generally accepted among academics, as long as everyone is aboveboard about the sponsorship; indeed, it's often encouraged by universities, in that it builds profitable ties with industry, gets more exposure for its faculty, and lessens pressure on schools to provide big salaries and funding to its researchers. Encouraged by his sponsor at HP to keep the budget extremely low, and assured there was no pretense of trying to obtain scientifically valid, peer-reviewable, journal-publishable results, Wilson dragged eight students into a quiet room one at a time and gave them a standard IQ test, and then gave each of them another one—except that the second time, he left either a phone ringing continuously in the room or a flashing notification of incoming e-mail on a computer monitor in front of them. And what do you know? The students scored a bit lower while hounded by the constant noise or flashing light. "It didn't prove much of anything, of course," Wilson told me. "But Hewlett-Packard seemed happy with it, and I thought that was the end of it."

No one was more surprised than Wilson when the story exploded in the media, fueled by an HP press release that gave no hint of the crudity and tiny scale of the experiment but that did provide reporters with a wildly overreaching interpretation of the results, along with a bizarre comparison to the effects of marijuana. The story generated a stream of reporter interview requests to Wilson that, ironically enough, left his phone ringing and incoming e-mail notification box flashing nonstop for several weeks. Though Wilson tried to be a good sport about obliging, he had little luck in straightening the record. "It was awful," he said. "Embarrassing." Eventually even HP became alarmed by the extent of the coverage—it's a little hard to see why a PC vendor would want people to worry about electronic distractions in the first place—and asked Wilson to decline further comment. But by then the story had likely made its mark. About a year after the bulk of the news coverage, I happened to hear the bestselling get-organized guru Julie Morgenstern address a packed auditorium of business executives. "We used to think multitasking was efficient," she told the group, "but now we know it causes brain damage."

Infomania was a strange episode. Or was it? If such a flimsy, low-validity, non-peer-reviewed, journal-published "study" could get so much play in the legitimate press—much of that coverage twisted, exaggerated, and inaccurate—then should we be wondering about the general quality of the media's handling of expert findings? Of course we should. Most of the public doesn't read professional or research journals, or directly interact with high-powered researchers and other influential experts. Instead, people typically absorb expert wisdom via the mass media. If the result of our dependence on the media for the transmission of expert wisdom is to be susceptible to yet another layer of bias toward bad advice, and the distortion of what good advice is available, then clearly we're looking at an important part of the self-perpetuating problem of misleading expert pronouncements.

That conclusion probably won't come as a surprise to anyone. I found in talking to experts that they tend to reflexively blame the media for distorting their excellent findings in a way that only makes them *seem* to end up off track. (Though they usually have trouble sticking to that story when pressed.) And there appears to be no level of exaggeration, bad judgment, suspect motives, inaccuracy, or general untrustworthiness that the public is unwilling to believe of journalists. As the former journalist, publisher, and media watchdog Steven Brill has put it, "When it comes to arrogance, power, and lack of accountability, journalists are probably the only people on the planet who make lawyers look good."

It's no mystery what might cause the press to get into trouble with expertise. The media don't, by and large, exist solely to tell us what's right and true; they exist to get us to read about, watch, and listen to them, and that often means selecting and presenting expert findings in a way that is entertaining, provocative, useful sounding, and otherwise satisfyingly resonant. Claiming that journalists are devoted to bringing the truth to light is a bit like saying accountants are dedicated to upholding tax laws — it's often more about knowing how far you can go in the other direction without getting into real trouble. As we learned earlier, what newspapers, magazines, television programs, radio shows, and trade books look for from an expert and her findings — simplicity, controversy, color, broad appeal, a definitive answer, striking measurements — is virtually a recipe for bad advice. And the fact that the media often insist the experts they showcase wield academic credentials or other standard trappings of expertise, or that their opinions are backed by others in their expert communities, is hardly protection from wrongness.

Not that the media limit themselves to highlighting the wisdom of scientists and other high-level, authoritative experts. Even mainstream publications, programs, and websites seem willing to occasionally become unmoored from their normally already shaky standards of evidence. In one prominent segment in 2008, the *Today* show—watched by an average of more than five million people—featured the respected and popular correspondent and news anchor Ann Curry enthusiastically pushing photographic evidence (a patch of glare on a television monitor) of the curing of a terminal patient via the visitation of an angel to a hospital ward. Scientists and press critics, or at least those without strong religious beliefs, can sigh and roll their eyes over that sort of exotic, hard evidence–free claim, but there doesn't seem to be much of a point in confronting it head-on. People who believe such reports are probably not going to be much swayed by arguments based on logic and the need for experimental data—I doubt many believers in the Shroud of Turin's connection to Jesus have had their minds changed by carbon dating. But if scienceless claims sometimes get a free ride, claims based on junk science are another matter. The media, many critics charge, simply don't do a good job of filtering out the presumably bogus findings and opinions of nonmainstream experts who cloak themselves in the trappings of real science without actually performing real science, or at least without submitting themselves to what are accepted as the checks and balances of real science.

Among the many observers who make this charge is Tracey Brown, the managing director of Sense About Science, a U.K. nonprofit organization that focuses on countering media reports that lend credence to alternative health treatments or that alarm the public about such alleged dangers as carcinogens in plastic bottles, killer radiation from cell phones, toxins in water supplies, risks from genetically modified foods, and other claims often labeled as "junk science." (The "GM" food issue is one that hasn't received nearly as much attention in the United States as it has in Europe.) "In an effort to make it all more interesting for the public, they get away from good science," she says.

When I dropped in on Sense About Science's London headquarters just outside Piccadilly Circus, I was expecting a cramped warren of laid-back, T-shirted cubicle rats—in other words, something like those quarters of university science departments inhabited by graduate students toiling away on their bosses' research. But Sense About Science's offices could pass for those of a venture capital firm, complete with secretaries and assistants smartly sporting business noncasual, as was Brown herself. The upscale, corporate aura reminded me that Sense About Science is often dismissed by activists as an industry front that never met a chemical or electromagnetic wave it didn't love, and I delicately bounced that suggestion off Brown. She briskly fended off the charge with a firm smile, insisting that only 30 percent of the organization's funding comes from industry. The bulk comes from "foundations," she added after I pressed a bit, and then she changed the subject.

Brown explained that when signs of suspect science start reverberating in the media, her organization immediately mobilizes, barraging journalists with press releases containing what is presumably the straight dope right from the mouths or keyboards of some of the three thousand or so scientists who have agreed to make their wisdom available to Sense About Science. Brown often gets on the phone herself to offending and influential journalists to gently upbraid or enlighten, and offers to set them up with interviews with scientists on her list. As Brown sees it, prodding credible scientists to answer the call of duty in these cases is a critical part of Sense About Science's mission. "They feel they're not supposed to have to persuade anyone to believe them," she explains. And scientists have to be prepared to respond to a query within hours or even minutes, she adds, not the weeks or even months during which they might dialog with a journal editor. Sense About Science also tries to get the word out directly to the public, via brochures that explain why peer-reviewed publication serves as a seal of good science. More than sixty thousand people have requested and received the brochures, she boasts.

The notion that the media's transmission of bad scientific findings and opinions can be pegged to a failure to focus on "good" scientists was echoed to me by Tammy Boyce, who, at the time I met with her, was a journalism professor at the University of Cardiff in Wales. (She has recently become a research fellow at the King's Fund, a U.K. nonprofit that seeks to improve the nation's health-care system.) Boyce, who specialized in studying how journalists cover science, went even further than Brown, arguing to me that journalists should not only stick with the findings of peer-reviewed research but limit themselves to research from "better" peer-reviewed journals and universities. "There are too many journalists quoting research published in third-rate journals, authored by scientists from the University of Nowhere," she told me. It's these lesser scientists, with their sloppy studies, who provide journalists with the health scares and the illusion of controversy that the reporters need to sell papers, she said. If journalists would just say no to these inferior scientists and stick with the real deal, the public would be well informed.

But there are some real holes in these arguments. For one thing, what is dismissed by mainstream science as junk science sometimes turns out to be worth a closer look. Long berated by Sense About Science and many other groups as based on sloppy science, the concerns about the effects of Bisphenol-A (BPA) in some plastic bottles started crossing over into mainstream science in 2007. The mainstream medical science community has also been fairly relentless in jumping all over the validity of studies that purport to show alternative medical treatments as having more than a placebo effect, but in 2008 a large review study of twenty-five randomized controlled trials found that acupuncture as a treatment for headaches not only performed better than the placebo (yes, there are techniques for faking the placement of needles) but even performed substantially better than established medical treatments.[1]

With surveys by the U.S. National Institutes of Health and the Centers for Disease Control and Prevention indicating that 40 percent of U.S. adults have been turning to alternative medical treatments,[2] we might wonder whether these numbers are to some extent a gauge not simply of the public's gullibility and ignorance but also of people's awareness that mainstream modern medical science hasn't been as relatively effective and trustworthy as it often makes itself out to be. The point here isn't to turn people away from mainstream science or medicine — far from it. But it's a mistake to believe that the problem with bad expert advice can be *mostly* attributed to media coverage of substandard science. After all, even if the press were to do nothing but simply reprint the entire contents of the most respected research journals, we'd still end up with mostly wrong conclusions.

Still, it's likely true that what appears in the media in terms of science coverage is on average worse than what's in journals, in terms of findings and advice that will later appear to be refuted, exaggerated, misleading, or flat-out wrong. That's not entirely because reporters frequently draw from outside of credible, peer-reviewed research, as they did with the infomania pseudostudy; it's also because of how they draw from *within* it. Consider this excerpt from a short piece written in 2008 by Lucy Danziger, the editor in chief of *Self*, a magazine serving as a widely trusted journalistic source of health and fitness advice, and which is in a position to influence the dietary decisions of millions of (mostly) women. The article was posted online and received prominent coverage on Yahoo!'s home page, among other choice locations.

Skip the Diet Soda

Get ready to ditch your soda habit. I'm kicking Diet Coke—it takes time, and I'm down to five a week from a high of 12, but it's worth it.

Here's why: Recent research has shown that artificial sweeteners in soda may interfere with your body's ability to estimate how many calories you've ingested, so you eat more than you need....

Need more convincing? For every diet soda you sip daily, your risk of becoming overweight can rise by 37 percent, according to researchers at the University of Texas Health Science Center in San Antonio.

Danziger was reporting here on perfectly legitimate, peer-reviewed research that was covered by many news outlets. But she doesn't merely pass the findings on to us; she seems to accept them completely, and helpfully translates them into a firm call for a rather severe course of action—that of abandoning diet soda—in spite of the fact that the studies to which she appears to be referring are, as we saw earlier,[3] largely based on animals; don't rule out other reasons why consuming diet sodas might be linked to obesity; and directly conflict with other studies that don't observe any such link. In effect, this sort of coverage amplifies the likely wrongness of a finding by exaggerating its significance; ignoring the qualifications, limits, and uncertainties associated with the finding; and cheerleading for significant lifestyle changes based on it without further investigation or any real perspective.*

I don't mean to pick on Danziger or *Self* (for which I have written); there's a true embarrassment of riches when it comes to finding examples of questionable judgment on the press's part in selecting and presenting research findings from published, peer-reviewed studies. A few more examples:

• In September 2008, when New Orleans was reeling from Hurricane Gustav and bracing for three other hurricanes heading in its direction, and Sarah Palin and her family were at the Republican convention, threatening to change the face of American politics, the NBC *Nightly News* anchor Brian Williams gave a top-of-the-show headline to a story—"sure to be watercooler talk tomorrow," as he put it—about a study identifying the "monogamy gene" in men, said to determine their likely fidelity. In fact, the vast majority of the work on the gene had been done on rodents (voles, to be exact), while a single new study had attempted to apply the work to men, not by looking at how their infidelity or promiscuity or relationship status varied with the gene but rather by looking at only written quality-of-relationship tests (e.g., "How often do you kiss your mate?") taken by a group of married couples.[4] Another study, meanwhile, had already found no significant relationship between any single gene and monogamy, and refuted the notion that the vole studies applied to humans.[5]

---

* I tried to speak with Danziger about the piece—I was particularly eager to hear whether dropping Diet Coke effected the promised big improvement in her ability to estimate calorie intake—but *Self*'s PR crew turned down my request for an interview. Incidentally, journalists proved less likely to return my calls than any sort of expert I tried to reach for this book, including top scientists. I suspect many of us journalists know too much about journalism to want to risk being subjected to it—at least when we don't have a book to promote.

- The Associated Press distributed a 2008 story headlining the claim that not sleeping soundly through the night raises the risk of diabetes—based, as it turns out, on a study of nine young, healthy volunteers who were subjected to disturbing noises at night, apparently resulting in their experiencing fluctuations in blood sugar levels.[6]

- "Work Out and Drink Up," headlined *Time* magazine in early 2008, in uncritically reporting a Danish study's claim that it's okay for middle-aged and older folks to cut down on exercise as long as they replace the lost treadmill time with a daily alcoholic drink or two. The article also touted several other potential health benefits to regular drinking, including limiting stroke damage and the risk of diabetes. The article did take the trouble to warn off alcoholics or women with a family history of breast cancer but said nothing about the growing evidence in recent years that even moderate consumption of alcohol appears to be linked to other forms of cancer, or that the evidence about the relationships between alcohol and diabetes and brain health have been mixed (moderate drinking has, for example, been strongly linked to long-term shrinking of the brain),[7] or that there's a body of evidence that drinking alcohol simply doesn't translate into living longer, or that the association among health, longevity, and level of exercise is a far better-established one (even if cause versus effect is still debated).

I'm not saying the studies described in these news stories were bad or necessarily wrong, but they suffered from potential weaknesses, and their findings were at odds with those of other studies, leaving much room for interpretation and skepticism. Yet the findings were reported much as if they were proven facts, ready for application in our lives. There's no way of knowing how many restless sleepers have added fear of diabetes to whatever anxieties were already disturbing their repose, or how many women want to order up genetic fidelity tests on their prospective mates, or how many exercisers are cutting their workouts short to chug a beer, but if it's many more than zero for any of these cases, then that's a shame. And these news reports are absolutely typical of how the media essentially sell us on questionable research findings published in respected, peer-reviewed journals.

Of course, the mass media can also be champions of exactly the right expertise, too. The link between smoking and lung cancer didn't get much traction in the public until *Reader's Digest* reported on it in 1952—and when Americans promptly switched en masse to filter cigarettes in the belief that doing so avoided most of the risk, *Reader's Digest* again churned things up with an article in 1957 that convincingly showed filters offered little or no protection.[8] But more often the media simply draw the most resonant, provocative, and colorful—and therefore most likely to be wrong—findings from a pool of journal-published research that already has a high wrongness rate. What's more, the press's compliance when it comes to passing on dubious findings lies in sharp contrast to the way it tends to remain quite vigilant about the untrue and distorted assertions of politicians—every metropolitan daily newspaper of any reputation whatsoever routinely runs investigative pieces of city and state political corruption, bias, sloth, and ineffectiveness, and it has become commonplace now for the press to run "fact-checking" pieces reporting on the speeches, advertisements, or debates of presidential candidates. Why don't we see a hint of the same sort of skepticism applied to expert studies? Isn't it at least as important that we see through the questionable claims related to our health and well-being as it is that we see through the questionable claims related to taxes and campaign donations?

One reason for the discrepancy is that while the public generally expects political reporters to take a jaundiced view of what politicians claim, hardly anyone seems to worry about the fact that science reporters tend not only to trust but to idealize and even idolize scientists. In 2008 Dennis Overbye, a celebrated science writer for the *New York Times*' "Science Times" section—one of the most respected mass-media science publications—compared in an article the virtues of science to those of democracy, stating that scientists' "values, among others, are honesty, doubt, respect for evidence, openness, accountability and tolerance and indeed hunger for opposing points of view." I've heard much the same privately over the years from many science journalists, and have on occasion echoed those sentiments myself. One science journalist once told me that whenever a scientist says something that he realizes might look bad in print, he stops her and asks her to reconsider whether she really wants to go on the record with the comment. When journalists are convinced prima facie that their sources are mostly paragons of honesty and trustworthiness, and may even see part of their role as making their sources look good in print, well, the risks are obvious.

In addition, while it's much more fun to read about the ways in which a politician has slipped up or bent the truth than it is to read about one who is operating as he should be, the opposite is usually true for science: there typically isn't much of a good read to be had about how a study's findings may not be trustworthy. "Once a reporter starts to back away from supporting what the expert is saying, the editor will start scratching his head over why they should be running the piece," I was told by Scott Maier, a longtime newspaper reporter and now a professor at the University of Oregon's School of Journalism and Communication. "We want to look at the positive aspects of medical breakthroughs, we want stories that pay off with some dividend. If you want the story to have its fullest impact, you're more likely to exaggerate what the expert says than you are to question it." This notion would help to explain, for example, why *National*

Geographic, on the strength of one expert's opinion, ran a story in 1999 proclaiming a bizarre fossil to be that of a creature representing the missing link between birds and dinosaurs, even though others in the field felt sure the fossil was an absurd hoax. (It was.) And it would help to explain why the *New York Times* ran a piece in 2008 singing the praises of five weight-loss books written by research scientists whose "recommendations are based on sound studies and clinical trials that have yielded a better understanding of what prompts us to eat more calories than we need and, in particular, more calories from the wrong kinds of foods"—even though the diets pushed in these books haven't been clearly shown to work better than other diets and in some cases go against findings from other studies.*

We probably shouldn't expect most reporters to have the scientific or other specialized knowledge sometimes needed to spot the subtle or technical flaws in studies, especially when scientists' own colleagues often can't spot them. It's hardly shaming to say of the typical science journalist that she probably can't interpret particle-accelerator wire-chamber readouts, or analyze metabolic pathways, or recheck complex statistical analyses. But reporters often seem unwilling to undertake even the most perfunctory checks of whatever dubious numbers they're handed. In early 2009 the AP ran a story announcing that a swimmer had covered a record-setting 2,100 miles in twenty-five days—which would have merely required that she swim at the pace of an Olympic 100-meter champion for twenty-four hours a day for the better part of a month. (It turns out she had been hanging on to the back of a boat for most of the journey.) And a sports measurement is a lot

---

* For example, the evidence for the frequent claim that calories from one sort of food are more conducive to long-term weight loss than the same number of calories from another type of food has long remained convoluted and contradictory, though a large study released in early 2009 seemed to shoot the idea down convincingly.[9]

more likely to be double-checked than a medical finding. "Reporters almost never question numbers from scientists," says Maier.

But, more important, the media consistently fail to highlight how untrustworthy studies turn out to be *in general*. Consider these three article headlines and excerpts, presented here as they appeared together in the "Health" category of the home page of Google News on March 28, 2008, meaning (if you accept Google's ability to judge webpage popularity) that these were, at the time, the three most widely read health-news stories on the Internet:

"FDA Reviewing Asthma Drug, Suicide Link"
Boston Globe
WASHINGTON—Merck & Co.'s Singulair may be linked to suicide and changes in mood and behavior, US regulators said yesterday in disclosing a review of the company's top-selling asthma drug.

"Study Hints of Gene Link to Risk of Schizophrenia"
New York Times
A new study has found that rare and previously undetectable genetic variations may significantly increase the risk that a person will develop schizophrenia.

"When the Waist Widens, Risk of Dementia Rises"
Los Angeles Times
People with high abdominal fat were found three times more likely to develop dementia, adding to previous studies showing that people with large abdomens face a greater chance of diabetes, stroke and heart disease.

Each of these articles, appearing as they did in three of the United States' most respected newspapers, was on the whole quite good, reporting accurately on the research and mentioning various limitations of it. But none of them even came close to clueing the reader in to the basic fact that there's an excellent chance none of these conclusions will hold up in the long run. I've already mentioned that drug-suicide links are usually based on self-reporting in a way likely to distort the picture and that gene-link studies depend on techniques and assumptions that have proven unreliable. The fat-dementia study was an epidemiological study, and we know that these are rarely highly trustworthy—though they account for a large proportion of the flashy health stories pumped by the press.

Most science journalists seem to believe that all problems with studies disappear if you stick to randomized controlled trials, in spite of the fact that these studies, too, often go very wrong. The Science Literacy Project, a well-regarded program aimed at sharpening the skills of radio journalists who cover science and run by a group that specializes in producing science pieces for public radio in the United States, offers via the Internet a series of "tip sheets" for science journalists. Here's an excerpt:

Learn the Basics of Study Design

Many stories in the media fail to point out that while a study result is intriguing, it may be far from certain because of the way the study itself was conducted. Most of the time we report these things as fact—then come back two weeks later and report a completely contradictory finding, also as if it were scientific fact. No wonder people get frustrated with us! Avoid this problem by learning enough about how studies are designed and conducted to be able to tell your listeners how solid the research really is. As a bonus, this can help you weed out a lot of nonsense research that probably shouldn't be reported on in the first place. The gold standard is a randomized, double-blind, controlled trial. Other kinds of studies…can provide intriguing hints but not firm evidence.

So there you have it: journalists should be skeptical of study findings—unless they're from an RCT, in which case all is well. Not only does this piece of expert advice invite journalists to treat potentially highly misleading RCT findings unskeptically but it encourages them to downplay or even ignore what may in fact be important and relatively trustworthy evidence that happens to not come from RCTs. If journalists had been strictly following this advice for the past five decades, most of us would believe today that no one has ever produced "firm evidence" that smoking is bad for you, that seat belts save lives, or that the HIV virus is transmitted by unprotected sex, none of which was established via RCTs. The fact that many journalists do subscribe to the myth that RCTs are unassailable is one reason we've been presented with "firm evidence" that fat is bad for you, fat is good for you, carbs are good for you, carbs are bad for you, it doesn't matter which foods you eat as long as you control calories, and you shouldn't focus on controlling calories as long as you eat the right foods.

Some science and health journalists are aware that study findings of *all* types are often contradictory, muddled, misleading, refuted, and otherwise untrustworthy. Nick Bakalar, a reporter who regularly covers medical study findings for the *New York Times'* "Science Times," told me he doesn't discriminate between studies by study design as much as by whether or not they avoid setting off certain alarm bells—he rarely touches animal studies, early-phase clinical drug trials, and studies that make "big or scary claims," even if they are RCTs. Still, he acknowledged that in the end there's little he can do to avoid plying the public with findings that may well prove misleading, short of offering sharp, blanket reader warnings that would make the story sound pointless and fail to get past editors.

But the problem with media coverage of expert studies goes beyond simply passing on to the public the misleading results from journals. Reporters often add their own bias, error, exaggeration, and distortion to the package, often in a quest to capture the provocative. In late 2008 the media widely showcased a study, complete with outraged quotes from consumer experts, that found half of U.S. physicians regularly prescribe placebo treatments—almost universally failing to mention that these "placebos" were mostly the pain relievers and antibiotics we expect our doctors to prescribe for us, not sugar pills. Similarly, the media went to town on a 2008 study that supposedly proved via brain scans that bullies enjoy seeing people suffer—when in fact the study had shown only that eight teenagers exhibiting aggressive, and not necessarily bullying, behavior seemed to experience either pleasure or displeasure at others' suffering. In translating a 2007 report that showed blood flow can affect brain cells, the U.K. *Daily Mail* ended up with the caption "Standing on your head could be used to help treat diseases such as Alzheimer's."

You might think you'd be in safer territory with a mass-media account of a published study if it includes a quote from one of the authors explaining the significance of the study in her own words. But journalists can be quite good at twisting the arms of even the most circumspect interviewees into making statements that pry their tongues from their better instincts—indeed, it's a journalistic core competence. Gabor Forgacs, the University of Missouri biophysicist, told me he had been besieged with calls from reporters when he published his research on a device that presses human tissue cells onto special paper for drug-testing purposes. "Every single one asked me to say when we'll be ready to manufacture full organs that can be transplanted into humans," he said.

"No reputable scientist would answer that question." Forgacs was brave to hold out, but he is wrong on that last score; trust me, reputable scientists are prodded by journalists into answering those sorts of questions all the time.

But if a reputable expert does refuse to give up the goods to a reporter determined to get a colorful quote, no problem—there's a vast army of other experts who will be willing to stand in and spew titillating sound bites. When the former model and actress Christie Brinkley went public, during her divorce trial, with her husband's pornography habits, ABC's *Good Morning America Weekend Edition* was among the many media institutions to take the opportunity to explore the topic of sex addiction, trotting out a psychologist who directed a counseling center. ABC's website quoted the man this way: "Anyone who is married to Christie Brinkley and has to masturbate at all is probably a sex addict"—a remarkable statement revealing in one breath a spectacular disregard for almost everything known about sex addiction, marriage, and masturbation, and which, if taken seriously, must have generated thousands of pointlessly worried calls to sex-addiction hotlines. Of course, a journalist may have little way of knowing whether an expert's opinion reflects sheer genius and a wealth of evidence or just sloppy thinking and opportunism. "I guess sometimes we just have to trust them," the *New York Times'* Bakalar told me. "I'm not the expert in these situations—they are. How do you get through life if you don't accept some expertise?"*

Still, it doesn't help if you can't get your facts straight. Reporters assigned complex stories with tight deadlines simply

---

* It's hard to blame the editors of *Time*, for example, for not more closely vetting the aforementioned article pushing the health benefits of alcohol—the byline belonged to Sanjay Gupta, who is not only a popular media commentator but a respected physician who was widely reported to have been offered the U.S. surgeon general's job by the Obama administration in early 2009. (He turned it down.)

don't always have time to cross-check information. The University of Oregon's Maier found in a study of newspaper articles that half of the stories contained at least one factual error, and in another study found that in 60 percent of the target articles, at least one person interviewed for the piece claimed the reporter didn't get the story straight.* And, as with academic research, there has been an impressive array of cases of what appear to have been brazen fabrications among notable reporters and columnists at respected publications. The *New York Times* (and, separately, its magazine), *USA Today*, the *Boston Globe*, the *Village Voice*, the *Sacramento Bee*, the *Detroit Free Press*, *Wired*, the *New Republic*, and *The New Yorker* were all among those esteemed newspapers and magazines humbled by highly visible cases over the past decade. Even the dean of Northwestern University's highly regarded journalism school faced charges of fabricating quotes for an article in 2008. (He was cleared by an investigating committee, which cited a lack of evidence, though the sources of the quotes were never located.) But as with research fraud, the hoopla over these public cases often has the paradoxical effect of lulling us into believing that all is well with the mainstream — these are supposedly the exceptions that prove the rule. Not likely.

Even were journalists to avoid less trustworthy studies, and manage to accurately convey their findings, and point out that the conclusions shouldn't be regarded as sure things even if they come from RCTs or review studies, the reporters would still usually be providing the public with a distorted view of expert findings. That's because journalists rarely fully transmit to readers

---

* Sources often claim they were misquoted or "quoted out of context," when the truth is they didn't like the quote the reporter picked out or the point it was used to support. But such a high discomfort rate from sources hints at some level of real carelessness on the parts of journalists.

the various uncertainties that arise from all the corrupting factors we've looked at. "Scientists understand that uncertainty," says Maier, "but I'm not sure it's clear to the media, and it isn't necessarily conveyed to the public." Indeed, whose job is it to bring these uncertainties to light?* Researchers say they don't need to spell them out in their published research, since they're publishing for one another. Journalists could reasonably claim that they can't be blamed for not reporting aspects of research that researchers don't mention.

But regardless of who may or may not be to blame, these uncertainties surely matter. In the short term, not knowing about them causes us to place undue faith in ultimately misleading findings that can affect our lives. In the long term, after we have seen countless flip-flops and have been repeatedly burned when attempting to extract reliable guidance from experts, we may simply stop trying.

---

* It would be helpful if journalists, with the assistance of more forthcoming researchers, were able to point out which studies were more susceptible to these troubles, and which were less so. But failing that, perhaps all mass-media coverage of expert studies could, like cigarettes, come with a boilerplate warning.

CHAPTER EIGHT

The Internet and the Technology of Expertise

Dopeler effect (n): The tendency of stupid ideas to seem smarter when they come at you rapidly.
— ENTRY IN 1998 *Washington Post* CONTEST
ASKING READERS TO INVENT WORDS

C lothes made from recycled materials can, as it turns out, be a little itchy. But Jackie Stewart is determined to dwell on the positive and therefore is chatting engagingly about the dress she's wearing, pointing out that in addition to striking a blow for Mother Earth, it fits well and is brightly colored. The dress does, in fact, look great on her, though Stewart would probably make a dress put together from inner tubes look smart. She's so comfortable talking up Green style that it's easy to forget she is being filmed on a set, until the director, Damian Weyand, interrupts to suggest she not flourish her arms to call attention to the dress. "It's a little too *Price Is Right*," he explains. "We just want you to be Jackie, not spokesy."

Just being Jackie isn't the sort of thing normally asked of Stewart. She's a professional model in the stable of Ford Models, the storied agency. Ford is producing this short video, one of hundreds it has put together featuring its models applying their shopping savvy at the racks in boutiques, sweating through what-it-takes-to-look-like-a-model workouts, and dishing backstage secrets at fashion shows and photo shoots. The videos became something of a new media hit in 2007, turning up all over the Internet and sending a stream of traffic to Ford's website. In particular, they scored big on YouTube, where, within six months of their appearance, some of them garnered more than half a million views apiece, making the Ford videos, for a time, the third most popular destination of YouTube visitors.

Could the Ford videos also represent the future of expertise? Ford's fare offers a form of expert advice that's tailored, personal, searchable, monetizable, cheap to produce, free to access, user comment–friendly, and open to a vast class of potential advice givers we might call micro-experts. You could also argue it's inane, at least compared to the sort of expertise we've been considering so far, but who would you be to judge? To some people, finding out how to get a good deal on a pair of jeans that fit might far outstrip the importance of advice on how to avoid cancer, head off global warming, or elude the devastation of retirement savings. As Mitch Grossbach, who directs Ford's digital efforts, told me, "It's hard to be a fifteen-year-old girl competing to be popular in Louisville."

To put it another way, this form of expertise is democratic. Thanks to the Internet, anyone can in theory get precisely the expert advice they want and need, and anyone can in theory be the expert who provides it. Or so argues a legion of Internet boosters, who claim that by wrenching control of expertise from the elitist clutches of universities, research institutes, consultancies, big corporations, government agencies, and the mainstream press, and outsourcing it to the billion or so people on the planet with Internet connections, we can raise the usefulness, relevance, cost-efficiency, and even trustworthiness of expert advice. You'd need a pretty wide shelf to hold just those popular books that have made one aspect or another of that case in recent years—works whose titles include *The Long Tail*, *Wikinomics*, *Here Comes Everybody*, *The*

Wealth of Networks, *Smart Mobs*, *Everything Is Miscellaneous*, and *Infotopia*, among many others.

What to make of the fact that the authors of most of these books, along with many of the other persuasive voices pushing the wonders of online distributed expertise, are academics, high-powered consultants, influential print journalists, captains of industry, and other types of conventional mass experts? At first it might seem as if, in calling for a more egalitarian take on wisdom, these experts are boldly hastening their own professional downsizing for a good cause. But the truth is, they've latched on to a very good thing for themselves—one of the best ways to sell books and magazines, get published in journals, make it onto the first business page of newspapers, excite investors, and thrive on the speaking circuit is to push a clever take on the growing inferiority of, as compared to what can be done online, books, magazines, newspapers, journals, traditional businesses, and real-time, verbal communication between colocated human beings. Still, even if becoming an old-fashioned expert on the triumph of new-fashioned expertise may be self-serving, that doesn't make these folks wrong, and anyway it's not as if they're the only ones talking up the Internet. Perhaps a better reason to be at least a little skeptical of their claims is that while it's undeniable there's a staggering array of expertise and advice waiting to be tapped online, there seems to be a certain amount of magical thinking behind the notion that somehow we can be connected to exactly the *right* expertise.

Oh, wait—that's what Google is for. There are plenty of other search engines, but in the United States about two-thirds of all Internet searches are via Google, and the percentage is even higher in most Western European countries, leaving other search engines to fight over relative scraps of user attention. (Google's numbers tend to be quite a bit lower in Asia.) Googling is a nearly unrivaled activity online, with half of all Internet users performing a search on an average day—a number that's been growing steadily. Google can point you to any of more than one trillion webpages, and that number is rapidly increasing as well.

There's no question that Google is an extraordinarily useful resource, but what's often overlooked is that Google frequently does a terrible job in getting us the information we need, and the failure is even more glaring if we're looking for trustworthy expert advice on a complex subject. The fact is, most of what Google returns in such a search is likely to be irrelevant or wrong. Google's CEO, Eric Schmidt, may have articulated the problem as clearly and concisely as anyone: the Internet, he has said publicly, is in danger of becoming a "cesspool" of false and misleading information. The reason is straightforward enough: anyone can post anything they want online, without having to present credentials or meet some editor's or anyone else's standards, and Google will dutifully and democratically index it as it would an article from *Foreign Policy* or the *New York Times.* Thus, in Google's results, good advice tends to be swamped by an exponentially larger array of useless, misleading, and generally subpar stuff.

In theory Google's famed ranking algorithm should help bring the more useful webpages to the top, but in practice it tends to not work out that way. That's partly because the algorithm is severely limited in its ability to assess how suitable a webpage is to what a user might be looking for, but it's also because the ranking scheme is highly susceptible to being gamed by people who master the art of manipulating webpage language, code, and links so as to boost a page's ranking far above what its usefulness, relevance, or popularity might reasonably merit—as, for example, when pranksters have brought George W. Bush's or, more recently, Barack Obama's website to the top of Google's results for searches on the word "failure." Of course, people who operate highly useful websites could work as hard and as sleazily as anyone else at the optimization game, but judging from the number of spam and otherwise quality-information-poor webpages that pop up high in the results, we find that it doesn't seem that they always do. Indeed, a small "reputation management" industry has sprung up not so much to raise the Google rankings of clients' existing pages but rather to bury often highly relevant pages under specially designed, less informative ones simply because their clients—for example, corporate executives embarrassed by coverage of their misdeeds—don't want the world to see the whole story.

This frequent failure of Google's results to provide links to trustworthy advice can be frustrating. Like so many others, I'm constantly turning to Google to try to dig up some wisdom on my problem of the day, be it a rattle in my car, an ache in my abdomen, a confusing tax form, a concern about a child's college applications, or a lousy snowboarding technique. The immediate result is typically a rat's nest of conflicting and dubious pronouncements. As a small example, I recently wondered if it would be safe to give my dog a bit of acetaminophen (Tylenol) for a paw she was suddenly favoring. The veterinarian wasn't available, so I hit Google and found, high up in the results, this wisdom from a columnist who regularly writes about pets: "A reader e-mailed me and asked me to remind dog owners that acetaminophen is toxic to both dogs and cats....Just about every Web site for animals warns pet owners about the danger of acetaminophen for pets." She's right about the websites; there's fairly strong agreement, at least among the higher-ranking Google results, that you'd be putting your dog at mortal risk to slip it even a small piece of a Tylenol tablet. That seemed convincing. But buried farther down in the Google results was the website of a veterinarian who claims that acetaminophen is not only safe but actually the safest of all pain medications for dogs, when given in weight-appropriate doses—he routinely prescribes it for his canine patients and has never witnessed a negative reaction. The widespread notion that the drug is unsafe for dogs, this vet suggests, is due to confusion related to the fact that acetaminophen can be dangerous for *cats*, which lack a key enzyme. That sounded pretty convincing, too, leaving me little enlightened after ten minutes of searching. But I kept hunting and eventually discovered an online version of the American Veterinary Medical Association Pet Poison Guide, which more or less backed up the vet. In the end, I had doggedly tracked down what seemed to be the good advice I was looking for. But as a journalist, I'm sort of a professional information searcher. I doubt a large percentage of online users have my experience and persistence. (And even then, I imagine that I'm still taken in quite often.)

Having to sift through contradictory and often inappropriate online medical advice has become a sort of public health problem in its own right. Some 160 million Americans looked for medical information online in 2007, according to one survey.[1] A 2008 study by Microsoft researchers found that one out of fifty Internet searches focuses on health and that a third of Internet users who looked into a health question followed up with searches about a serious illness.[2] No wonder: the study found that health searchers tended to focus on only the top few results, and these results often highlight rarer, more serious diagnoses of common ailments—such as headaches (brain tumor!) and chest discomfort (heart attack!)—over far more likely possible explanations (such as stress and heartburn, respectively). It's hard to find clear, consistent advice online about whether or not it's okay for adolescents to pop their pimples, never mind questions about urinary tract problems, mysterious lumps, changes in appetite, or dizziness. One of the best things that can be said about Google and the hunt for expert wisdom is that the search engine typically points to hundreds or even thousands of pieces of obviously conflicting and lousy advice, instead of just one or two morsels of less obviously bad advice that might more easily be mistaken for the final word on the subject—though the latter situation might as well be the case if people are looking only at the top results.

To balance my slightly cranky view of online wisdom, I visited William Dutton, the director of Oxford University's Internet Institute. The Internet Institute is not to be mistaken for one of the shabby operations set up by many otherwise good schools primarily to reap profits from the purveying of high-fee, low-cost online classes; it's a well-funded academic research department of Oxford, housed in substantial and elegant digs. Dutton argued to me that the search for online expertise ought to be evaluated not in absolute terms but rather in how it compares to the quality of advice people end up with off-line. After all, we're not exactly getting consistently sterling advice from television and print publications. In the case of medical questions, for example, we ask our doctors—and Dutton notes that patients often feel far less than fully satisfied by the quality of their doctors' responses. "There's a tendency to romanticize the doctor-patient relationship, but doctors are notoriously bad communicators," he told me. Nor should Internet advice necessarily be evaluated on a stand-alone basis, he added; it can be a valuable complement to off-line advice. "You can take the information you get online and bring it to the doctor's office, so you can ask better questions," he said. "The doctor doesn't have to agree with all of it." Off-line as well as on, Dutton argued, extracting better expert advice from the junk requires "critical reading skills." But he conceded that the higher ratio of lousier to better information likely found in a Google search compared to, say, the table of contents of an established magazine makes those skills even more, well, critical. "It's the same old issues, but it's becoming more important on the Internet," he told me. "For less-critical readers, the online world could create more serious problems." This observation, which Dutton and other academics refer to as the "knowledge gap hypothesis," essentially counter-intuitively associates the democratization of media with a rich-get-richer outcome—as more information becomes available to more people, those who are already better educated and better informed are better able to take advantage of it, while everyone else becomes only more likely to drown in a sea of second-rate information. One way to cope with the problem, Dutton added, would be to tailor the way online information is presented to people with different needs, skills, and backgrounds—but how this mechanism might work, and who would decide the appropriate sort of tailoring, he couldn't say.

Search services like Google's may be distorting not only the way in which we're exposed to expert advice but also our ability to process it. The journalist Nicholas Carr, a perceptive critic of many aspects of our increasingly computer-centric world, has been among those who have argued that by dishing up a large number of websites in response to queries, Google and other search engines have turned us into skimmers of information instead of careful, deep readers.[*,3] The claim that Googlemania may be having a deleterious effect on how we acquire and absorb information is to some extent supported by an in-depth 2008 University College

---

* Perhaps, Carr has contended, Google is even altering our brain chemistry to make it difficult to concentrate for extended periods of time. That's not a new notion; Kurt Vonnegut contended that the advent of television curtailed the development of "imagination circuits" in young brains, and indeed at the birth of all new media there have been older-media types who foretold a consequent rotting of minds. I have no strong opinion on whether or not our dependency on Google is wreaking significant physical changes inside our skulls, though I do worry generally about the sheer amount of time more of us are spending focusing on one sort of screen or another throughout the day, and how that may be distancing us from the physical world around us in ways that are impoverishing. The fact that London has found it necessary to embark on a program to place padding around its lampposts in order to protect the heads of peripatetic text-messagers is not a good sign.

London study of online search behavior.[4] The study found that 60 percent of people visiting electronic publications viewed three pages on average and then left, most of them never to come back to that site during the course of the study. Most of the pages viewed represented tables of contents and abstracts, leading the study authors to note, "It almost seems that they go online to avoid reading in the traditional sense." In addition to observing this "flicking" behavior, as the authors call it, the study also found that young people in particular seemed hard-pressed to determine the relative relevance of the webpages presented to them by Google and other search engines, and often ended up simply indiscriminately printing off a number of them. Yet these younger surfers seemed baffled by online resources organized in more conventional, librarylike ways, and generally gravitated to search engines for their "familiar, if simplistic solution."

Might there be a better way to search out advice? Yahoo! and Microsoft, as well as Google, have been working on search algorithms that do a better job of understanding what you're looking for, whether it's by being able to interpret complete questions, prompting you to more clearly specify your goals, or even taking into account what else you've been up to on your computer. "What you're doing should inform the search about your intent," the former Microsoft search chief Brad Goldberg told me, suggesting that a search on the word "Coke" might return financial information on the Coca-Cola Company to an accountant crunching stock data on a spreadsheet, while a student writing a term paper on health and diet might get the nutritional rundown on a can of soda. Meanwhile, venture capital firms injected some $350 million into seventy-nine search-related start-ups in 2005 and 2006 alone, and Charles Knight, a search-industry analyst who runs a website called AltSearchEngines, tracks no fewer than one thousand search contenders, including splashy entries such as

Powerset (which handles Wikipedia queries written in plain English) and Wolfram/Alpha (which spits out more fully formed answers to queries rather than simply pointing to websites). Some of these companies are trying to tackle the problem of poor search results from the other end—that is, by doing a better job of understanding the content of the webpages they index, rather than simply looking for specific keywords. "In most cases the document you want won't contain all your search terms," I was told by Rohini Srihari, a University of Buffalo computer scientist and the CEO of Janya, an Amherst, New York, company specializing in powering government searches for counterterrorism leads. "And if you're looking to discover who or what has suddenly become a hot topic, you won't even know what search terms to use."

But why depend on keywords, link counts, or even sophisticated concept matching to turn up a list of possibly useful websites, when hundreds, thousands, maybe even hundreds of thousands, of people could be available to creatively chip in to the task of coming up with the good advice you need, or at least of pointing you in the right direction? As social networks such as Facebook and LinkedIn surge in popularity, it's inevitable that we try to tap into the online wisdom of crowds. Several websites, including NosyJoe, Wikia, Squidoo, Mahalo, Sproose, ChaCha, Knol (run by Google), and Delicious (bought by Yahoo!), serve as crosses between search engines and social-networking sites by allowing either selected human guides or simply any old user to help determine which webpages are most useful, or to create or aggregate content on a particular topic. But other than the fairly popular but somewhat limited Delicious.com, which enables anyone to submit favorite bookmarks of webpages so that others can search through them, none of these sites has so far made even a tiny dent in the traditional search business. However, there are other, non-search-engine-based, potentially more interesting ways to put social networking to work in tracking down expertise. Wikipedia, for example, represents a radical rethinking of the nature of authoritative information by shoehorning mass collaboration into an encyclopedia format, resulting in a sort of consensus expertise. Though it has been predictably plagued to a certain extent by inept contributors, marketers, and vandals—some of the latter have become so adept at their game that they have managed to destroy the accuracy of several pages a minute during extended attacks—Wikipedia has held up surprisingly well in studies that compare its accuracy to that of traditional encyclopedias, thanks in part to a dedicated corps of volunteer editors, as well as tightened rules of contribution aimed at weeding out the lesser and more annoying contributors. Even so, it seems to me the bar is relatively low for Wikipedia, given that, appropriately enough for an encyclopedia, it merely seeks to survey and briefly represent the various points of views that may be out there on any particular question, rather than actually having to create wisdom or even to choose from and prioritize others' ideas in order to offer real guidance. You might feel more informed after reading a Wikipedia entry on a particular vitamin, diet, or financial strategy, but you probably won't feel you've been steered through controversy and contradiction toward a solution, or even presented with any genuinely new ideas. That means it's hardly a replacement for advice from any sort of expert.

To my mind, the single greatest opportunity for social networking to revolutionize advice seeking is with sites that allow users to post specific questions that other users can answer. In its simplest incarnation, such an approach is embodied in the classic online user forums that have been around in one form or another since the 1970s. I utilize these forums all the time, and I've found them to be absolutely the most useful and enlightening, and simultaneously the most undependable and frustrating, way to get guidance on the Internet. Let me give you a few simple examples:

- Every few weeks the low-oil-pressure warning light would come on for a minute in my 80,000-mile Volkswagen Passat and then turn off, even though there was plenty of oil and the oil pump tested fine. After searching at some length through several automotive forums, I dug up three scattered postings from Volkswagen owners that told remarkably similar stories: the light occasionally flashed on, dealer mechanics told them the oil pump was fine but replaced any number of other components at significant cost and with no useful result, and then after a few months the oil pump suddenly failed catastrophically and the entire engine had to be replaced. The next day I had my mechanic swap out my oil pump at around one-tenth of the cost of a rebuilt engine, even though he felt the pump seemed to be working perfectly. The light never came on again, and the car ran like a top for three more years, until I sold it. I'm convinced the forum advice saved me thousands of dollars.

- I added a bit of weight lifting to my modest exercise regimen and after a few months developed severe pain in multiple tendons in my arms. The online advice in forums was pretty much unanimous: stop the weight lifting and don't start again until the tendons heal. I followed the advice, along with the ice, heat, and massage that various online experts advocated, and a few months later the tendons were still as sore—it hurt terribly just to lift a grocery bag. I mentioned it to my doctor during my annual physical, and she advised me to get back to the weight lifting in spite of the pain, but to ease up a bit on the amounts lifted—advice that I never saw anywhere online. I tried her suggestion, and the pain was mostly gone within a month and hasn't returned, enabling me to slowly build back up to previous levels of weights (such as they are).

• My son wanted to transfer some of the music he had bought on Apple's iTunes website store to a non-iPod device, but some of them were "M4P" or "protected AAC" files purposely scrambled by Apple to prevent illegal sharing. I hit music and computer forums to find a solution and found them teeming with similar pleas for help with this obviously common problem. Many of these requests had simply been ignored, and the vast majority of responses that did get posted were absolutely wrong, insisting either that these files simply can't be transferred or recommending various file-conversion programs that, as I can assure you now from considerable personal experience, don't work with these files and don't even claim to. I eventually found what proved to be the right answer buried deep in the heap: you can either burn the protected tunes onto an audio CD (not an MP3 CD) and then rip them back from the CD into MP3 files (you can also get software to automate this somewhat time-consuming and slightly quality-degrading process) or, if you're up to an advanced hack, you can generate "user encryption keys." (I'm clueless about the legality of these techniques.)

This last example probably best typifies the forum experience: there's likely good advice in there somewhere, but you need to have the patience and search skills to locate it, as well as the experience and judgment to distinguish it from the junk, and even then you have to be prepared to suffer through some potentially bad tips. That is, you need a certain level of meta-expertise to hook up with good expertise on these forums. But how nice it would be if sites could somehow provide that meta-expertise on your behalf, either bringing the best answers directly to the fore or providing you with tools for identifying those answers. And that's just what a number of sites are trying to do now, by employing various sorts of evaluation mechanisms. Many are essentially conventional subject-oriented forums that have simply added the ability for visitors to rate answers or to see how often a particular answer-poster has usefully contributed to the site, providing in theory some guidance as to where the most useful and trustworthy advice can be found. Other sites, such as Help.com and PeopleJam, are more closely designed around such ranking features so that frequent contributors and highly rated answers get clearly called out in one way or another. On the WikiAnswers website, anyone can post a question, but only one answer can be posted, which anyone can subsequently edit—essentially crossing the forum approach with the Wikipedia consensus model. That approach must have something going for it; with nearly 600,000 WikiAnswers users contributing answers to close to two million questions, WikiAnswers racked up the fastest-growing visitor count of any major website in 2008, according to Internet market-research firm comScore.

Aside from the fact that videos can in general be more appealing, attention-grabbing, and personal than written information, especially for younger people, some advice topics really do call for visual representation. Though YouTube isn't primarily known as an expert wisdom–dispensing site, it has become one. I recently learned how to sharpen a pair of scissors, how to reset the throttle body on a Saab, and an easier way to transfer home-brewed beer into bottles, and none of this advice would have been nearly as enlightening in nonvideo form. In fact, I suspect more advice of one sort or another may be dispensed through YouTube than through any other single source of expert advice of any type anywhere, with the exception of Google—and, as discussed, Google (which owns YouTube) doesn't really provide advice; it only points to it on other websites, if you're lucky.

The popularity of Ford's videos is not about ogling hot models—well, there's a bit of that, to judge by the user comments, but mostly the viewers are looking for tips about clothes, hair, makeup, the modeling business, and the fashion industry. And it's not just models being turned into new-media celebrities by the Ford videos. Johnny Lavoy, a hairstylist with the agency, has been in a number of spots, including an enduring "sexy beach hair" segment, though he was at first skeptical. "I thought to myself, *Who watches these things?*" Lavoy told me. "I thought I'd get a couple of hundred people here and there. But one of my videos has hit four hundred fifty thousand views. It's insane." Lavoy now sometimes gets stopped walking down the street by fans who recognize him from the videos. Of course, advice on achieving the perfect hair curl, or blending tan lines, or selecting the right top for black jeans, or buying a purse, or exfoliating lips, is available from any number of magazines and even some television shows. But the Ford videos have a more candid, friends-sharing-secrets feel that somewhat paradoxically lends authority. "This is stuff our models know about," says Liz Edelstein, Ford's video-talent coordinator. "They can explain why one top works and another doesn't. There's takeaway." Because total production costs for Ford dip as low as mere hundreds of dollars per video, the company can afford to churn out one or two per day, on average. That, in turn, means there's plenty of opportunity to focus videos on topics that appeal to narrow constituencies—how to make up Asian eyes, how to arrange African-American hair, yoga for fuller-size women, diet tips for vegetarians. "This isn't one size fits all," Ford's president, John Caplan, told me.

Videos aren't necessarily the last word in improving the individualization and immediacy of online advice. LivePerson.com makes some thirty thousand people available to chat live online as experts, including therapists, doctors, chemistry tutors, business consultants, software analysts, and more, typically at per-minute rates that work out to between $30 and $180 per hour, and all the experts are rated by users to help you get the most bang for your buck, at least in theory. And if you're so unevolved as to actually prefer a physical presence, you can still rely on crowd wisdom to help find and screen candidates, thanks to online services that let users rate locally available experts of all sorts, including Yelp (best known for restaurant reviews but which allows ratings of any service, from psychiatric to accounting) and Angie's List (which is focused mostly on the odd combination of home-contracting services and doctors).

But the majority of the questions to which I want answers turn out to have received little or no attention from contributors and raters on most of these and similar sites, and what little wisdom is posted tends to cry out for intelligent consolidation from an editor. And while Ford Models may have done a good job in meeting the demand for fashion advice (I'm not really in a position to judge), most of the searches I do on YouTube to locate expertise yield nothing of much use. Of course, if I ultimately come up with a solution to my problem, I could easily throw together a video to help out the next person, just as I could help out with the gaps and shortcomings on any of the various sites I visit, but I haven't been moved to do so, and apparently most other visitors aren't either. And that's probably the crux of the difficulty. As George Bernard Shaw put it, "There are not competent people enough in the world to go round." Or at least there aren't enough competent people who are also sufficiently motivated and possessed of enough time on their hands to visit these sites and help out with useful, wise answers and reliable ratings. The University of Copenhagen researchers Timme Bisgaard Munk and Kristian Mørk produced a simple but interesting illustration of the situation in a study of how users of the shared-webpage-bookmarking site Delicious.com come up with descriptive tags for the sites they share. The study found that most users enlist tags that cover broad categories, such as "food," while more descriptive tags, such as "tofu," are employed even far less frequently than their specificity would dictate—even though narrower tags are much more helpful in enabling Delicious.com users to zero in on webpages of particular interest. The reason, concluded the study, is that coming up with more descriptive, less obvious tags requires more thought than most users are willing to put into the process—Munk and Mørk call it "cognitive economizing"—and that in turn limits the ability of Delicious .com to point people to the right webpages.[5] In the case of websites that allow many people to contribute advice on a topic or in response to a question, the problem of a shortage of wise people generous with their time is compounded by the fact that there is often a surfeit of less wise or at least less helpful people who are plenty eager to contribute. The result is that what good advice there is on the site is drowned in the flood of misguided or otherwise unhelpful blather. The widely respected website usability consultant Jakob Nielsen has asserted that "in social networks and community systems, about 90 percent of users don't contribute, 9 percent contribute sporadically, and a tiny minority of 1 percent accounts for most contributions." The wisdom of the crowd is considerably less formidable when fully 99 percent of the crowd is either silent or, worse, distracting.

Adding to the problem is that advice-giving sites face a tricky scaling problem. When the communities using these sites are small, they're more likely to attract a core of sincere, motivated contributors—but a small crowd can't provide wisdom to a large number of problems. On the other hand, as a community that's working well swells and attracts the attention of the masses, the influx of freeloaders (like me), dilettantes, cranks, and wise guys can easily outpace the growth in the number of people willing and able to give considered, well-informed advice. What's more, while it's easy for a modest number of professional or volunteer editors to clean up after a small crowd of contributors, or for raters to bring the best of a modest pool of stuff to the top, such low-key policing and ranking aren't likely to be able to remain as effective with tens of thousands or even millions of contributions, especially if the contributions are of more wildly varying and lower average quality. In broader, academic terms, as expressed by Helga Nowotny, a well-known social-science researcher at the Swiss Federal Institute of Technology and vice president of the European Research Council, "the societal distribution of expertise, while displaying emancipatory features of empowerment of citizens, also raises issues of quality control."[6] As whatever rating and editing systems are in place struggle to keep up with an ocean of inferior and irrelevant advice, users become less and less likely to be able to plow through it to locate the bits they really need. The prominent high-tech news website CNET reported thusly on the growing popularity of Twitter at a large 2009 interactive-media conference: "It's never been harder to find what you're looking for amid the flood of posts about the panels, barbecue, Web celebrity spottings, and deep thoughts about social media." Welcome to the new world of popular, advice-spewing social networks.

It doesn't help that on most advice-oriented sites there's usually no meaningful penalty for giving bad advice. The Zurich University economist Ernst Fehr, who conducted the trust-drug-up-the-nose study mentioned earlier, has also run experimental games in which subjects can choose to enforce or not enforce penalties for cheaters and noncontributors. Most subjects reflexively prefer to operate without punishments but quickly become frustrated with the inevitable sleazy, parasitic members of the community who take advantage of the laxity, with the result that most players end up as enthusiastic punishers.[7] It's not hard to see how social-network-advice sites might feel similarly frustrating and chaotic to users, especially to that minority of them who conscientiously and usefully contribute to advice and ratings. You might not think there'd be much opportunity to "cheat" on advice networks, but in fact there is. Take, for example, the well-known Experts Exchange site, aimed at allowing computer hardware and software professionals and enthusiasts to get help from the community with sticky technical problems. People who post advice on the site earn points that are good not only for recognition but also for discounts on membership fees. But complaints have surfaced that many members of the Exchange have learned to game the system by quickly posting vacuous solutions cut-and-pasted from help files on other websites or otherwise tossed off that often look good enough at first glance to garner points; the more valuable task of cleaning up after such lousy advice then falls on the shoulders of more dedicated and talented contributors, who may not earn as many points for their efforts. The result is that some of the bigger point-winners are some of the less useful members of the community. The competition to rack up impressive quantities of advice, without necessarily having much regard for quality, can take place on any site that gives users a chance to crow about their numbers. On Amazon and Yelp, for example, book and restaurant reviewers, respectively, get to see impressive review counts on display, and some reviewers have worked hard enough to drive their "score" into the hundreds or beyond. The New York–based "Andy 'Daddy-O' H." had been, as of early November 2009, posting Yelp reviews at an average rate of almost exactly two a day for seventeen months, and it's not hard to find people who occasionally submit a dozen or more Yelp reviews overnight. It's possible that the sorts of reviews that emerge from such frenzied one-upmanship are consistently useful and reliable — some of Andy H.'s reviews seem perceptive enough — but it's not likely to be the rule. An extensive study by the Cornell researchers Shay David and Trevor John Pinch backs up the notion that user reviews are in fact rife with abuse and distortion.[8]

That the ratio of useful advice givers to less helpful people tends to be small wouldn't be as big a problem if the simple systems for ranking or rating advice and advice givers—such as clicking on one to five stars, or voting on a best answer—were reliable in bringing the minority of wise advice to the top. But even as straightforward a crowd-wisdom mechanism as rating runs into trouble. For one thing, while ratings are obviously a crude form of wisdom that in their simplest incarnation carry relatively little information, one of their most glaring omissions is usually overlooked. While ratings can clearly express a "valence"—that is, they can indicate whether the rater wishes to express a positive or negative assessment—they lack a means for raters to express their confidence in their own ratings. You might suppose the two are roughly related, so that people who give a very high or very low rating tend to feel more strongly about their assessment than people who give middle-of-the-road assessments, but the Stanford Business School researcher Zakary Tormala studied the relationship between confidence and valence in online ratings and found little correlation.[9] And when you think about it, that's not so strange. For example, someone might buy a new tool that works well on a first usage, so she throws up a great review—even though she knows it's a quick and dirty assessment that may not hold up after the tool is tried out on many different tasks. Someone else might rate the tool as so-so after months of experience that have left him highly confident of his neutral rating. This obscuration of ranking-confidence levels can lead to skewed, misleading average rankings. In fact, I see this problem come up all the time in rankings on major websites—for example, I recently took a closer look at the many reviews for a highly ranked bicycle sold on Amazon and realized that a large number of gushing reviews from inexperienced buyers thrilled to get a nice-looking bike that seemed to ride fine at an affordable price were swamping a smaller number of far more insightful pans from knowledgeable cyclists who were able to detail the serious reliability issues with the cheap components.

Ratings are also easily corruptible by various biases. EBay's ratings of buyers and sellers have long been notoriously unreliable because users have often hesitated to put up negative ratings, fearing "retaliatory" negative ratings from the other parties. (EBay finally moved to address this severe problem in 2008 by prohibiting a seller from posting a negative review of a buyer who has just given him a negative one.) And on eBay, Amazon, and other sites, there's little to stop people from surreptitiously raising their own ratings by recruiting friends, family, and colleagues, or even setting up multiple accounts to rate themselves. Studies suggest such manipulation is a serious problem—in 2009 an enterprising employee at the electronics manufacturer Belkin even went so far as to openly solicit positive reviews for one product in exchange for payment.[10] Or ratings can just be biased by such mundane phenomena as the fact that some people tend to give better ratings to brands they like—Apple fans, for example, tend to be highly forgiving of the company's stiff prices and product weaknesses—or to products that are more expensive, reasoning (perhaps unconsciously) that if they cost that much, they must be high-quality. A study of the website Rate My Professors by the Central Michigan University finance professor James Felton and his colleagues found that professors are more likely to win ratings as good teachers if they're seen as "hotter" and easier.[11] And numerous studies have found that people tend to think more highly of whatever everyone else thinks highly of, whether there's a logical reason to join in on the positive assessments or not. For example, a 2007 study by a University of Rome researcher and his colleagues found that voters tend to pick politicians based on their popularity rather than their policies.[12]

Perhaps the biggest problem with ratings is that most people just don't bother to provide them. Looking through the fairly popular Yahoo! Answers websites, where people can post questions to or answer questions from the community and anyone can rate the answers, I found that the great majority of questions attract answers that only one or two people, if anyone, end up rating. Even on Amazon, top 100–selling books often get only a handful of reviews, and many products remain unreviewed. That people aren't motivated to spend just a moment or two to register their opinion, thereby helping to ensure that these systems are useful, must come as a disappointment to those who would like to put their faith in online community advice, but it shouldn't be surprising. It has long been established that when people are part of a crowd in which they're anonymous, they tend to behave less conscientiously than when they're identifiable, or dealing with one or a few people, or engaging in face-to-face contact. Fifty years ago researcher Leon Mann showed that people were more likely to maliciously encourage a prospective suicide jumper to take the plunge if they were in a large crowd, if the jumper was too high up to clearly see them, or if it was nighttime. Paul Schwerdt, the cardiac interventionalist I mentioned early in the book, told me that the average time it takes for a victim of cardiac arrest to receive attention from a bystander is inversely proportional to how many people are around—in other words, you're better off dropping in front of a handful of people than in front of hundreds, apparently because people stand out enough in small groups to feel the pressure to act decently. If people in big crowds are comfortable ignoring a person dying at their feet, we can hardly expect people in big online crowds to feel particularly guilty about not contributing ratings.

Can more sophisticated models for collecting, filtering, and accessing online wisdom save the day? For example, there are the so-called recommendation engines employed by Amazon, Netflix, and other retail sites that serve to suggest products you might be interested in. These engines generally employ data about your previous purchases and established preferences to identify other customers with comparable interests, and then pull up suggestions for you from the list of items these other customers have bought or highly rated. I could imagine these sorts of tools being applied to identifying people who have appreciated similar sorts of advice, in order to come up with suggestions for advice for new problems. Unfortunately, these engines haven't proven particularly effective even in the more cut-and-dried realm of purchasing books or renting movies. I'm a steady customer of both Amazon and Netflix, and I find almost all of their recommendations useless—somehow the choices served up strike me as being worse than I would expect from random recommendations, as if whatever patterns appear to be emerging in my selections are in some way not only unhelpful but actively misleading, at least when compared to other customers' patterns. I've talked with and read comments from people who swear they often find these recommendations useful, but that doesn't seem to be the rule—the fact that Netflix was moved to offer a prize of $1 million to anyone able to improve the hit rate of the company's recommendations by 10 percent hardly suggests widespread delight with the current state of the art. (The prize was claimed in June 2009, after three years of feverish global competition.) And advice is likely to be harder to successfully match than are movies. The recent work of the former University of California–Los Angeles social-networks researcher Jennifer Chayes, now director of the Microsoft Research New England lab, doesn't provide a rosy outlook for highly effective recommendation engines. Chayes and her colleagues studied the different characteristics that a recommendation engine would have to incorporate to get the job done, and ended up with a mathematical proof that "there is no possible recommendation system that has all these desired properties."[13]

Another possibility might be "prediction markets," a much-talked-up approach to tapping into crowd wisdom in which participants essentially bet real money against one another that certain outcomes will obtain in some arena. Most often employed to come up with predictions for political elections or world events—the U.S. government tried to set up a website-based market to predict terrorist attacks, but too many critics loudly pronounced it to be in bad taste—prediction markets seek to harness that special brand of human insight and ingenuity that supposedly emerges when cash is on the line. Most problems for which we seek expert advice don't readily lend themselves to being posed as prediction contests, but some do. For example, we want experts to predict which investments are most likely to appreciate, which medicines will prove safe and effective, which lifestyle changes will buy us extra years, which professions will best pay off down the road, and so forth. Other than investments, such topics haven't been much put to the test in the context of prediction markets. And even though everyday financial trading is the prediction market on which all others are based, the complete failure of financial markets to usefully anticipate the recent global near collapse of most forms of investment makes it harder to establish firm faith in this method of producing reliable expertise.

Even forgetting financial markets, we find there's little other evidence that prediction markets are particularly effective. The notion that prediction markets might do a better job of producing weather forecasts than conventional meteorologic expertise has been explored by the Pennsylvania State University economist Anthony Kwasnica, who oversees a pool of weather-forecast "traders" consisting of sixty Penn State graduate and undergraduate students, about half of whom are studying meteorology and thus represent experts. The students are given small amounts of cash, after which they stake out bets among themselves as to what the temperature will be in five days, and they're free to continually rejigger the bets as the day approaches and the weather conditions change. I spoke to Kwasnica about the ongoing study, which as of 2009 was in its third year, and he told me the results so far haven't been especially encouraging: the predictions are on average no more accurate than conventional forecasts, and the fact that they aren't less accurate is owed entirely to the expertise of the meteorology students. "Novices generally don't make much of a contribution," Kwasnica told me. "They lose all their money to the pros, and I have to replace them every few weeks." He added that he still hopes the market will prove useful, if not in coming up with predictions, then in assigning confidence levels to predictions—for example, distinguishing between a shaky average forecast of 70 degrees when the traders wildly disagree, and a take-it-to-the-bank average forecast of 70 degrees when there is broad consensus. So far, though, even that angle hasn't produced practical results.

In theory, a social network such as Facebook or LinkedIn can give you access of a sort to hundreds or even thousands of people who might be friends of friends of friends, but can you use that network to locate reliable expert advice? Different social networks provide various means for searching through people's posted biographical and other information, or for broadcasting a plea for information through a network, but neither approach is an effective way for hitting up just the right person to help solve a problem. After all, "about me" statements are generally neither complete nor dependably accurate, and genuinely useful advice givers aren't likely to repeatedly drop everything they're doing to respond to each of a flood of pleas from strangers careening blindly through a large network. But an interesting possibility in wringing better expertise out of these communities is being raised by new research in a long-standing field known as "organizational network analysis," which seeks insights into the routes information travels as it is exchanged among large groups of people. Conventional organizational network analysis tends to focus on identifying people in a network who informally serve as de facto "hubs" by swapping information with unusually large numbers of people in the organization. That isn't an especially fruitful line of attack when it comes to trying to match up advice seekers with the right potential advice givers. But more recently researchers have been trying to find ways to automate the process of figuring out which people in a large network seem the best sources of what sort of information by analyzing the nature of data running around the network—a sort of network fMRI that could be a real boon to those seeking expert advice from online crowds. Several software companies are working on various incarnations of this approach, including Aptima and Tacit Software (acquired by Oracle).

But there's a big catch: to understand what you know and what you need to know, the software has to keep an eye on what you do electronically, which can include poring over your e-mail messages, your websurfing, the data you keep on your computer, even your online calendar and task list—as Aptima's CEO, Dan Serfaty, pointed out to me, you can't be very useful as an expert if you're buried by work, meetings, or travel. Employees may have little choice about submitting to such scrutiny if the companies they work for decide to install such software (at least in the United States, where courts have repeatedly ruled that employees have few rights to privacy on company-owned computing and communications systems), but more widely accessible social networks such as Facebook and LinkedIn aren't likely to get away with keeping close tabs on everyone's communications. In fact, Facebook has repeatedly tried to grant itself those sorts of privileges and has repeatedly been forced to back down by appalled users. And even if this sort of software did become widely installed and was allowed to watch over everything we do at our keyboards, there's no strong evidence yet that it's really capable of understanding what it observes well enough to successfully match advice seekers with potential advice offerers. As with an fMRI, it would be easy to read too much into the pictures it produces.

On June 10, 2005, five-day-old Sarah Jane Donohue was shaken by a babysitter in her New York City home violently enough to break both her collarbones and multiple ribs, and to severely damage her brain. Her father, Patrick, stunned and devastated in the following months to learn how little useful knowledge the medical community seemed to have accumulated about such "pediatric acquired brain injuries," and how few mechanisms existed for pooling advances in that knowledge, set up the Sarah Jane Brain Project website in 2007 to try to remedy the situation. The website allows clinicians, researchers, therapists, and anyone else to freely access Sarah Jane's complete medical records, invites the families of other children with brain injuries to post their records, and encourages anyone with any relevant skills and knowledge to help the project build a closely collaborating network of experts and expertise on pediatric acquired brain injuries. "The doctors said that if I could get fifty, or a thousand, families to post their medical records, it could fundamentally change the way brain-injury research is conducted," Donohue told me.

In a sense, Donohue is trying to turn the wisdom-of-crowds model upside down. Instead of bypassing conventional experts to bring individual problems to the crowds, he wants to bring a mass of problems to conventional experts so that they can gain more insight. Whether the approach can work with brain injuries and, even if it does, whether it would apply to other problem domains are both open questions. But the effort at least serves as a reminder that just because the online world hasn't yet been able to reliably muster crowd wisdom to replace conventional experts, that doesn't mean that conventional experts can't leverage online communities to improve the wisdom they produce, or at least to improve the world's access to their wisdom.

One obvious way to take advantage of the Internet with an eye to improving expert wisdom would be to try to mitigate the deficiencies of the journal-publication system. As we saw earlier in the book, many of the biases, distortions, and corruptions in expert findings stem from the intense competition to get articles placed in leading journals. Because journals tend to favor filling their highly limited publication slots with positive, exciting results, we end up with pervasive publication bias, and because articles have to survive peer review, they are subject to the whims of potentially cranky, biased, self-serving, agenda-wielding reviewers. One possible solution is represented by *PLoS ONE*, a generally well-regarded online-only research journal that uses more or less conventional peer reviewers—but only to screen out technically flawed research. Every article submitted to *PLoS ONE* ("PLoS" stands for "Public Library of Science") that doesn't turn out to have clear methodological errors is published, without regard to impact or whether the findings are positive or interesting. That means thousands of research findings that might otherwise have been stuck in file drawers, or published only in obscure journals read by almost no one, now find a home in a visible and highly accessible journal.

The flip side of the coin, of course, is that being published in a journal that publishes almost anything generally doesn't come off as much of an achievement for an expert, which means that the majority of researchers will continue to compete to publish in more established journals, using *PLoS* as a backup for getting their findings out there when other journals turn them down or aren't a realistic option. That means, in turn, that established journals will continue to draw the more impactful and exciting work that will get the most attention from the media and therefore from the public, and publication in these journals will still determine tenure, funding, and status among researchers. Thus researchers will continue to feel the same pressures that lead to bias, distortion, and corruption of findings.

Many researchers and observers are now advocating using online resources to improve the research-publication process by approaching the problem from the other direction. That is, instead of enlisting conventional peer review to support an open-access online journal, online expert crowds can be enlisted to replace conventional peer review at established journals. Why place the fate of a research paper in the hands of a few anonymous (authors are given peer reviewers' comments but not their names), status-quo reviewers who may have territory to defend or axes to grind, when a community of experts can be tapped to forge a consensus on the value and promise of a research effort, drowning out individual biases, shortsightedness, and grudges? What's more, we've seen that peer reviewers tend to miss most errors in research papers—but we have an impressive role model for error identification in the world of open-source software, where anyone can contribute their programming skills and in which it has been well established that crowds are especially adept at ferreting out subtle problems, or "bugs," that are invisible to any small number of individuals. As the open-source guru Eric Raymond has famously put it, "Given enough eyeballs, all bugs are shallow." Chris Anderson, the editor in chief of *Wired* magazine and author of *The Long Tail* and *Free*, has argued strongly for "open peer review" in the pages of none other than *Nature*. Describing Google as the "closest thing to an oracle the world has ever seen," Anderson goes on to state, "It's now possible to tap such collective intelligence online by doing to scientific publishing what the web has already done to mainstream media: democratizing it."

Well, "democratize" would be one verb to describe what the online world has done to mainstream media. And I have to point out that Anderson has never met a crowd he didn't think capable of solving any problem, and that finding various ways to say so in his magazine and books has made him quite a prominent mainstream-media figure, one who reportedly pulled in $2 million in speaking fees in 2008. I personally would also find his argument more convincing (or at least more convincingly sincere) if he led the way to open peer review by turning over the editing of *Wired* and his books to the crowds. But none of that means he's wrong. Besides, there's a better way to assess the merits of open peer review: *Nature* tried it out over a four-month period in 2006, offering the authors of all submitted papers that weren't immediately rejected by editors (as most are, remember) the option of having their candidate papers posted online for public comment in addition to being sent to conventional anonymous reviewers. Of those 1,369 eligible papers, the authors of only seventy-one of them—about one out of twenty—agreed. Thirty-three, or just under half, of the publicly posted papers received no comments at all. The rest received a total of ninety-two comments, more than half of which were attached to eight papers, and one of those eight papers received ten of the comments. Bearing in mind that the great majority of authors in the experiment received either zero comments or one comment—and more often zero than one—the authors mostly claimed they felt pretty good about the whole thing, with three-quarters agreeing that the process had improved their papers. Well, sure; given the normally prickly nature of peer review, I suspect these authors saw it as a no-news-is-good-news situation that left them relieved to get little attention. The journal's editors, who were asked to more formally evaluate the quality of the posted comments, were less sanguine, rating the editorial quality of the notes an average 2.6 out of 5, and the technical quality 1.8 out of 5; all of the editors insisted the comments didn't inform their decision as to whether or not to publish any of the articles. The editors further reported that getting established researchers to comment was "like pulling teeth," that authors in competitive areas of biology "did not wish to be involved," and that most of the comments that did come in were "general comments, such as 'nice work.'" Some senior researchers reported that they would probably ban lab members from participating in any way in open peer review. Charles Jennings, the MIT neuroscience research administrator and former *Nature* editor, wasn't surprised at the results. "The idea that the world will just step up and provide analysis and commentary and apply the wisdom of crowds to determining the quality and importance of a piece of work is just nonsense," he told me. "Scientists are sufficiently busy that they aren't motivated to troll through the Web to write commentaries on whatever catches their fancy. There's nothing that compellingly suggests it could do a better job than handpicked experts working under a deadline and a well-defined process."

But even if researchers don't seem ready to warm to open-access journal publication and open peer review, you might think they'd at least be enthusiastic about the opportunities the online world opens in terms of collaboration. And, in fact, numerous organizations have sprung up to provide researchers with frameworks for sharing information in various fields, including websites and data standards. But John Wilbanks, who runs a prominent effort along those lines called the Science Commons, which boasts an executive team that includes two Nobel Prize winners, has complained publicly about the research community's reluctance to open up its work. "Right now, it's still in scientists' interest to follow the classical model of one scientist working alone," he told

Popular Science in 2007. "In today's system, you don't get rewarded for sharing — no one gets tenure for choosing to publish preprints of their papers in molecular biology, or for spending weeks making cells for other labs to do research. And you sometimes get ahead by deliberately withholding. If you think you can squeeze more papers out of your data, you might not share it even if it takes years for someone else to replicate the research you've written about." Clearly groups such as Wilbanks's hope to change that culture, and they might, but so far there's been relatively little obvious progress.

What about simply informally sharing thoughts and ideas in open online communities? There are any number of forums in which researchers can do so, perhaps most prominently on the websites associated with established journals and professional science magazines. One of those sites is run by the well-regarded magazine *The Scientist*, whose editor in chief, Richard Gallagher, described his goals this way when he introduced the forum in a statement in the magazine in 2008:

> What if, instead of being a passive consumer of *The Scientist*, our readers played a role in shaping the content? We could have 700, or 7,000, minds thinking up and debating great story ideas, instead of just seven. Such a community could identify breakthrough research and commercialization opportunities before they received widespread attention. Or decide on the fields and firms that are being oversold. It could identify scandals, tag the unrecognized heroes and geniuses of science and business, and work out and test ways to communicate research. We now have the capability to do these and many, many other things.

I called Gallagher in 2009 to ask how that was working out.

"It's been a real disappointment in terms of members of the community posting on new topics," he told me. "Probably ninety percent of the new topics are raised by our staff." Traffic on the site is fairly brisk, he added, but only about 1 percent of visitors post a comment. What's more, he said, people who do post tend not to be established scientists and are usually less interested in discussing research ideas than career issues such as academic honesty.* One scientist who contributes to the magazine warned Gallagher it would be an uphill battle in trying to get credible researchers to take the trouble to post anything of substance on the site. "She told me she just has too much to do, and if she has a good idea she wants to save it for publication, not just throw it onto a forum," he explained. Gallagher admitted that he could empathize; he frequently visits a forum for fans of a Glasgow soccer team but has never posted a comment. I asked him if he knew of any open online forums where scientists were more forthcoming, but he didn't. "There may be some closed groups where people are swapping information, but I think for the most part they're just sticking to e-mail and face-to-face contact," he said.

In the case of some researchers, it also may be that they're too busy blogging. Could blogs ultimately be the best forum for expert idea-sharing? Whether it is in general a good thing to tap into experts' thinking by having them make their cases on their blogs—without the benefit of any sort of filter, be it peer reviewers, editors, reporters, or a community of commentators—would make for a lively debate. But it may not be worth staging that debate yet, since only a small percentage of established researchers have active blogs. As *Nature* noted in a 2009 editorial, blogging is "on the fringe of the scientific enterprise. Blogging will not help,

---

* Scientists and academics are appalled and often combative when anyone publicly questions the general integrity of research but actually do so all the time among themselves.

and could even hurt, a young researcher's chances of tenure. Many of their elders still look down on colleagues who blog, believing that research should be communicated only through conventional channels such as peer-review and publication."

From the public's point of view, the fact that the online world may so far have largely failed to help experts arrive at more reliable findings, to promote wider collaboration, or to create new arenas in which they are willing to express their ideas doesn't mean that we can't get better expert advice out of the deal. If nothing else, those of us who are purely consumers of research findings now have unprecedented access via online sources to those findings in a variety of forms, from journal papers to abstracts to mass-media articles, as well as to background material on whichever topics and researchers interest us, and all generally at no hard cost beyond what we pay for Internet access. What's more, this access can in principle enable us to more critically examine what even highly credentialed experts claim—and don't think they don't know it. "My students are checking out my CV online while I'm lecturing to them," Oxford's Dutton told me. "They find views that are contradictory to mine and challenge me with them. It makes for a much more stimulating class and holds me accountable for what I say."

On the other hand, let's not forget that journal papers and university faculty CVs are but an infinitesimal pimple of information on the cheek of cyberspace compared to everything else that's online, volume-wise, not to mention the fact that there's a difference between the googling talents of Oxford students and those of the average joe. In other words, we're back to that problem of whether most people in the public are equipped to track down high-quality information on the Internet, as opposed to ending up with advice that may look convincing but is in fact junk. Sheldon Krimsky, an environmental policy researcher at Tufts University, studied in 2007 the different websites that turn up when one goes googling for information on perfluorooctanoic acid, or PFOA, which is used in manufacturing Teflon and other nonstick materials and which has been the subject of some controversy with regard to environmental risks. Krimsky found that Google's top results tended to be dominated by what is essentially propaganda from interest groups, pro and con, disguised as objective information rather than by unsponsored academic studies or any information that could reasonably be considered objective.[14] More so than with traditional media, such tainted information about possible health and environmental risks, when presented on the Internet, is more likely to slip past people's defenses, Krimsky found. "All risk websites are potentially equal in Cyberspace," he concluded, "constrained only by the skill of the web designer. It levels the playing field to a public that does not understand the hierarchy of expertise.... The Internet can also be used quite effectively to mobilize public fear in the face of half-baked scientific information and speculative hypotheses."

Or, as the Science Commons founder John Wilbanks put it, "Google doesn't work as well for finding science as it does for finding pizza."

CHAPTER NINE

Eleven Simple Never-Fail Rules for Not Being Misled By Experts

No lesson seems to be so deeply inculcated by the experience of life as that you never should trust experts.
— LORD SALISBURY

I f Alex Trebek is your idea of a brainy game-show host, you ought to meet Harry Collins. Collins presides over his game in a slightly tired office at the University of Cardiff, Wales, but what the setting lacks in glamour the host more than makes up for in captivating patter, and of an unusually substantive sort. As perhaps the world's best-known expert on expertise, Collins masterfully wields anecdotes of epic feuds between leading minds and outsize personalities, the disastrous scientific follies of African despots, and political jousting that risked compromising the health of large populations. It's expertise as high soap opera.

And as competitive sport, too, thanks to the Imitation Game. The rules of the game are simple. One main player is kept separate from a "tacit" expert in a particular area—where "tacit," as per Collins's extensive typology of expertise, denotes the sort of facility one can attain in some domain only by being actively immersed in it for years. The domain could be organic chemistry or medieval German literature, but it isn't restricted to academic fields or even to cable network show–level expertise such as cooking or car restoration. Instead, the Imitation Game often zooms in on some of the ordinary sorts of expertise we all take for granted—expertise at being a college student, for example, or a parent, or a female.

When I played, the expertise at question was British life; that is, the expert had spent most of his or her life in Britain. The twist, though, was that there was another sequestered "expert" in the game, and this one was a phony—a non-Brit. My job as a player was to be the "judge," coming up with questions for the two candidates that would help me determine which was the real deal.

Sitting at a computer linked to a console in the room with the "experts," I submitted my first question: **What foods are typically served with tea?**

After a minute, the answers popped up on my screen:

Expert #1: If it's tea in the sense of afternoon tea, then cake and cookies are appropriate.

Expert #2: Sandwiches and hopefully some cake, unless it's tea with the evening meal.

My second question: **What would you bring to a football match to show your support for the home team?**

Expert #1: I'd wear my local team shirt.

Expert #2: It depends on whether or not I'm an away fan.

My third question: **Why didn't Diana fit into the royal family?**

Expert #1: Her social background made it hard to fit in.

Expert #2: Neither her husband nor mother-in-law seemed that fond of her.

Hmmm. As is typical for a nonexpert trying to evaluate someone who supposedly is, I didn't actually know what would constitute solid, legitimate answers to the questions I'd asked. Also typically, I had mistakenly assumed I would be able to operate on an "I'll know it when I see it" basis—that the answers coming back from the real expert would be so impressively detailed and authoritative-sounding that they would be beyond suspicion, while those from the faker would strike me as vague and improbable. After mulling it over, I decided I liked Expert #2's answers a bit more—he or she mentioned sandwiches, which I recalled being present at a formal afternoon tea I had been served in a restaurant; in differentiating between home and away games, he or she played into my belief that showing certain types of support for an away team among the sometimes violent fans at a British football match is probably a risky proposition; and I hazily recalled that Diana came with impeccable high-society credentials, casting some doubt on Expert #1's "social background" complaint. I reported my choice to Collins, who then, in the best tradition of game-show hosts, built the suspense, asking me if I was confident in my answer. Only moderately, I confessed, at which point he told me I'd missed something in the responses that should really have given it away. After giving me a moment to ponder my oversight in vain, Collins stabbed his finger at the word "cookie" on the screen. *Doh!* Even *I* know that "cookie" is strictly an American word—the British say "biscuit." The good news, though, was that the unnoticed howler came from Expert #1, which means I was right. Collins passed the word to the two "experts" to come on down, and in strode the East German graduate student and faux Brit Martin Weinel, along with Robert Evans, a thoroughly British colleague of Collins's who works closely with him on expertise research. Weinel, though surprised to learn about the inappropriateness of "cookie," was pleased to hear he came close to taking me in despite boasting only a few years of British life under his belt, or as much British life as a hardworking graduate student in Wales can find time to soak up. In fact, players much better steeped in their assigned subjects than I was are fooled all the time in the game by "experts" who are anything but, and in domains you might think it would be nearly impossible to fake expertise. For example, a blind person has successfully passed for an "expert" in sight, and Collins himself notoriously managed to fool a panel of physicists into believing he was an expert on gravity-wave physics, an especially knotty, arcane subfield of that generally daunting branch of science—a branch whose practitioners, by the way, tend to look down on sociologists such as Collins.

Collins developed the game to show that the line can blur a bit between those who have genuinely mastered an area of expertise and those who might know merely enough to put up a good front. In other words, if someone is determined to pass herself off as an expert, it can be quite difficult to ascertain that she actually doesn't entirely know what she's talking about. All of which raises this question: if it's so hard to spot blatant nonexpertise even when we know there's a 50 percent chance it's phony, how are we supposed to distinguish the good stuff from the not so good among genuine, highly credentialed experts whose findings are affirmed in prestigious research journals, leading newspapers, and trusted news shows? Faced, for example, with the expert claim that housing prices will soon rebound, or that it's healthier to eat earlier in the day than later, or that playing with a toy computer is good for your toddler's educational prospects, we would seem to have precious little to go on when it comes to deciding whether or not the advice is likely to be trustworthy.

Small but high-powered communities of philosophers, sociologists, and other academics have been working overtime on the problem of assessing the trustworthiness of expertise for quite a while, and have come up with fascinating insights and in some cases impressive solutions. Unfortunately, the insights often deem the problem unsolvable, and the solutions tend to directly contradict one another. Back in the eighteenth century, Immanuel Kant urged independence of expert opinion via his celebrated maxim "Think for oneself." But the philosopher John Hardwig has called that simple advice "a romantic ideal which is thoroughly unrealistic and which, in practice, results in less rational belief and judgment." Nevertheless, he concedes, recognizing that we'll do better with expert advice than we will on our own is one thing, while figuring out who can be trusted as an expert is quite another. Without special knowledge of how an expert has come to his advice, he writes, most of us are "in no position to determine whether the person really is an expert."[1]

Collins's Imitation Game gives us a fair shot at smoking out nonexpertise but under unrealistic conditions. Is there at least in principle a way laypeople could test expert thinking in real-world situations to see if it's as sharp as claimed? Nope — not even in principle, concluded the Northwestern professors Wojciech

Olszewski and Alvaro Sandroni.* The lack of any sort of reliable test for genuine expertise would help explain how, for example, the president of a Texas drug-testing laboratory was able to provide apparently credible testimony in a prominent 2009 trial after being accepted by the court as an expert medical witness by virtue of his medical degree and three professional certifications relating to assessing clinical data — none of which actually existed, according to evidence presented to the court later on.[2] It would also help explain how a woman who had faked all of her undergraduate and graduate degrees rose through the ranks of academia to become the longtime and widely respected dean of admissions at MIT, of all places, where until being unmasked in 2007 she was a nationally quoted critic of student résumé padding.

If it's hard to distinguish the pronouncements of real experts from those of outright fabricators, we can't expect the picture to be much clearer when we're faced with conflicting pronouncements from multiple experts whose bona fides are, well, bona fide — even if the pronouncements come from experts on expertise. The University of Tasmania philosopher David Coady maintains that laypeople may be able to do fairly well at picking out the more trustworthy expertise if they simply follow the crowd, because when large numbers of people put their support behind an expert, it's usually for a good reason. No way, counters Alvin Goldman, a Rutgers professor of philosophy and cognitive science. Goldman insists that the existence of a large number of supporters for a claim tells you very little, as witness the many examples all around us of popular but dubious beliefs. (In the mid-2000s, at least, following the crowd certainly

---

* They enlisted a long, dense train of formal logic to prove that the lousy predictions of bogus, highly biased, or otherwise inferior experts have a good shot at passing any test anyone can come up with, unless the test is made so formidable that even the wise predictions of top-notch experts might not pass it.

seemed in retrospect to have been toxic to financial health.) To assess the validity of an expert's claims, Goldman says, you have to look at how many of the expert's *fellow experts* have independently decided to throw their support behind her thinking. Forget about it, says the Harvard Law School professor Scott Brewer; he concludes that laypeople simply can't be expected to figure out which expert to believe, no matter what technique they employ. (Now that you've heard the experts on expertise weigh in on the question of conflicting experts, what would you take away from a *Washington Post* article in late 2008 that quoted the president of the American College of Cardiology as saying that new study results clearly indicate many patients whose cholesterol levels are normal should immediately start taking cholesterol-lowering statins anyway to reduce heart-disease risk, just before the article quoted a prominent Stanford University heart researcher as warning that prescribing statins in this way would be risky?)

John Ioannidis half kiddingly suggested to me that we ought to keep score of experts' rightness. Well, is that such a bad idea? Of course, we'd first need to decide what sort of "rightness" would win points. Should you get points if your published research isn't refuted? But a lack of refutation might not mean much, given that we've seen most research isn't refuted simply because no one bothers to put it to the test. And just because a paper draws a refutation doesn't mean it's wrong—refutations are often followed by refutations of the refutations. Should an expert get partial credit for a finding that's only partly refuted? What if a researcher is "right" because his claim is so vague that it can't really be pinned down as wrong, a trick perfected by fortune-tellers and horoscope writers? (Think of child-raising experts promising good results to parents who are "responsive to the child's needs.") Should an expert get points if her conclusion is something we all believed anyway? (There are many studies that conclude we ought to exercise, have a healthy diet, and not smoke.) How about points for a conclusion that ultimately proves wrong but that took a good stab at a very difficult problem, leaving us with a better understanding of it? (History makes clear we can expect the vast majority of novel approaches to curing cancer to end up not working out, but surely we want researchers to keep trying, eliminating dead ends along the way.) Or maybe we could give points according to how useful other researchers find the research. Oh, wait—experts already keep score among themselves that way via citation counts, and a fat lot of good that's done for the rest of us.

You'd think in the realm of investment wisdom, at least, it would be easy to keep score: just tally up the money won or lost. And, in fact, we do have an unambiguous winner in this realm, to judge by more than a decade of bottom-line figures running through 2008: a hedge-fund operator by the name of Bernard Madoff, who turned in a by-all-accounts unmatched steady and generous return on investment—assuming, of course, there wasn't some sort of measurement problem associated with that data. Unfortunately, investment decisions can't always be that cleanly judged. Numerous analysts have looked at the hypothetical returns from Jim Cramer's stock picks, for example, and though each has been able to come up with a clear conclusion, the conclusions sharply conflict, ranging from confirming his genius to ascertaining that one could thrive by doing exactly the opposite of whatever Cramer recommended. Among the vagaries in such analyses: there's no clearly appropriate way to determine exactly what sort of advice constitutes a genuine "buy" recommendation, as opposed to an off-the-cuff positive comment; the results can sharply differ depending on what period of time they are measured over; and there's no universally accepted way of taking into account the risks associated with a portfolio of investments along with its expected and actual payoffs—that is, an expert such as Cramer may seem "right" in the sense that his recommendations would have on average made an investor some money, but "wrong" in the sense that the strategies would have entailed risking unacceptably heavy losses. If I urged all elderly couples to go out and invest their entire savings in lottery tickets, some of them would end up thanking me.

The problem of a lack of a clear yardstick for rightness is one that the Berkeley political science and psychology professor Philip Tetlock was forced to confront straight off when he undertook an extensive study of political expertise—a study that served as the foundation of his marvelous 2005 book, *Expert Political Judgment*, in which Tetlock explores the question of what characteristics distinguish political pundits and prognosticators who are more likely to be right from those who are more likely to be wrong. Being an academic and all, Tetlock was compelled to come up not only with a precise definition of rightness but also with one that would allow qualitatively measuring that rightness. (In other words, he needed to find a streetlight to look under.) In the end he decided to give all his experts questionnaires that demanded clear, specific predictions of the outcomes of various then-in-flux political situations, and later, when the real-life political outcomes were in, he checked to see who got it right. Tetlock himself takes pains to make it clear that it was a far-from-definitive means for assessing rightness. Is an expert "right" if she calls an outcome correctly but for entirely the wrong reasons? (Imagine, for example, someone who predicted Obama would be elected U.S. president only because Obama would be seen as stronger than McCain on national security.) Is someone a poor excuse for an expert if he blows a bunch of cut-and-dried prediction challenges on a questionnaire, even though he's known for occasionally coming up with fairly accurate predictions in particularly complex, ambiguous situations that tend to stump other experts?*

You can see why claims such as "Eleven Simple Never-Fail Rules for Not Being Misled By Experts" ought to set off alarm bells. In the end, I don't think we're likely to have a formal scorecard for expertise, or at least one that's widely accepted as effective. And that in and of itself may be at least a partial explanation of why expertise tends to fail. As the University of San Diego law professor Frank Partnoy has put it in the context of the business world, "A company that is paid regardless of its performance is a company that will eventually underperform." In other words, it may well be that in neglecting to tie the career advancement and status of experts to their rightness, we virtually ensure that rightness will end up being somewhat neglected by them. Instead, experts are more likely to become quite good at that which more directly and clearly pays off: getting published, getting cited, and getting attention, for example, with all the rightness-degrading biases that the drive to maximize such outcomes can entail.

If we just can't really be sure which, if any, experts are right, then what's the point of this entire exercise? Are we any better off for having explored the magnitude and sources of expert

---

* Tetlock concluded from his data that what makes some political prognosticators more likely to be right largely comes down to their being "foxes" instead of "hedgehogs"—a metaphor originally dating back to an ancient Greek poem and which holds fox-people to be flexible, adaptive, and aware of complexity, while hedgehog-people are ideologues whose predictions are based not so much on evidence but on a rigidly held and relatively simplistic set of beliefs. I'm not sure most thinking people needed a big study to recognize that ideological rigidity is not highly conducive to rightness, but if nothing else Tetlock's book is a must-read for its extensive, enlightening, and entertaining tour of cognitive biases, a subject on which he is one of the world's foremost authorities.

wrongness? Quite a bit, actually, or so I would argue. I didn't say I don't have *any* tips for getting better expert advice; I just said I don't have any *simple* ones.

I once sat in on another sort of expert game show, and one that is not always for the fainthearted. It is perhaps the longest-running game show in the world, having debuted in 1900, and it is still held in the same place—an auditorium at the Massachusetts General Hospital in Boston, where anyone can walk in and be part of a sometimes large and enthusiastic audience. (Well, partly enthusiastic. Some of the attendees are highly overworked and sleep-deprived interns and residents who look as if they wouldn't be roused by an onstage raising of the dead.) In the *New England Journal of Medicine*, which has published an account of the production in most weekly issues since 1924, the show is entitled "Case Records of the Massachusetts General Hospital" but is recognizable informally to most doctors as "grand rounds" at Mass General. A more descriptive and layperson-friendly title might be: "The Bafflingly Deathly Ill Patient Challenge." If the X Games had a medical-knowledge component, this would be it.

The presentation opens with a physician-host who comes onto the stage to describe the true-story experiences of a patient at Mass General. The details can be horrific, typically entailing hair-raising symptoms, a string of nonilluminating test results, and a fusillade of increasingly desperate and ineffective treatments, all capped off by, in many cases, the patient's death. (I just looked up the as-of-this-writing most recently published case. It begins: "A 79-year-old woman was admitted to the burn unit of this hospital because of a blistering cutaneous eruption," after which things rapidly go downhill.) Unflinching as the account is, the host omits from his narrative what we most want to know: what strange ailment was causing all this suffering and medical confusion? Guessing the answer is the job of the show's guest star, a visiting and highly prominent physician-researcher who is duly led out onstage to take a stab at a diagnosis, after which a pathologist comes out and reveals the correct answer. The whole thing is a bit like a cross between *House* and *Who Wants to Be a Millionaire*. (Most university-affiliated hospitals—Mass General is a Harvard teaching hospital—run grand rounds, often on a departmental basis, but none comes close to achieving the status and showmanship of Mass General's.)

The guest star often gets it right—the fellow on the hot seat the day I was there nailed a child's near-fatal woes as stemming from a rare form of asthma. Such diagnoses are unquestionably astonishing displays of expertise. But I also think grand rounds serve to hit home how much the experts on which we often depend are up against. Producing a right answer is in many ways far harder for these everyday experts than it is for the guest stars on grand rounds, who after all are choosing between known, if sometimes obscure, disorders, and who have a blizzard of presumably relevant and accurate data at their fingertips—the very fact that the producers of Mass General's grand rounds have selected a particular case for the show is pretty much a guarantee that a clear answer is lying within reach somewhere in that data, in that the show wouldn't be enlightening if the cases were truly indecipherable. Public experts, on the other hand, don't get to take this sort of multiple-choice, open-book test. They are typically trying to forge insights into matters that have never been clearly understood, or in some cases even well characterized, and that for all we know are of such complexity that the right answer won't be known for hundreds of years, if ever, if indeed there really can be said to be a right answer at all, and they must depend for guidance in this daunting quest on information that is almost always mismeasured, biased, incomplete, or otherwise misleading. What's more, they face this challenge knowing that should they manage to come to a correct conclusion, they might not be acknowledged or rewarded for it, and might even be penalized, should the conclusion be considered boring, or unappealing, or improbable, or threatening in some way to other, influential experts or to communities of experts.

Fully appreciating all that stands between mass experts and reliable advice gives us our first, and probably most potent, weapon in trying to avoid being misled: an appropriate level of wariness with regard to any expert pronouncement. When we can watch the claims of medical or parenting or financial experts on the *Today* show, or read them in the *New York Times*, and think to ourselves not "Wow, I better make some serious changes to the way I eat / talk to my children / use my credit cards" but rather "Hmmm, I wonder how likely it is that this advice will turn out to be worth following," then we are already way ahead of the game.

On the other hand, while our being keenly aware of how likely experts are to be at least partly if not completely wrong may protect us from dangerous gullibility, it can also tempt us to shrug off all expert advice. Even if we are reconciled to the notion that experts turn out to be at least partly wrong or in strong disagreement the great majority of the time, that still leaves us with dozens or possibly hundreds of cases in which they are mostly in agreement and seem highly likely to be right, and in which we can pay a big price for not following their advice. I discussed this aspect of the expertise problem with the almost frighteningly polymathic Charles Ferguson, a political science PhD who, in addition to academic gigs at MIT and the University of California–Berkeley, has also founded a massively successful software company, authored several books on a variety of subjects, and written and directed the award-winning 2007 documentary film *No End in Sight*, which makes the case that the Bush administration had ample warning about the challenges it would face in rebuilding postinvasion Iraq from experts who were in a good position to know. The main way Bush's team got into trouble, Ferguson argues, was by simply ignoring all that good advice. "The point isn't that you should always do what the experts say," he told me, "but rather that making giant, sweeping decisions without listening to them at all is really dumb."

What is apparently true for world leaders surely applies to the rest of us in our everyday lives. At the very least, more of us ought to be following consensus expert advice that seems well supported, is not terribly burdensome to implement, and appears to have little downside, such as eating fish (or taking fish oil), not eating large quantities of saturated fat, getting exercise, putting aside money into tax-deferred savings plans, employing encouragement with children much more often than browbeating, keeping our minds active as we move into older age, keeping our eye on the golf ball as we swing, and so on. And yet many of us manage to avoid following advice that not only is espoused by a wide range of experts but seems so basic and well proven that to mistrust it would appear to defy all logic. This isn't merely the behavior of the uneducated, antisocial, and dysfunctional we're talking about. The smallish town in which I live was recently shocked by the loss via car accident of a mother of three who at the time of the crash apparently was text-messaging while driving and, as per habit, wasn't wearing a seat belt—she was on her way home from her job leading a major physicians' group at a world-class hospital. I chose the quote at the top of this chapter so I can pointedly take issue with it here: while it's clearly true that you should never trust experts *blindly*, there are many situations in which you should and even must trust them, and in which to do otherwise is nothing other than reckless behavior.

But even those of us who are determined to follow what might be seen as clearly good advice from experts are still left in a quandary when we come up against new, disputed, or back-and-forth pronouncements among experts, whether the pronouncements are about diets, sun exposure, real-estate investments, the effect on children's minds of video games, and so forth. In many of these cases, we can't simply avoid making a choice—we all have to eat *something*—and it is sensible to make the choice at least knowing what experts have to say about the matter, in the hope that we can spot some clues as to which of the pieces of advice is more likely to be right or more applicable to our individual situations. I think the path to many such clues runs through the observations we've made throughout the book about the problems with expertise. So let's pull some of those observations together here to see if we can't extract practical if rough guidelines for navigating the trickier waters of expert advice.

Typical Characteristics of Less Trustworthy Expert Advice

Expert advice with a higher-than-average likelihood of being wrong is often given away by any number of tells. Be extra wary if the advice fits any of these descriptions:

It's simplistic, universal, and definitive. We've discussed the mismatch between the complex, subtle problems that mass experts tackle and the more cut-and-dried conclusions we push them to give us. When advice is of the sort that promises broad benefits and can be described in a sound bite or headline—"Drinking Coffee Extends Life Span!"—chances are good that either it's coming from an expert who has wandered off track through mismeasurement, bad analysis, or bias, or something has been lost in the translation as the findings made their way through research journals and the mass media. And remember that the conclusions of even the most careful studies are typically based on averages that pretty much ensure the findings won't neatly apply to most people.

It's supported by only a single study, or many small or less careful ones, or animal studies. Any advice based on one study should be regarded as highly tentative, no matter how good the study seems. The more studies, the better, as a rough rule, but even a series of big, rigorous studies can occasionally produce wrong conclusions. The risks of error are higher with research conducted with mere dozens of people (though statistical flukes can take over even in studies with thousands of people), or that isn't controlled and randomized (which means that confounders can take over), or that is limited to certain specific types of subjects such as students or very sick people (which means the results may not be relevant to anyone else). And such errors often can't be corrected by combining the results of many lower-grade studies, claims to the contrary notwithstanding—putting together several pools of bad data sometimes just creates one really large pool of bad data. I recommend treating as interesting fantasies any claims for human health or behavior that are based entirely on animal studies. And don't swallow the line that animal evidence has been shown to "translate" to humans because it has been backed up by one or two small or less formal human studies; lousy human evidence is lousy human evidence, regardless of what the animal work has indicated.

It's groundbreaking. For one thing, most expert insights that seem novel and surprising are based on a small number of less rigorous studies and often on just one small or animal study. That's because big, rigorous studies are almost never undertaken until several smaller ones pave the way, and if there had already been several studies backing this exciting finding, you probably would have heard about it then and it wouldn't seem novel now. Or consider the simple, if nonintuitive, logic asserted by Ioannidis and other Bayesians: a novel finding is by definition one that hasn't previously been clearly observed, and a typical reason why something has never before been clearly observed is that it isn't real.

It's pushed by people or organizations that stand to benefit from its acceptance. All experts stand to benefit from their research winning a big audience, of course, and that's well worth remembering, but in some cases the potential conflict of interest is more likely to be corrosive. That's especially true when the research is coming out of or being directly funded by individual companies or industry groups whose profits may be impacted by the findings. Corporate sponsorship doesn't mean a study is wrong, but there's simply no question it sharply raises the risk of serious bias; tobacco companies, for example, were always able to find physicians and researchers willing to come up with "evidence" that smoking might be getting a bad rap. And remember that study after study has shown that many potential conflicts of interest are not clearly revealed in expert reports and are sometimes actively obscured, which means that digging or reading between the lines may be required. Government-sponsored research is generally more trustworthy, though not always—there were widespread charges of research corruption under the George W. Bush administration, which by most (but not all) accounts saw research spending in part as a means to advance an ideological agenda. High-powered consultants, meanwhile, tend to employ mass advice as a way to market their services, leaving the advice approximately as trustworthy as any other form of advertising.

It's geared toward preventing a future occurrence of a prominent recent failure or crisis. This is the "locking the barn door" effect: we're so irked or even traumatized by whatever has just gone wrong that we're eager to do now whatever we might have done before to have avoided the problem. It's about as smart a strategy as standing on a twelve in blackjack with the dealer showing a face card, just because you've busted twice in a row. But experts will oblige by dispensing such already obsolete advice, as when, for example, we are encouraged to be ultrafastidious with our food handling after an outbreak of food-borne bacteria (bearing in mind that the problem of drug-resistant bacteria has been exacerbated by overuse of antibacterial cleaners) or to build up our savings after a national borrowing binge has crashed the economy (bearing in mind that a widespread shift to savings can stifle recovery).

Characteristics of Expert Advice We Should Ignore

Expert claims often draw our attention and win our credulity via factors that don't really give us good reason to trust them. It's not that we should hold it against expert advice if it employs these factors; rather, the information simply doesn't tell us much one way or the other.

It's mildly resonant. We've seen that some expert advice just sounds right to us—it fits well with our view of the world, it appeals to our common sense, it's amusing, it makes life easier for us, it offers a solution to a pressing problem. Too bad none of that improves the chances of an expert conclusion being true. In fact, these factors if anything tend to speak to the untrustworthiness of advice, in that they represent temptations for twisting conclusions to make them resonant or that they can point toward publication bias.

It's provocative. We love to hear an expert turn a conventional view on its ear: Fat is good for you! Being messy can be a good thing! We're tickled by the surprise, and at the same time it may ring true because we're so used to finding out that what we've all been led to believe is right is actually wrong. The conventional view is indeed often wrong, or at least limited, but look for good evidence before abandoning that view.

It gets a lot of positive attention. The press, the online crowd, your friends—what do they know? The coverage drawn by an expert claim usually has more to do with how skillfully it has been spun or promoted, combined with its resonance and provocativeness, rather than how trustworthy it might be. The discovery in May 2009 of a forty-seven-million-year-old fossil, apparently that of a primitive lemurlike primate, generated more than 750 news articles within a few days, according to Google News, most of which faithfully aped the tune sung to the press by the discovering scientists and their academic institutions, which claimed the fossil—resonantly nicknamed "Ida"—represented the long-sought "missing link" between primitive primates and more modern ones, including humans. (Ida was even incorporated into Google's home-page logo for a day, the Internet equivalent of a Nobel Prize.) Underneath all the spotlights and the tie-in television documentary and the Ida book were the little-heard voices of several highly credible experts, including the scientist who heads up vertebrate paleontology at the Carnegie Museum of Natural History, complaining that Ida did not in fact appear to unambiguously represent as important a link as argued. Ida may turn out to be what its advocates claimed, but there was ample reason to bipedal with caution.

Other experts embrace it. Well, this one shouldn't really be ignored, just carefully put into perspective. As mentioned previously, a good case can be made that the wide support of fellow experts in some circumstances can speak to the credibility of an expert claim. But we've also seen that communities of experts can succumb to politics, bandwagon effects, funding-related biases, and other corrupting phenomena. It's also often hard for laypeople to tell if most of the experts in a field do in fact support a particular claim—press reports may be presenting a biased sampling of experts. Interestingly, a 2009 Wharton study that looked at more than a century of data on the popularity of first names in the United States and France found that the more widely and quickly a name rises to popularity, the more widely and quickly it is likely to fall from favor, and the study authors suggested that the same basic principle appears to apply to the adoption of ideas.[3] We've already seen that management advice tends to be highly faddish, and it may be reasonable to wonder if all sorts of expert claims follow faddish cycles. In that light, the immediate, wide support of a community of experts for a new claim might be seen as a warning sign rather than a recommendation. More trustworthy, by this reasoning, would be support that gradually builds among experts over a longer period of time.

It appears in a prestigious journal. Surely you'll never fall for that one again.

It's supported by a big, rigorous study. Yes, a large, randomized controlled trial is in general more trustworthy than most other types of expert studies, but as we've seen, that isn't saying all that much. No study, or even group of studies, comes close to giving us take-it-to-the-bank proof. When several big, rigorous studies have come to the same conclusion, you'd be wise to give it serious consideration—though there may still be plenty of reason for doubt, perhaps on the grounds of publication bias (the dissenting studies may have been dropped somewhere along the line), sponsorship corruption (as when a drug company is backing all the studies to bolster a product), measurement problems (as when questionable markers are involved), flawed analysis (as when cause and effect are at risk of being confused), and more.

The experts backing it boast impressive credentials. We've seen that some of the baldest cases of fraud oozed out of Ivy League campuses, world-class hospitals, and legendary industrial labs—where competence and standards may be sky-high, but so are the pressures to perform, along with freedom from close oversight. If überexperts can cheat, they certainly can succumb to bias, gamesmanship, sloppiness, and error. And they do—all the time. A trickier question, though, is this one: when highly credentialed experts face off against not very highly credentialed experts, should we back the folks with the big reps? I think most of the time we should lean that way, because whatever biases, errors, and distortions scientists, megaconsultants, top government advisers, and other impressively credentialed experts wrestle with, the problems are likely to be that much worse with pop, self-proclaimed, or lay "experts." When parents put their autistic children on exotic diets touted by well-meaning celebrity moms instead of immediately getting them into the intensive behavioral therapy urged by virtually every academic specialist on autism,* they've catastrophically failed to cut a safe path through the jungle of advice.

But I don't think informal expertise should be dismissed out of hand, even when it is in conflict with that of formal experts. Most formal experts are compelled to focus on amassing precise data and then rigorously analyzing the information to make their

---

* At least in the Western world, not counting France.

cases, and we've seen how that process can actually carry experts away from the truth. The fact that informal experts can rely on less meticulous but potentially more relevant real-world observations and that they're free to enlist experience and common sense to assess them occasionally works in their favor. A simple example: the 2004 *Physicians' Desk Reference* advised that anabolic steroids don't enhance athletic performance—thanks to the fact that no one had been able to design an ethical study able to effectively test this claim out, probably supplemented by a strong bias against the casual use of these drugs. Meanwhile, coaches and athletes everywhere had long had all the evidence they needed to know the truth, which is that anabolic steroids can have an *enormous* impact on performance, a notion that the medical community now acknowledges.

Some Characteristics of More Trustworthy Expert Advice

The following elements are often tip-offs that extra care, integrity, and perspective have gone into the making and reporting of an expert pronouncement. Some of these factors involve not so much the nature of the advice itself but rather the information with which it's presented.

It doesn't trip the other alarms. Knowing now the characteristics of less trustworthy advice, we can obviously assume that expert advice not exhibiting such traits is likely to be more trustworthy. In other words, we ought to give more weight to expert advice that isn't simplistic; that is supported by many large, careful studies; that is consistent with what we mostly believe to be true; that avoids conflicts of interest; and that isn't a reaction to a recent crisis.

It's a negative finding. As we've seen, there is significant bias every step of the way against findings that fail to confirm an interesting or useful hypothesis—no one's going to stop the presses over the claim that coffee doesn't stave off Alzheimer's disease. There isn't much reason to game a disappointing conclusion, and anyone who publishes one or reports on it probably isn't overly concerned with compromising truth in order to dazzle readers.

It's heavy on qualifying statements. The process by which experts come up with findings, and by which those findings make their way to the rest of us, is biased toward sweeping under the rug flaws, weaknesses, and limitations. What can experts, or the journals that publish their work, or the newspapers and television shows that trumpet it, expect to gain by hitting us over the head with all the ways in which the study may have screwed up? And yet sometimes journal articles and media reports do contain comments and information intended to get us to question the reliability of the study methodology, or of the data analysis, or of how broadly the findings apply. Given that we should pretty much *always* question the reliability and applicability of expert findings, it can only speak to the credibility of the experts, editors, or reporters who explicitly raise these questions, encouraging us to do the same.

It's candid about refutational evidence. Claims by experts rarely stand unopposed or enjoy the support of all available data. (A saying in academia: for every PhD, there's an equal and opposite PhD.) Any expert, journal editor, or reporter who takes the trouble to dig up this sort of conflicting information and highlight it when passing on to us a claim ought to get a bit more of our attention. But don't be impressed by token skeptical quotes tossed into media reports in the name of "balance"; nor by the brief, toothless, pro forma "study limitations" sections of journal articles that listlessly toss out a few possible sources of mild error; nor by the injection of contradictory evidence that seems to have been introduced just to provide an opportunity for shooting it down. The frustration of on-the-one-hand-but-on-the-other-hand treatments of an expert claim is that they may leave us without a clear answer, but sometimes that's exactly the right place to end up. And, once in a while, watching the negative evidence take its best shot leaves us recognizing that the positive evidence actually seems to survive it and is worth following.

It provides some context for the research. Expert findings rarely emerge clear out of the blue — there is usually a history of claims and counterclaims, previous studies, arguments pro and con, alternative theories, new studies under way, and so forth. A finding that seems highly credible when presented by itself as a sort of snapshot can sometimes more clearly be seen as a distant long shot when presented against this richer background, and it's a good sign when a report provides it. Andrew Fano, a computer scientist at the giant high-tech consultancy Accenture, put it to me this way: "The trick is not to look at expertise as it's reflected in a single, brief distillation but rather as the behavior of a group of experts over a long period of time."

It provides perspective. Expert claims are frequently presented in a way that makes it hard to come up with a good answer to the simple question "What, if anything, does this mean for me?" We often need help not simply in knowing the facts but also in how to think and feel about them. I've already mentioned that more trustworthy pronouncements tend to more clearly spell out the limitations in their relevance — that a treatment has been tried only on animals or on healthy people, for example, or that a shift in real-estate prices has been clearly observed only in higher-end homes or in one part of the country. But experts and those who pass along their findings can and often should go further and suggest some clearheaded, practical, bottom-line meaning to a claim—a meaning that can otherwise be lost in a study's details, in the hype that might build around it, or in our own tendency to jump to conclusions. Such meta-findings might take the form of "Though the effect is interesting, it's a very small one, and even if it isn't just a fluke of chance, it probably doesn't merit changing behavior"; "Chances are slim this will apply to you"; "While this seems to be an important observation, there is yet so much un-certainty surrounding it that it shouldn't be taken seriously until much better evidence comes in"; or "This is only one of several strategies for achieving this goal, and it's not clearly better than the rest of them." Experts, journal editors, and journalists might reasonably argue that their audiences shouldn't need these sorts of reminders, that the facts should speak for themselves, that it's not their place to interject such semi-subjective commentary. Well, fair enough, but I'd assert that those who go ahead and do it anyway ought to be rewarded with a higher level of trust, in that it demonstrates they're willing to sacrifice the potential impact of an expert claim to help out the rest of us in knowing what to make of it. The need for such explanation is particularly acute when research involves statements about probabilities and risk, which the public has a terrible time interpreting (as do many experts). A University of Washington study found that one out of two peo-ple doesn't understand everyday weather forecasts well enough to make informed decisions based on them—many people think a 30 percent chance of rain means it will rain over 30 percent of the area, while others think it means it will rain 30 percent of the day.[4] And yet as fundamental as statements about risk are to medical and financial advice, rarely do reports of expert claims fully make clear their significance or lack of significance.

It includes candid, blunt comments. We're all aware that good political reporters work hard to get officials to drop their prepared remarks and talking points and start saying what they really believe, but good science and financial journalists struggle in the same way, or ought to. I don't think you can be confident of really understanding the reliability or significance of an expert claim unless you've heard the expert herself or other well-informed experts express their doubts and skepticism. The best places to look for such comments, in my experience, are in longer magazine articles, in letters to journals, and occasionally in radio interviews. (The Internet abounds with such forthright assessments but tends to be so clogged with contentious complaints about every claim made by anyone that it's hard to recommend it as a reliable source of insight.) I don't mean to hold up longer media interviews and journal correspondence as beacons of truth—they are often themselves highly biased—but I believe they're well worth taking into account and offer at least a shot at getting at the real and often hidden ins and outs of an expert pronouncement.

All this requires work. Do I really expect everyone to go through a long checklist, complete with hunting down supplemental information, every time they're presented with an expert claim? No, not most people, and not most of the time. Part of the whole point of having experts is to relieve us of much of the responsibility for really having to do our homework on these matters. Nature seems to have programmed into us a knack for that "cognitive economizing" I mentioned earlier on; an Emory University brain-imaging study found that the sections of our brain that seem charged with decision making become significantly less active when we're presented with what we're told is expert advice, regardless of how bad the advice is.[5]

But not all of us. In 2009 a high-school senior in Sammamish,

Washington, decided to second-guess the string of doctors who told her that her severe and ongoing digestive discomfort wasn't caused by Crohn's disease, which is treatable. She finally brought her own intestinal tissue samples into school and stuck them under a microscope, where she promptly spotted the Crohn's-specific inflammations known as granulomas, a diagnosis later seconded by a specialist. Most of us aren't likely to be that enterprising when it comes to standing up to formal expertise. But at least being willing to go through the trouble of keeping a checklist for assessing expert claims in the back of one's mind could allow immediately filtering out some of the advice that's least likely to hold up. And surely many people will find it worth the effort to look a bit more closely into matters when considering adopting advice that can lead to better health, major lifestyle changes, organizational shake-ups, altered child development, and substantially larger or smaller 401K accounts.

If you're not formally trained in science or haven't soaked a lot of it up in some other way, you'll probably find research journals tough going. I've been told by dozens of highly regarded scientists, including two different Nobel laureates, that they have trouble understanding many of the journal articles that are in their field but outside their immediate area of focus. On the other hand, it isn't always hard to spot some of the potential shortcomings of a journal study, such as small numbers of subjects drawn from narrow populations, or the use of dubious surrogate measures such as those used in psychiatric studies to infer the emotional states of animals.

Besides, there's always the hope that putting some effort into learning how to vet expert claims will over time lead to the development of a more intuitive sense of when a finding ought to be regarded with extra suspicion. Our brains are marvelous pattern-recognition machines, and just as good doctors learn to accurately diagnose illnesses with scant information, I think most of us, too, can become moderately competent assessors of expert pronouncements, and without always having to bury ourselves in research. In 2007 the *New England Journal of Medicine* ran the story of a Providence, Rhode Island, nursing-home cat that seemed able to identify patients who were close to death—whenever it showed sudden interest in curling up beside a patient, that patient usually turned out to have little time left on Earth, and apparently it wasn't always patients whom the doctors had recognized as being at death's door.[6] You don't have to fully buy that story to know there may be ways of sensing complex truths that don't require years of formal training and intense experience. We can't always trust our common sense, and we don't always know good advice when we hear it, but if we work at it in a well-informed way, I think most of us can move at least a bit in that direction.*

---

* Unless, of course, this book is itself mostly wrong and has misled you. I remind you yet again that I've explored this possibility in Appendix 4.

A Tiny Sampling of Expert Wrongness, Conflict, and Confusion

Are violent video games harmful to children's development?

"Most of the alarmism about violence is based on a profound misunderstanding about the social and emotional function of games. Games allow people who are midway between childhood and adulthood to engage in fantasies of power to compensate for their own feelings of personal powerlessness. This role-playing function is important for children of all ages."
—One of thirty-three researchers and psychologists
filing a 2002 court brief opposing a law banning minors
from obtaining violent video games

"Violence in video games appears to have similar negative effects as viewing violence on TV, but may be more harmful because of the interactive nature of video games. Playing video games involves practice, repetition, and being rewarded for numerous acts of violence, which may intensify the learning. This may also result in more realistic experiences which may potentially increase aggressive behavior."
—2005 American Psychological Association press release

"The real puzzle is that anyone looking at the research evidence in

this field could draw any conclusions about the pattern, let alone argue with such confidence and even passion...."
—British psychologist and researcher commenting
on the conflicting findings on the impact of media
violence on children

Does choice of college affect earning power?

"Our research found that earnings were unrelated to the selectivity of the college that students had attended among those who had comparable options."
—A widely quoted 2000 study by researchers at Princeton
and the Andrew W. Mellon Foundation

Median starting salaries are 32 percent lower for top liberal arts college graduates than for Ivy League graduates. Median midcareer salaries are 34 percent lower.
—Results (paraphrased) from a widely quoted 2008
survey conducted by compensation research
firm PayScale, Inc.

Should I try to get eight hours of sleep every night?

"In general, most healthy adults need seven to nine hours of sleep a night. However, some individuals...can't perform at their peak unless they've slept ten hours."
—National Sleep Foundation website

"Studies show that...people who sleep 8 hours or more, or less than 6.5 hours, don't live quite as long. There is just as much risk associated with sleeping too long as with sleeping too short. The big surprise is that long sleep seems to start at 8 hours. Sleeping 8.5 hours might really be a little worse than sleeping 5."
—Sleep researcher quoted in *Time* magazine, 2008

Can "biofuel" made from corn and other crops help the environment?

"When compared with the life cycle of gasoline and diesel, ethanol and biodiesel from corn and soybean rotations reduced greenhouse gas emission by nearly 40 percent...."
—Announcement of results of research study
by the U.S. Department of Agriculture and
Colorado State University, 2007

"Corn-based ethanol, instead of producing a 20% savings, nearly doubles greenhouse emissions over 30 years and increases greenhouse gases for 167 years."
—Research study published in the journal *Science*, 2008

"On the basis of our own analyses, production of corn-based ethanol in the United States so far results in moderate [greenhouse gas] emissions reductions."
—Response to *Science* study by U.S. Department of
Energy researchers, 2009

Should I stay out of the sun?

"Exposure to the sun's ultraviolet (UV) rays appears to be the most important environmental factor involved with developing skin cancer.... It's always wise to choose more than one way to cover up when you're in the sun. Use sunscreen and put on a shirt.... Seek shade and grab your sunglasses.... Wear a hat, but rub on sunscreen too. Combining these sun protective actions helps protect your skin from the sun's damaging UV rays."
—U.S. Centers for Disease Control and Prevention website

"UVR exposure is a minor contributor to the world's disease burden.... A markedly larger annual disease burden [including potentially fatal cancers]... might result from [too little exposure to UV rays]."
—Research cited in 2006 World Health Organization (WHO) report

Is being a nice guy good for romance?

"The nice guy cares too much, too soon. He has made the woman too important and too valuable and it shows in everything he says and does. He is too available, too eager to please, too accommodating, and he gives too much—all without getting anything in return. By doing so, he has made himself appear desperate, insecure, needy of this woman's attention, affection, and approval—and he has stripped himself of any value in her eyes."
—Relationship advice expert April Masini, aka the
"New Millennium's Dear Abby" and author of four
popular books on dating

"That's where you come in, Mr. Sweet Guy. Because you're the guy we really want for the long haul. Here's my advice for all the nice guys: Remember what we were wearing on our first date. Give romantic gifts on birthdays and anniversaries (and remember flower-mandatory holidays such as Valentine's Day). Get what we're all about. Let us know what you're all about. Kill any bugs that sneak into the kitchen. Give us your coat when it gets chilly outside."
—Relationship advice expert Lisa Daily, author of a syndicated
column appearing on more than fifty websites and of the
popular book *Stop Getting Dumped!*

Are fertility treatments effective?

"The latest figures (2006) show that 23.1% of all [in vitro fertilization] treatments resulted in a live birth."
—Website of British fertilization regulatory agency

"None of the treatments studied had any significant benefit over no treatment at all."
—Lead author of a 2008 *British Medical Journal* study of the two most popular infertility treatments, quoted by the Associated Press

Are pets good for my health?

"Several studies have documented that pet animals also can have an important supportive role and a positive influence on the health of their owners. Pet ownership is a significant predictor of 1-year survival after myocardial infarction. Relative to the support of friends and spouses, the presence of a pet elicits significantly lower blood pressure and heart rate reactivity during mental stress. In addition, elderly individuals with pets are buffered from the impact of stressful life events and make fewer visits to physicians...."
—2001 study published by the American Heart Association

"Pet ownership was associated with poor rather than good perceived health."
—2006 Finnish research study

How should I break in the engine of my new car?

"The break-in period is supposed to be a time in which you drive gently and allow the rings to 'seat,' or mold themselves perfectly to the exact shapes of the cylinder walls."
—Ray "Clack" Magliozzi, of the famed *Car Talk* radio show, in 1997

"During break-in... the only thing to be concerned with is to vary the speed every 10–15 minutes and avoid full throttle acceleration and hard braking."
—Pat "Goss's Garage" Goss, whose car advice has appeared
regularly in the *Washington Post* and on PBS, in 2005

"What's the best way to break in a new engine? The short answer: Run it hard!...If the gas pressure is strong enough during the engine's first miles of operation (open that throttle!!!), then the entire ring will wear into the cylinder surface, to seal the combustion pressure as well as possible."

—Pat "MotoMan" McGivern on his "Mototune USA" website,
which, along with his twelve-thousand-subscriber newsletter,
is often quoted by car and motorcycle enthusiasts

Is it okay to let my child sleep in my bed?

"Although taking your child into bed with you for a night or two
may be reasonable if he is ill or very upset about something, for
the most part this is not a good idea."
—Dr. Richard Ferber, in the 1985 edition of his bestselling
book *Solve Your Child's Sleep Problems*

"If bedtime is happy and the kids go willingly, it doesn't make a
lot of difference where they go to bed."
—Dr. Richard Ferber, speaking on the *Today* show in 2006

Should I drink a lot of water when exercising?

"Two hours before physical activity, drink two cups of water,
drink one cup immediately before and a half cup every 15 minutes during, and at least two cups after. Don't wait until you are
thirsty. By then you are already on your way to dehydration and
poor physical performance. Always stay ahead of your thirst."
—Nutritionist in a 2001 online publication of the
Medical University of South Carolina, echoing
near-universal advice at the time

"Hyponatremia [a potentially fatal low-sodium condition that can
be caused by drinking too much water when exercising] occurs in
a substantial fraction of nonelite marathon runners and can be
severe."
—*New England Journal of Medicine* study, 2005

"Athletes are still told, 'Stay ahead of your thirst,' which is terrible
advice."
—Exercise researcher quoted in the *New York Times*, 2006

Is "educational television" good for children's development?

"*Sesame Street* and...*Blues Clues*...are examples of shows that started learning epidemics in preschoolers, that turned kids on to reading and 'infected' them with literacy."
—Malcolm Gladwell, journalist and author of *The Tipping Point*

"Exposure to television programming from age 6 months to 30 months was significantly related to vocabulary and expressive language development, with the majority of children's programming positively impacting development."
—2005 study by University of Pennsylvania and
University of Kansas researchers

"Watching even really good educational shows...is bad [for children under three]."
—Coauthor of study published in the *Journal of Pediatrics and Adolescent Medicine*, 2005

"Among infants (age 8 to 16 months), each hour per day of viewing baby DVDs/videos was associated with a [substantial drop in language and communications skills]. Among toddlers (age 17 to 24 months), there were no significant associations between any type of media exposure and [language and communications skills]."
—2009 study by the director of the Center for Child Health,
Behavior and Development at Seattle Children's Hospital

Do cell phones emit harmful radiation?

"There's really no biological basis for you to be concerned about radio waves [from cell phones]."
—Director of the International Epidemiology Institute,
commenting to the press after a 2006 Danish study of
420,000 cell phone users concluded that cell phones
don't cause cancer, and echoing the near-universal
opinion of the scientific community at the time

"The study indicates that during laboratory exposure to [cell phone–type] wireless signals, components of sleep, believed to be important for recovery from daily wear and tear, are adversely affected. Moreover, participants that otherwise have no self-reported symptoms related to mobile phone use, appear to have more headaches during actual radiofrequency exposure as compared to sham exposure."
—2007 multiuniversity research study

"Although the evidence is still controversial, I am convinced that there are sufficient data [on the link between cell phones and cancer] to warrant issuing an advisory to share some precautionary advice on cell phone use."
—Director of the University of Pittsburgh Cancer Institute,
in a widely publicized 2008 memo to faculty and staff

Have experts learned how to avoid a repeat of the financial turmoil of recent years?

"We will learn an enormous amount in a very short time, quite a bit in the medium term, and absolutely nothing in the long term."
—Widely respected U.S. investment manager Jeremy Grantham

Is medical science steadily progressing toward curing or preventing most diseases?

"This is a really dramatic result. It makes you step back and worry, 'What do we really know?'"
—University of North Carolina researcher, commenting
on a new study highlighting the failure of colonoscopies
to detect many tumors

"We progress, not along straight lines, but in wavelike alternations of improvement and stagnation or retrogression."
—Editorial in the *Journal of the American Medical Association*, 1909

The Evolution of Expertise

Every epoch, under names more or less specious,
has deified its peculiar errors.
— PERCY BYSSHE SHELLEY

Are vegetarian diets healthier than diets heavy in meat? To find out, one proponent of the less-meat-is-better view convinced the military to sponsor a study in which two groups of people were each restricted to one of the diets for a period of time, after which the health of all the subjects was assessed. Though the results were deemed by the backers of the research to support the greater healthfulness of vegetarianism, the experiment didn't really settle the question. The study, as described in the Bible,* was conducted around 600 BC, and today, countless studies later, expert advocates of both types of diets insist the data support their points of view.

---

* "Daniel spoke with the attendant who had been appointed by the chief of staff to look after Daniel, Hananiah, Mishael, and Azariah. 'Please test us for ten days on a diet of vegetables and water,' Daniel said. 'At the end of the ten days, see how we look compared to the other young men who are eating the king's food. Then make your decision in light of what you see.' The attendant agreed to Daniel's suggestion and tested them for ten days. At the end of the ten days, Daniel and his three friends looked healthier and better nourished than the young men who had been eating the food assigned by the king." — Daniel 1:11–15

For better or worse, experts, along with their dubious pronouncements and supporting research, have been with us quite
a while. Fossil and other archaeological evidence reveal early
development of various specialized skills, be it related to tools,
hunting, combat, shelter, or art—for example, unearthed sculp-
tures of the human female form complete with striking fertility
symbolism date back as far as 35,000 years. While opinions may
differ as to where exactly to draw the line between ordinary and
higher-level, community-influencing forms of expertise, we can
reasonably assert the world had seen the latter by at least 12,000
years ago, the age of the earliest-known archaeological evidence
for shamanistic burial rituals. Held by the community to have
special understanding of and even influence over nature and su-
pernatural entities, shamans can rightly be considered religious
figures, but their role in prehistoric times would also have been
something roughly akin to scientists, in that they would have been
the trusted source of wisdom on weather, on the rise and fall of
animal and plant populations critical for food, and especially on
health. Eerily well-preserved 5,000-year-old cadavers, chipped in
recent decades out of icy graves, show clear signs of having been
ministered to by medical experts of a sort—experts who in many
cases must have inflicted considerable harm and suffering, not to
mention death, with their bold, creative, and intricate techniques,
including the airing of brain matter via the sawing of holes in the
skull, various types of amputations, and the treating of chronic
pain with tattoo needles. Whether submitting to such shamanistic
wisdom would have on average increased one's chances of survival
is an interesting question. It's possible the inclination to trust experts was hardwired into our brains through straightforward evolutionary pressures rather than having arisen as a glitch or as a
side effect to other evolutionary traits. On the other hand, there's
always the possibility that the tendency to trust even expert advice

that ultimately proves catastrophically bad helps prune whatever genes contribute to dangerous levels of gullibility.

By 2500 BC, Egypt had seen the development of something beginning to resemble mass expertise—that is, experts who are in a position to transmit their wisdom to large or influential chunks of the population. The region already had at that time some three millennia worth of heavy construction savvy under its belt, but now significant progress was under way in mathematics, medicine, and astronomy. The experts of Ancient Egypt would, in the coming centuries, reckon that the Earth was a spinning globe that orbited the sun, and that the positions of the stars could be charted so as to allow predicting when the Nile would flood. Though there wasn't much difference between a scientist and a priest, the outline of what we would come to think of as the scientific process—that is, gathering data from observation and matching it to theory—was fitfully taking shape. Babylonia, too, was making this sort of progress, but Egypt gave us what may well be the earliest identifiable public expert, or at least the first who wasn't also royalty and whose name and achievements survived into distant posterity: Imhotep, who was especially accomplished as an architect and engineer but also arguably a founding father of modern medicine, in that he achieved an understanding of some aspects of human anatomy and of the diagnosis and treatment of various ailments that was in some cases not too far out of line with what we know today. Inspired if not directly guided by Imhotep's findings, Ancient Egyptian doctor-priests operated on tumors, cauterized wounds, dispensed hundreds of mostly herbal prescriptions, counseled the use of sunscreen and laxatives, fought infections with bread mold (a possible source of penicillin), and fashioned prostheses, all to the frequent betterment of patients. Well, not always betterment: many of the prescriptions were for such potentially harmful agents as animal dung and blood;

treatment relied heavily on incantations and charms; and anatomical insight was surprisingly vague given Egyptian mastery of tricky, mummification-related organ-removal procedures, which were performed through orifices and small incisions almost as per today's laparoscopic surgery. Still, Imhotep made enough of a positive impression on Egyptian society to end up with the sort of lasting acclaim normally accorded to only pharaohs, including deification. (His reputation has suffered more recently at the hands of Hollywood, which portrayed him as the eponymous ghoul in the 1932 movie *The Mummy* as well as in the 1999 remake.)

That the names of other nonruling experts mostly haven't survived from this ancient era may tell us that there weren't many of them. Or perhaps there were plenty of them, but their fame proved fleeting. Ancient Egypt's, and indeed the world's, first recorded death sentence was for a young fellow convicted of "magic," which may well have consisted of an attempt at healing or prediction that went awry. Those responsible for foretelling the Nile's floods are also believed to have risked death over miscalculation. Our forefathers were sometimes a lot harder than we are today on those whose bold claims of insight don't pan out.

Critically for the evolution of public expertise, the Ancient Egyptians developed the means for preserving what wisdom was produced by writing it down on sheets of hardy papyrus, which would eventually lead to the establishment of a library in Alexandria that grew to contain what may have been as many as several hundred thousand scrolls before it was destroyed under Roman rule. Medical insights long believed to have been originally authored by Imhotep himself (though that authorship is disputed today) were recorded around 1600 BC, and the resulting text yet endures at the New York Academy of Medicine. We might even claim that Ancient Egypt produced the world's first research journal, thanks to the editorial ambitions of a man named Ahmes, who, though not known to have been a producer of wisdom himself, dutifully recorded in the seventeenth-century BC the mostly mathematical discoveries of others in a text, now at the British Museum, entitled *Directions for Knowing All Dark Things*—a title that serves as a reminder of the then fine line between magic and science. But these one-off texts, significant as they may be, hardly constitute mass media, and though the names of leading experts might have been known to segments of the public at large, it was only royalty and others among the most influential pockets of society who would have had routine access to their wisdom. But at least these documents would have facilitated the training of other medical caregivers, enabling Ancient Egypt to boast not only general practitioners but also specialists in ophthalmology, proctology, and dentistry, among other domains.

Mass expertise made an extraordinary series of leaps in classical and early Hellenic Greece (between about 600 and 200 BC) that would come to define much of the modus operandi of highly credentialed public experts even as we know them today, as well as to lay down a foundation for many of the subjects these experts would explore. The fact that the world around us is composed of invisibly tiny atoms, the difference between matter and energy, the origins of our planet and the life on it, the way we take in information through our senses, the relationship between language and thought, how to apply rigorous logic, the need to establish cause and effect, the nature of categorization, the subjectivity of truth, the importance of learning by questioning—all of this was tackled *before* most of Ancient Greece's big-gun philosopher-scientists entered the scene. Throw in the contributions to mathematics, physics, epistemology, medicine, and even psychology of Pythagoras, Hippocrates, Socrates, Plato, Aristotle, Euclid, and Archimedes, and the depth and breadth of the expertise transformation become hard to exaggerate.

It wasn't merely the conclusions, pronouncements, and proofs of this parade of early intellectual giants that made them so influential to the development of mass expertise. Rather, it was the way in which they approached problems. For one thing, in general they tended to push religion away from the spotlight and into a corner of the expert conversation (though Pythagoras for one managed to blend the two in a way that didn't prevent him from making important strides in math). In addition, they established a formal tension between observation and theory, sought to uncover simple rules that underlay what seemed to be a messy and complex world, raised questions about the limits of knowledge, highlighted the role that the mind can play in interpreting reality, and insisted that arguments and claims be buttressed by clear logic. Equally important, at least in terms of what we're considering in this book, these Greek titans established certain key career-management strategies for public experts. Specifically, some of them seemed to appreciate the importance in a fairly democratic society of becoming influential with the masses via highly resonant ideas and pronouncements; they came up with bold, novel assertions and then defended them intensely and uncompromisingly for the rest of their careers; they established intellectual alliances that served to marginalize other experts who might have threatened the dominance of their thinking; they became closely associated with academies that provided credibility, avid supporters, a ready pool of student labor, and a steady income; they (especially Archimedes and, separately, the leading Sophists) became adept at raising substantial funds through government contracting or commercial consulting; and some of them tended to place a heavy emphasis on publication. Archimedes's written works still yield surprises today, as with the 2009 discovery that he invented a rough, limited form of calculus about two millennia before anyone else would get on its trail.

Perhaps most significantly, the great Greek thinkers proved that expert influence and general success have almost nothing to do with actually being right most of the time. Pythagoras insisted that we harbor hidden memories of past lives and that all phenomena could be broken down into relatively simple relationships between numbers. Hippocrates focused on diagnosis and treatment of disturbances in the balance of the body's "humors"—various fluids said to rule emotions. Zeno, immortalized through the various paradoxes he proposed, argued that physical motion was an impossibility and therefore an illusion. The somewhat antidemocratic Socrates believed that virtue was an inherent quality that couldn't be learned and claimed he was ordained by the gods to make these and other points clear to humanity. Plato dismissed observation as a means for getting at truth, arguing that the nature of the world could be discovered only through internal reasoning and intuition. Archimedes, who was on safe ground when he stuck to modest engineering projects that could be easily tested, proposed building giant banks of mirrors to turn the sun's rays into enemy-ship-incinerating weapons, never mind the ready availability of less flashy but effective flaming arrows. Even Euclidean geometry could be said to be wrong, at least in a strict sense, in that it is predicated on assumptions about parallel lines that turn out to not hold in some important cases. But it was Aristotle more than any classical Greek thinker who managed to throw much of the world off, thanks to a series of extensive, firmly argued, meticulously recorded, and impressively wrongheaded pronouncements. For example, he declared, in defiance of what a few minutes of careful observation in and around one's home might suggest, that like materials attract, and unlike materials such as air and water repel, and that moving objects screech to a halt if they're not being actively pushed. Aristotle also concluded that the celestial bodies were propelled around the Earth at constant speed in perfect circles by the hands of a prime mover, in contradiction of the fluky planetary motions that even by then had been documented. Alas, his fractured view of physics and astronomy, unencumbered by any compulsion to carefully check it against reality, would hobble Western science for more than seventeen centuries.

After the lights dimmed in classical Greece and scientific progress in the Western world was mostly put on hold, China and the Islamic world made important contributions both to science and to the influence of experts. By the first-century AD, acupuncture was on its way to becoming an established and widely available treatment in China, making it one of the first major medical practices to survive more or less intact to the present day. Papermaking was established in China in the eighth century, finally providing a relatively economical and reliable way to record expertise. (The development of inkable stamps around the same time allowed the printing of books, although the vast array of such stamps that was needed to reproduce thousands of Chinese characters limited the technique's practicality, and texts mostly remained laboriously handwritten.) Meanwhile, Islamic thinkers busily translated the classic Greek texts, which—thanks to papermaking techniques imported from China—had finally become widely circulated. These Islamic scholars, adopting an emphasis on observation and experiment over reasoning and intuition, were in some cases able to go well beyond the Greeks to build up an impressive body of credible work in astronomy, chemistry, medicine, and physics— insights that would anticipate and inform the coming scientific revolution in Europe. Researchers such as the eighth-century chemist Jābir ibn Hayyān and the eleventh-century optics pioneer Ibn al-Haytham are perhaps fairly categorized as the world's first true scientists, opening an important new chapter on expertise.

By the end of the eleventh century, it was Europe's turn, via the founding of the University of Bologna, arguably the first institute in the world to at least roughly fit our modern conception of a university as a non-church-run haven of research and learning empowered to grant formal credentials of expertise—in law in the beginning, and later in a range of arts and sciences. The first of Oxford University's colleges and the University of Paris–Sorbonne were founded in the thirteenth century, and Europe was off and running, university-wise. The printing press came along in the mid-fifteenth century, just in time to feed a growing interest on the part of the quickly expanding ranks of university researchers to promulgate their theories and findings to their colleagues. Among those peers, they might variously find enthusiastic support or vigorous rebuttal. But such print-abetted debate sometimes ran counter to the influence of existing social and political institutions, and in particular that of the church.

That clash would come to a head in the field of astronomy. At the end of the fifteenth century, a young law and medical student at the University of Bologna named Nicolaus Copernicus started thinking about the movements of the planets and became convinced that those motions could be better explained by a model of the solar system that had the planets orbiting the sun rather than the Earth. He cautiously kept his theory away from the printing press until the end of his life, when it was finally published—to the profound irritation of the Catholic Church, which insisted that Aristotle and the Bible had it right in putting the Earth at the center of the universe. The first scientist who loudly stuck up for Copernicus was burned at the stake. When at the beginning of the seventeenth century the Italian polymath Galileo Galilei embraced and publicly advocated Copernicus's theory, however, the church wasn't so quick to stack wood. The problem was that Galileo's groundbreaking work in devising simple, elegant physics experiments that made clear some of the laws governing the motion of objects, as well as his skill in wielding a primitive telescope, had led to his becoming a new sort of scientist: one with a popular following. As a result, instead of the stake, he was let off with life-time house arrest.

One scientist who had provided important public support for Galileo was the German astronomer Johannes Kepler. Kepler went on to add crucial insights of his own into the rules that governed the shapes and speeds of the planets' orbits, as well as into the relationship of the moon and the Earth's tides, and was the first to propose the concept of gravity as we know it today. But as an early instance of the sometimes fine line between collaboration and competition among experts, Galileo refused to return the favor and endorse Kepler's brilliant work, slowing its acceptance.

Isaac Newton's uncovering in the seventeenth century of the laws of motion and gravity, along with the almost incidental invention of calculus to support them—all largely accomplished while hanging around the farm for two years after graduating college—may forever be seen as the single most dramatic and influential leap of expert insight the world has ever known. And the nature of the fallout from Newton's breakthrough was almost equally groundbreaking: while it had taken Aristotle about a thousand years to become the first global celebrity expert, Newton became the second in less than a year, thanks in large part to the power of academic publication, and perhaps more important to that of a newly emerging popular press that sought to thrill the coffeehouse crowd.

While rivalry among experts was well known to exist among the classical Greek thinkers, and for that matter was probably an issue going back to shamanism, expert rivalry became more intense in Newton's time, and for a simple reason: swept along by faster, tighter communication links and an accelerating pace of discovery into increasingly complex and specialized problems, different experts at different institutions were for the first time likely to focus on exactly the same problems. In other words, not only did experts have to contend with competitors whose ideas clashed with theirs but they also had to race their rivals to the finish line and deal with those who claimed they thought of the same idea first.

The potential thorniness of this problem was brought to light in a spectacular way by Newton's invention of calculus. Calculus resisted discovery for thousands of years' worth of mathematics (though, as noted earlier, Archimedes brushed up against it), but within about eight years—exact dates remain unclear—of the time Newton claimed to have taken it up, the German mathematician Gottfried Leibniz made a comparable breakthrough. Leibniz staunchly insisted he had no foreknowledge of Newton's discovery, and quite credibly, since Newton had at first felt no rush to formally publish his work. Newton's low-key approach to expert communication, however, allowed Leibniz to get early versions of his insights into print first, forever establishing a question mark over who should get credit for the discovery of what is perhaps the single most important mathematical advance ever.

From experts' point of view, the moral of the story was clear: the way to make sure you got credit for your groundbreaking work was to get it published. And yet rushing to publication wasn't as straightforward a prospect as might be assumed. For one thing, not all forms of publication were equal; in Newton's world, for maximum credibility and attention, one wanted to be published by a reputable press, and preferably under the auspices of the Royal Society or its emerging counterparts in other countries. That meant one had to survive the judgment of editors and peer review. If you were an established scholar respected by the members of the applicable society, you weren't likely to be rejected. But if you were an up-and-coming scientist with new ideas—the very sort of ideas that might be most valuable to the world—it could be a different story. For example, the very concept that there was an invisible force called "gravity" that emanated in all directions from all matter to tug on distant objects was openly ridiculed by some prominent scientists when Kepler proposed it. Indeed, the Royal Society at first hesitated to admit Newton when he applied as a young scientist because his work on optics (a field to which Newton would make substantial contributions) conflicted with the ideas of the Society member and acclaimed scientist Robert Hooke. Newton, an extremely eccentric fellow, was peeved enough at the near rejection to wonder for a time if it was even worth the effort of trying to share his discoveries with the world. We'll never know how many experts with exciting ideas simply kept their mouths shut after being snubbed by their peers.

And there was another complication. The strategy of publishing a scientific insight as soon as possible so as not to get scooped sometimes ended up inviting exactly the opposite result. Putting a less than completely nailed down solution into print risks tipping off previously clueless competitors to key ideas that they might then perfect, leaving them with most of the credit. And if your idea is submitted to peer review and rejected, then all you've done is provide potential rivals with a full accounting of your efforts, without anything to show for it. Hooke himself was forced to contemplate the perils of early publication when he came up with the important insight that the force exerted by a spring is proportional to the distance by which it is compressed or stretched. He finessed the situation the way many scientists, including Leonardo da Vinci and Galileo, had in the past century: he published his finding in code, so that he could continue refining the idea in secrecy but would in theory be able to preserve his claim to primacy should someone else stumble on the same discovery and publish it. (He needn't have bothered; he published first, and today students learn about "Hooke's law" early on in high-school physics.)

Newton's triumphant discovery of the laws of motion and gravity had yet another major effect on expertise. Though it may seem self-evident today, scientists before Newton had no reason to be certain nature operated according to straightforward "laws," or rules. Who or what besides God would have made and enforced such rules? And if God were directly pulling the strings, what would have obligated him to do so in a simple, mathematically analyzable, universally applicable, consistent way? But once Newton had shown that something as complex as the motion of the entire zoo of celestial bodies—and, indeed, of every particle in the world around us—could (apparently) be entirely and precisely characterized by a few simple equations, the very nature of expert inquiry seemed ripe for transformative breakthroughs. If such simple laws underlie mechanical physics, there must be others that underlie optics, and chemistry. In fact, they probably underlie everything one would care to study! A new game was afoot; experts in all fields came to chase after simple laws that would explain the complex-seeming phenomena we observe, and then test them with experimental and observational data.[1] Among the thinkers who would explicitly seek such simple, neat Newtonian order in their fields were medicine's François Magendie, who in 1817 wrote of the need for "an intellect of the first order to come and discover the laws of the vital force in the same way Newton made known the laws of attraction"; Thomas Jefferson, who applied a scientific bent to politics, writing, "Nature intended me for the tranquil pursuits of science, by rendering them my supreme delight"; and Henri de Saint-Simon, the late-eighteenth-century cofounder of socialism, who wrote that he envisioned God wanting society ruled by a council dedicated to discovering "a new law of gravitation applicable to social bodies." In medicine, economics, and government, a mania emerged to move away from conjecture toward the amassing of facts, precise measurements, and

statistics and to applying those data to developing and confirming simple, elegant—and respectably publishable—theories that
would influence how populations might be healed, educated,
and governed. In the nineteenth century, for example, Florence
Nightingale would be among those prominent expert figures who
loudly pushed for developing formulas that would tie medical
practices to population studies and other data.

That same sort of sensibility would soon come to be applied
to business management, parenting, psychology, romance, and
much more. Never mind that Sir Francis Bacon, who back in the
late sixteenth century codified what is still today taken to be the
"scientific method" for wringing conclusions from careful observations, warned of "humans' tendency to perceive more order
and regularity in systems than truly exists." This sentiment would
be echoed by the Prussian general Carl von Clausewitz, who in
the early nineteenth century literally wrote the book on war (it's
called *On War*) and who is still regarded by many as the greatest expert on military theory who has ever lived. "All principles,
rules and methods," he wrote, "increasingly lack universality and
absolute truth the moment they become a positive doctrine." It
was a caution that would end up surprisingly relevant to Newton's
laws themselves, not to mention the far shakier conclusions that
experts would wrestle into publication in the softer sciences and
especially with regard to human behavior.

Even as experts were off and running in an effort to uncover
simple, exciting, publishable findings, newspapers were becoming
an ever more influential medium capable of quickly stirring the
public up with reports of breakthroughs. Due to the good press
he garnered, Benjamin Franklin was perhaps the first expert accorded what we would recognize today as something like pop-
superstar status, complete with public throngs jostling for a view
of him when he toured. By the early nineteenth century, the power

of mass media–borne expertise was such that wide swaths of the U.S. population, and eventually much of the world, little hesitated to accept the *New York Sun's* breathless reports of the leading British astronomer John Herschel's telescopic spotting of life on the moon, including goats, pelicans, and winged moon men, details of which the newspaper claimed to have pulled from research published by Herschel in a scientific journal. It was a blatant hoax on the paper's part—Herschel did happen to believe absolutely in the presence of life throughout most of the bodies that can be seen in the sky, including the sun, but never claimed to directly observe it—and it took some doing for Herschel to set the record straight with those tens of millions who had embraced the absurd claims, including science reporters at the *New York Times*.

Meanwhile, the close relationship between universities and mass expertise continued to evolve. Before the eighteenth century, professorships were often awarded on the basis not only of scholarly achievement but also of connections, religious ties, fame, and wealth. What's more, professors were expected to focus their energies on teaching students. But soon universities around the world were jostling to achieve the sort of prestige that would lure the best—and, more important, highest-paying—students. That meant pressuring professors to concentrate on churning out attention-grabbing research, with higher salaries and generous funding being an incentive to those professors who could produce. Graduate students, too, were expected to contribute to publishable research projects, and their degrees often became contingent on it. By the nineteenth century, governments were starting to put money into university research, in the belief that scientific and other breakthroughs would not only benefit society but also provide economic and military advantages—a trend that would lurch into much higher gear in the United States after World War II. As rivalries between researchers at different institutions became ever more intense, professors and students formed teams in imitation of the research labs that were springing up in large chemical and other industrial companies. Nevertheless, the academic community was able to increasingly shield itself from external influence, as the peer-review process was applied not only to publication decisions but also to those of promotion and funding.

Not that the population at large would come to consistently trust the claims of scientists and other highly credentialed researchers over those of less formally vetted experts. Indeed, with much of society, the pronouncements of alternative-medicine advocates, charismatic journalists, self-help gurus, and religious leaders frequently trumped those of top-shelf researchers, and that would remain the case to the present day.

A Brief Sampling of Contemporary, High-Powered, Apparent Scientific Fraud

Note: It's not completely clear what really happened in all of these and in many other cases of apparently falsified data. Confronted researchers don't always confess, and sometimes various investigative bodies lack the hard evidence they feel they need to conclusively state that the bad data was intentionally fraudulent and not simply extremely careless work. It's also often hard to say exactly which of the several authors of a study may be the guilty party.

• In the early 1990s the Canadian surgeon Roger Poisson was found to have falsified data on ninety-nine patients in fourteen large patient studies of cancer treatments, including six patients in one of the most influential breast-cancer studies ever undertaken—a thirteen-year-long study in which the results, when published in the *New England Journal of Medicine*, had led doctors to recommend to tens of thousands of women that they forgo mastectomies for early-stage breast cancers in favor of lumpectomies and radiation.

• In 1995 the Harvard surgeon and researcher Andrew Friedman confessed to making up patient data to support some of the fifty-eight research studies he published on gynecology and reproductive biology, many in top journals.

• The Emory University historian Michael Bellesiles was found to have falsified records in his book *Arming America*, published in 2000, which argues that pre–Civil War Americans didn't have much to do with guns.

• Jan Hendrik Schön, a young physicist at the storied Bell Labs, became a scientific superstar around 2001 with a startling, nonstop series of papers in top-of-the-heap journals, including über–science journals *Nature* and *Science*, that demonstrated how certain types of molecules could be made to act like electronic switches, promising revolutionary new generations of cheaper, faster, smaller electronic devices. It turned out he had been making up much of the data.

• The award-winning Harvard malaria researcher Ali Sultan was discovered to have falsified data on applications for federal funding in 2004.

• The MIT associate professor of biology Luk Van Parijs was dismissed in 2005 after confessing to falsifying data in highly regarded studies of immune system cells.

• In 2005 the prominent Frankfurt University anthropologist Reiner Protsch von Zieten was found to have been purposely misdating ancient human fossil remains for three decades, forcing the field to rejigger its conception of some thirty millennia's worth of human history.

• The prominent obesity researcher Eric Poehlman confessed in 2005 to having made up data in some seventeen applications for U.S. government funding and in ten published papers while a professor at the University of Vermont College of Medicine.

• The Wake Forest researcher Gary Kammer, a leading lupus expert, was deemed in 2005 to have simply invented, on applications for federal funding, ill patients and even entire families.

• The India-based researcher Pattium Chiranjeevi managed to publish more than seventy fraudulent papers between 2004 and 2007, even though, according to an article in *Chemical & Engineering News*, some of the research he published relied on data from equipment he didn't have access to, and violated accepted chemical principles.

• The Norwegian researcher Jon Sudbø confessed in 2006 to having made up approximately nine hundred patients for a study on how painkilling medication affects the risk of oral cancer in smokers, published in the British top-shelf journal *The Lancet*. More than thirty of Sudbø's published papers were thought to be affected by these and other fraudulent data.

• Kazunari Taira, a prominent chemist at the prestigious University of Tokyo, was dismissed in 2006 for fabricating the data behind at least twelve published papers describing his seemingly groundbreaking work in isolating a bacterial enzyme capable of altering some key types of RNA.

• In 2008 an important *Nature* paper by the Nobel Prize–winning Harvard researcher Linda Buck and her colleagues, which focused on mapping regions of the mouse brain dedicated to smell, was retracted after it became clear some of the data in the paper had been falsified.

Is This Book Wrong?

*The longer I live the more I see that I am never wrong
about anything, and that all the pains I have so humbly
taken to verify my notions have only wasted my time.*
— GEORGE BERNARD SHAW

All books like The Tipping Point *or articles by academics
can ever do is uncover a little piece of the bigger picture,
and one day — when we put all those pieces together —
maybe we'll have a shot at the truth.*
— MALCOLM GLADWELL

M y father was a research chemist for Dow Chemical, which installed him not at the company's headquarters in the factory city of Midland, Michigan, but in a small laboratory plunked down on a large, hilly, idyllic tract tucked away in tony, ex-urban Wayland, Massachusetts. The location enabled him to recruit and collaborate with faculty and graduate students at any of the half dozen superb universities within half an hour, and indeed for most of his career he was largely free to pursue his scientific curiosity much as any academic researcher might. Many years later, after he was retired and the lab was closed, the Dow land was discovered to harbor buried drums of toxic chemicals—it spent years languishing as a hazardous-waste site. But when my father worked there, the property seemed to me a big, pleasant park, with a pond and ducks.

The lab was quite high-tech for its day—it was active mostly in the 1960s and early 1970s—and for a visiting kid it was an arcade of wondrously menacing apparatuses, including bubbling beakers sealed in Plexiglas tanks accessible only via thick, black, arm-length gloves mounted in the sides; lab bench–lined nooks backed by metal sheeting that advertised in large letters the sheeting's ability to channel away the forces of explosions; and eye-bath stations for removing the acids that I imagined might at any moment charge into the air from experiments gone awry.

In comparison, my father's office was a letdown: just a desk, some bookcases, and a few shelves lined with models of molecules made from the toylike kits that chemists used to rely on for 3-D visualization in the days before desktop computers. As an eight-year-old, I paid little attention to the lone framed item hung in the middle of the only expanse of wall in that small room, except to notice that it was a page from one of the scientific journals that were often lying around the house, and that his name was in the text. I knew that he "published papers" and that this was an important part of his job, but that's as far as my knowledge and curiosity went. It was only on a visit some five years later that I took a minute to actually try to read this journal page that seemed to have pride of place in his office. I couldn't much understand it—it was mostly equations and formulas—but was able to surmise that this wasn't one of his articles at all but rather a letter to the journal written by another scientist who was pointing out an error in an article my father had previously published in the journal—an error that apparently torpedoed my father's results. Shocked and embarrassed for him, I asked why he would put such a thing on his wall.

"It reminds me how easy it is to be wrong," he replied.

I've thought of that journal letter on the wall many times while working on this book, in part as a means of prodding myself to stay attuned to the ways in which I might be going wrong, and in part to remind myself that I'll probably go wrong anyway. Of course, you probably don't need me to tell you that there's something a bit askew about a book about wrongness. Perhaps you didn't even make it past the subtitle before wondering, *If expert advice is usually wrong, then why wouldn't advice about expert advice likely be wrong?* In other words, why wouldn't the pronouncements of this book fall prey to the very distortions they seek to characterize? But if they do, and this book is wrong about experts suffering from all this trouble with wrongness, then perhaps this book doesn't suffer from problems with wrongness either—in which case this book might be right after all about experts having a lot of trouble with wrongness, which means this book ought to be wrong, too, which means...

There's actually a long, rich history of philosophers and others struggling with the knots into which logic seemingly gets tied when some statement or argument or system of knowledge ends up compromising itself. Eubulides of Miletus kicked things off twenty-five centuries ago in Greece by asking what we ought to make of someone who says, "I am lying." As generations of school-children have gleefully realized, the statement suggests that the person is actually telling the truth, which means she is lying, which means... and so on. The trail runs through Bertrand Russell, who at the turn of the twentieth century found a way to embed a roughly similar sort of apparently paradoxical claim in the rigors of formal logic, and thence to Kurt Gödel, who in the 1930s proved that what had until then seemed an interesting thorn in the side of clear-cut reason was in fact a jagged gash in the fabric of what we can claim to know. Gödel showed that all of mathematics, our purest form of understanding, is inescapably (though far from fatally) hobbled by the consequences of self-contradiction.

But if one can't escape self-negation when offering expert advice relating to the problems with expertise, then the study of expertise becomes a hall of mirrors, which leaves expertise itself in limbo. Can I dodge the doubt and confusion that mathematicians and philosophers cannot, and offer a solid argument that the expert advice in this book is in fact itself solid even as it tears into the nature of expert advice? Well, perhaps I can try arguing that I'm exempt from the problems of expertise, because I'm not really an expert, or at least not the sort of highly credentialed expert I've been focusing on. True, I occasionally play one on TV—I've been interviewed and quoted by the mass media many times, and often in exactly the way academic experts are featured, sometimes even alongside them. But that's really punditry. I could argue I'm not corrupted by expert biases because I don't have to publish in measurement-obsessed journals, avoid offending influential peer reviewers, navigate the politics of tenure and funding, win lucrative corporate contracts, come up with conclusions that please my sponsors, or hew to the agendas of government bureaucrats and elected officials.

On the other hand, we've already discussed the pressures on journalists to traffic in resonant, provocative, colorful claims so as to win readership, their frequent failure to fully grasp the concepts they're writing about, and their routine sloppiness with facts, all of which contribute to distortions that may be as problematic as, or possibly more problematic than, those that trouble expert claims. No, to say that you don't have to worry about my falling for expertise traps because I'm a journalist would be like a mugger offering the reassurance that she's no car thief.

So how can I make the case that this book isn't wrong? Actually, I think it's far more important to discuss some of the ways this book probably *is* wrong. For one thing, it's likely riddled with factual and conceptual errors of which I'm unaware. Some will have snuck in because I misheard or misread something, or took inadequate notes on it, or simply misunderstood it, and others because I've passed on flawed information from less trustworthy sources of information, such as mass-media reports. I know from my own record and from what I've seen of other journalists' experiences that even if I undertake fact-checking efforts that are fairly extensive by journalistic standards, I'll still end up with errors—and I suspect that time and other pressures will limit me to more ordinary levels of checking. The fact that I take reporters to task in the book for not scrutinizing the basic math in studies didn't inspire me to go over the math on more than a few studies myself. Why not? Lack of time, too much trust in experts' work, belief that someone in the crowd would have caught it—all the sorts of things I complain about in the book. Almost every time I read over a chapter, I find at least one point that suddenly sounds fishy to me, and sure enough, on double-checking many of these ostensible facts and insights turn out to call for some sort of correction or qualification. (A small but telling example: in the section where I point out how often the media get study facts wrong, I more or less by luck discovered I had slightly misreported the findings of the study results that seem to prove it.) That correction process will be far from complete when I'm finally forced to stop because the book is going to press.

I've often heard the comment that some particular journalist or publication always seems to get it right, with the exception of the time when that particular journalist or publication put forth an article that the commentator happened to know a lot about. Inevitably someone who knows a lot about one or more of the many topics I cover in this book will point out a handful of errors and claim that this book can't be trusted because I didn't get my facts straight.* Will that be fair? Maybe, but I don't think it's really worth dwelling on, because I doubt these errors are the most serious source of likely wrongness in the book.

---

* I look forward to framing at least one example of such criticism and placing it on the wall of my office, where I will make a point of inviting my kids to take note of it.

A more important issue is the distortion that comes not from my getting facts and concepts wrong but from the games I've played with the ones that may be right. I've probably spun, omitted, exaggerated, manipulated, and artfully selected facts and concepts in ways that bolster my case. That's because I'm biased. Given the title of this book, it would have done me little good to "discover" that experts do as great a job as can be expected, that the system in which they develop and present their advice works very well. I was convinced that there was far more to the story than that and set out to find it; my success with this project depended on it. And what do you know? I found the evidence I so badly wanted to find. Now, none of that is to say that my thesis is wrong, or that the evidence isn't real or even overwhelmingly solid and plentiful. But if my thesis *had* been wrong, and the evidence *had* been weak and scarce, I might well (as far as you know) have done whatever it took to make my case look strong.

For the record, just in case you care to take my word for it, I don't believe I would have ginned up that kind of crooked story if I hadn't uncovered the real deal, and, more important, I didn't have to. On the other hand, in going over this book and my notes with as critical an eye as I can force myself to bring to bear, I'm confronted with the various ways in which I've engaged in at least some fast footwork to make my points look sharper and cleaner here and there.* I also sometimes completely ignored studies that seem to contradict my arguments. For example, I spotted two findings in my notes that suggested medical studies do not become more biased toward favorable results when funded by companies, in contrast to the results I quote in the chapter about scientists.

---

* Small example: I light into the trustworthiness of fMRI "brain scan" studies at one point, but that didn't stop me from blithely citing fMRI study results elsewhere in the book when it supported a point I was trying to make.

I still claim that the evidence in favor of the corrupting influence of corporate funding is absolutely overwhelming, but I might have said *something* about the nonunanimity of the evidence. Of course, I could just go back and insert such a line right now, for whatever purpose that might serve, but I think it's more instructive to show you how the game is played. You ought to assume I do this sort of thing throughout the book, and perhaps in ways far more misleading than these small examples suggest, and perhaps to an extent far greater than I myself realize. Just as I apparently favored the studies that back me up, I likely favored the interview quotes that did my case the most good over those that might cause me problems, and may well have chased down the interviewees that would support my preconceived ideas. I can wave my hands all day in support of the notion that I wasn't so biased as to end up with genuinely misleading material, but bias is bias. Unlike George Bernard Shaw, I find I am wrong all the time, and often when I've been most confident. As a result, I'm certain that throughout this book, I've misled you. I will follow Thoreau's advice and chalk it up to being weak in the knees.

Even if I were able to offer convincing evidence that I'm some sort of mythical, above-reproach journalist who rarely makes significant errors and keeps his bias entirely in check, it wouldn't put me in the clear. That's because something along the lines of the liar's paradox would appear to be hanging over this book, thanks to the fact that I depend heavily on highly credentialed mass experts and their studies throughout to show why highly credentialed mass experts and their studies are generally not all that trustworthy. Why, if the claim is that experts and studies are so often wrong, should anyone accept the word of experts and their study results to back up that claim?

You absolutely shouldn't assume the experts and studies I quote in support of my arguments are highly trustworthy. These experts and studies are most certainly subject to the same biases and errors that plague experts and studies in general. There's evidence that this is so. A small example: I twice quote McMaster University's P. J. Devereaux, the cardiologist and biostatistics researcher, on how researchers often run into trouble when gathering data for their studies. But when Devereaux published a widely covered study in 2002 that seemed to show for-profit dialysis companies delivered care inferior to their nonprofit counterparts, he himself was loudly accused of having used obsolete and highly selective data in a biased way to produce that result. (Most of the objections happened to come from the dialysis industry or those with ties to it, but that doesn't mean they're easily dismissed.) And in fact I was able to turn up reasonable-sounding published objections, or stated limitations of one sort or another, to many of the studies I prominently cite as evidence of the problems experts run into. The popping up of study and researcher criticisms is par for the course when it comes to findings that hit home with any community, and it doesn't prove these studies are troubled, but it does suggest they aren't necessarily exempt from the very problems they seek to highlight.

Frankly, I would find it depressing if I've gotten so little across in this book that any of this comes as a big surprise. But having spelled out some of the traps this work has likely fallen into, let me explain why I don't think the whole effort is little more than a mass of contradictions and half-truths that ultimately says nothing coherent and believable about expert wrongness.

First of all, whatever my errors and biases, it seems to me a stretch to suggest they're of such a magnitude that they cripple the book's arguments. If I were that sloppy and manipulative a journalist, surely I'd have left some sort of easily googled trail of complaints, and I'll leave it as an exercise to the reader to confirm whether there's much to suggest I'm a complete hack. If you'll grant me at least modest competency and honesty, then what I most need to address is the problem of my relying on experts and studies to reveal problems with experts and studies.

Are the book's central claims mired in the liar's paradox? Actually, no. For one thing, I don't claim that all experts are always wrong. (Just as a technical aside, even that extreme claim wouldn't lead to a genuine paradox—it would simply be a provably untrue statement.) The strongest claim I make about expert wrongness is that there is some reason to suspect that most experts are usually wrong, and for the most part I really argue only that expert pronouncements are wrong a significant percentage of the time. I've been quite explicit throughout in saying that at least some experts are right at least some of the time. For my arguments to gain traction, it need be plausible only that many of the experts and studies I rely on to make my case are more or less right to an extent that outweighs the ways in which some of them may be wrong. To put it differently, this book slips out of the clutches of self-negation if the expertise it enlists has a somewhat higher rightness rate than the expertise it criticizes.

On what grounds would I claim that "my" experts and studies are less dishonest, biased, or error-prone than any other experts and studies? For all we know, experts who study expertise put their knowledge to good use by doing a better job of gaming results than do other experts. But I don't think it's unreasonable to suggest that in general, experts who study other experts' failings are better equipped and more highly motivated to avoid those troubles. Also, it seems to me there's an enormous convergence of evidence that the problems meta-experts point out and that are highlighted by their research are real. I think we've clearly seen that for decades, and in some cases for centuries, all sorts of meta-experts coming at the issue from a variety of angles have found the same troubles cropping up in different fields and in many ways over and over again, with relatively little evidence put forth to suggest these troubles are nonexistent. If the claims and studies of meta-experts seem to check out by every measuring stick we can hold up, then it is entirely reasonable to say that, yes, experts do seem to have a lot of trouble with wrongness—but that meta-experts seem to do better than most other types of experts.

Now obviously I haven't proven that this is true; I've merely been waving my hands to convince you it's not an unreasonable suggestion. At this point all I can really do is refer you back to the arguments I've been making throughout the book. Perhaps in the end I've accomplished no more than to have raised some issues that might be worth thinking about. Or maybe I've been adept and lucky enough to, as Gladwell put it, have uncovered a little piece of the big picture. Of course, others will point out flaws in my arguments and offer countercases, and you will end up, as usual, with conflicting pronouncements. But the fact that experts may duel over this matter—and that neither side can offer iron-clad proof—doesn't mean you are helpless to judge or even to come to at least a provisional conclusion. Look over the evidence, gauge the quality and breadth of support enjoyed by the different arguments, weigh the likely biases of the claimants, consider the qualifications and limitations to which each side admits or fails to admit, and take your best shot at deciding. No expert could do better.

ACKNOWLEDGMENTS

I'll never understand how my family is able to put up with me during the latter stages of book writing, especially when those stages last for a year. But they did put up with me — or pretended to — and more, and I'm wildly grateful. They all contributed ideas and helpful criticism, too. My brothers and extended family propped me up as well. Happy trails, B., thanks for being such an insistent pick-me-up and pal.

The following extremely bright people each served very brief stints as research assistants: Alex Freedman, Alex Kerr, Andrew Knippenberg, Andy Strong, and Catherine Yao.

My friend and agent Rick Balkin was, as always, wise, supportive, and helpful far beyond all norms of either friendship or agenthood.

There are very good reasons why Little, Brown has the reputation it does among writers, and two of them are Geoff Shandler and Liese Mayer. Their insight and patience were supersalutary. If any sentences in this book seem reasonably well turned, chances are the credit should go to Karen Landry's copyediting.

There are many friends and colleagues I could and probably should thank here for any of a variety of reasons, but I'll just give a shout-out to a representative few: Cam M., Dave A., Major W., Mike M., Fred G., Larry K., Mary W., and Phaedra H.

Steve Austad not only yielded a fascinating interview about the problems with forensic labs but also tossed in some feedback and perspective for the book as a whole.

As usual, many, many smart and busy people were good sports about submitting to interviews, only to end up being unmentioned in the book for any of a range of reasons having absolutely nothing to do with their not being insightful and interesting, and mostly in this case because the book was turning out too damned long and lots of stuff had to go.

SOURCE NOTES

I've tried to make it easy for the reader to distinguish between quoted or paraphrased comments that came from my personally interviewing a source and those that I picked up from that person's published work or from someone else's interview or account of the work. Most of the time I just spell out in one way or another that I was speaking with the person (as when I say, "she told me") or that the information came from an article (as when I describe or cite the article, or use the term "reportedly"). Occasionally I rely on common journalistic convention to differentiate: When I use attributions such as "he says," it generally means he said it to me. When I use more passive attributions, such as "she has stated," it generally means I've lifted the quote from somewhere else—though as I say, in most cases I've tried to make it explicit. I sometimes relied on handwritten notes of interviews, other times on recordings, and yet other times on notes typed directly into my computer. Surprisingly enough, I've never noticed a big difference in the results. I don't differentiate between phone and in-person interviews—sometimes I make it clear I was on the scene, but not always. I never relied on e-mail (or text-message, Twitter, or snail-mail) interviews without specifically pointing it out (as happens only once in the book). I didn't give any interviewees any approval or reviewing rights whatsoever, with two exceptions: Christian List and Berkeley's David Freedman were unyielding (though perfectly polite, and ultimately quite helpful) in insisting as a condition of meeting with me that I promise to give them each a chance to correct factual errors in any quotes of theirs I used. Freedman passed away not long after I interviewed him, well before I could show him anything, and I ended up not quoting List directly. (I take issue with science journalists who freely allow or even encourage the scientists they write about to review the work. Can you imagine political or business reporters doing that sort of thing?)

As is common in non–hard news journalism, I often mildly clean the spoken quotes of my interviewees—that is, I smooth out the rough edges around people's speech. I also sometimes string together spoken comments that were made a few seconds or even minutes apart. I'm careful not to do any of this in a way that, other than making people sometimes seem a bit more articulate and concise than they really are, changes the tone and especially the meaning of anyone's comments. All quotes are by the nature of quotation out of context, strictly speaking (and short of publishing a full transcript), but I'm careful to avoid selecting comments, even when quoted exactly as spoken, that don't reflect an interviewee's intended meaning, to the extent I can discern it. Which is not to say I've selected the quotes that the interviewee may feel best represents what she wished to get across in the interview—it's not my job to help anyone put her best foot forward, and in fact sometimes my job is to get at the sort of candid, dropped-guard quotes that an interviewee might *least* wish to be represented by in print. As long as the quote reasonably conveys the interviewee's meaning at that moment, it's fair game.

I haven't tried to approach scholarly (i.e., exhaustive) standards of citation of written works. If I felt I provided enough information in the main text (e.g., a quote from the material) to allow easy online searching (e.g., googling) of the material, then I didn't always provide a formal citation, especially in the case of mass-media articles. I also didn't always formally cite a work if my description of it in the text was based on what the author of the work told me about it in an interview. I often cite a single work that is meant only as a typical example of many articles that may be equally relevant to the issue at hand—I think it's usually clear in the text whether I'm referring to a specific article or a larger body of information. No doubt I've omitted some citations that belong here, and I'll try to correct for those omissions at www.wrongbook.com or www.freedman.com. I'll also try to respond via those websites to reasonable requests for further references on specific points from anyone who has found such references elusive or contradictory. (But please, young people, don't ask me to do your homework for you.)

INTRODUCTION
1. John P. A. Ioannidis, "Contradicted and Initially Stronger Effects in Highly Cited Clinical Research," *Journal of the American Medical Association* 294, no. 2 (2005): 218–28.
2. C. Arden Pope III and others, "Fine-Particulate Air Pollution and Life Expectancy in the United States," *New England Journal of Medicine* 360, no. 4 (2009): 376–86.
3. Elizabeth Cohen, "CDC: Antidepressants Most Prescribed Drugs in U.S.," CNN, July 9, 2007, http://www.cnn.com/2007/HEALTH/07/09/antidepressants/index.html.

1. SOME EXPERT OBSERVATIONS
1. Tara Parker-Pope, "Could a Defibrillator Have Saved Tim Russert?" *New York Times*, June 19, 2008.
2. Julie Steenhuysen, "Home Defibrillators Do Not Increase Survival," Reuters, April 1, 2008.
3. David Romer, "Do Firms Maximize? Evidence from Professional Football," *Journal of Political Economy* 114, no. 21 (2006): 340–65.
4. Steve Sternberg and Anthony DeBarros, "Hospital Death Rates Unveiled for First-Time Comparison," *USA Today*, August 20, 2008.
5. Richard Rosenfeld and Janet L. Lauritsen, "The Most Dangerous Crime Rankings," *Contexts*, winter (2008): 66–67.

6. Elissa Gootman, "State Puts 6 More City Schools on Failing List," *New York Times*, February 6, 2008.

7. Sarah E. Needleman, "Ivy Leaguers' Big Edge: Starting Pay," *Wall Street Journal*, August 1, 2008.

8. "Teenagers' Learning 'Dumbed Down,'" BBC, October 27, 2008, http://news.bbc.co.uk/2/hi/uk_news/education/7692843.stm.

9. "Conte's Prescription for Success," BBC, May 16, 2008, http://news.bbc.co.uk/sport2/hi/olympics/athletics/7403158.stm.

10. Henry Fountain, "Plugging Holes in the Science of Forensics," *New York Times*, May 12, 2009.

11. "Summer Play Can Bring Broken Bones," interview with the orthopedic surgeon Michael Piazza, KidsGrowth.com, http://www.kidsgrowth.com/resources/articledetail.cfm?id=260.

12. Claire Nee and Amy Meenaghan, "Expert Decision Making in Burglars," *British Journal of Criminology* 46 (2006): 935–49.

13. Janet Paskin, "10 Things Your Tax Preparer Won't Tell You," *SmartMoney*, February 21, 2008.

2. THE TROUBLE WITH SCIENTISTS, PART I

1. "$95 Billion a Year Spent on Medical Research," Associated Press, September 20, 2005, http://www.msnbc.msn.com/id/9407342.

2. Esther M. John and others, "Vitamin D and Breast Cancer Risk: The NHANES I Epidemiologic Follow-up Study, 1971–1975 to 1992," *Cancer Epidemiology, Biomarkers & Prevention* 8, no. 5 (1999): 399.

3. Cedric F. Garland and others, "The Role of Vitamin D in Cancer Prevention," *American Journal of Public Health* 96, no. 2 (2006): 252–61.

4. Joan M. Lappe and others, "Vitamin D and Calcium Supplementation Reduces Cancer Risk: Results of a Randomized Trial," *American Journal of Clinical Nutrition* 85, no. 6 (2007): 1586–91.

5. R. T. Chlebowski and others, "Calcium Plus Vitamin D Supplementation and the Risk of Breast Cancer," *Journal of the National Cancer Institute* 100, no. 22 (2008): 1581–91.

6. Jennifer Corbett Dooren, "FDA Questions Whether Avastin Benefits Breast Cancer Patients," *Wall Street Journal*, December 3, 2007.

7. Thomas H. Maugh II, "Patients Getting Aggressive Diabetes Treatment Had Higher Death Risk," *Los Angeles Times*, February 6, 2008.

8. "Mismanaged Measures," editorial, *Nature* 452, no. 7817 (2008): 504.

9. Lisa Nainggolan, "Cholesterol and Stroke: A Paradox," WebMD's *Heartwire*, November 29, 2007, http://www.medscape.com/viewarticle/566699.

10. Jim Schnabel, "Another Alzheimer's Drug Fails in Large-Scale Trials," Dana Foundation, June 30, 2008, http://www.dana.org/news/features/detail.aspx?id=12742.

11. Ganesh M. Shankar and others, "Amyloid-β Protein Dimers Isolated Directly from Alzheimer's Brains Impair Synaptic Plasticity and Memory," *Nature Medicine* 14, no. 8 (2008): 837–42.

12. Rowan Hooper, "Flirting Makes Up for Antisocial Tendencies," *New Scientist* no. 2623 (2007): 10.

13. C. L. Apicella and others, "Voice Pitch Predicts Reproductive Success in Male Hunter-Gatherers," *Biology Letters* 3, no. 6 (2007): 682–84.

14. Geoffrey Miller and others, "Ovulatory Cycle Effects on Tip Earnings by Lap Dancers: Economic Evidence for Human Estrus?" *Evolution and Human Behavior* 28, no. 6 (2007): 375–81.

15. J. Kiley Hamlin and others, "Social Evaluation by Preverbal Infants," *Nature* 450, no. 7169 (2007): 557–59.

16. Martin A. Nowak and others, "Winners Don't Punish," *Nature* 452, no. 7185 (2008): 348–51.

17. Veena Kumari, "Do Psychotherapies Produce Neurobiological Effects?" *Acta Neuropsychiatrica* 18, no. 2 (2006): 61–70.

18. Daniel Kennedy and others, "Failing to Deactivate: Resting Functional Abnormalities in Autism," *Proceedings of the National Academy of Sciences* 103, no. 21 (2006): 8275–80.

19. H. C. Breiter and others, "Functional Imaging of Neural Responses to Expectancy and Experience of Monetary Gains and Losses," *Neuron* 30, no. 2 (2001): 619–39.

20. B. B. Lahey and others, "Atypical Empathic Responses in Adolescents with Aggressive Conduct Disorder: A Functional MRI Investigation," *Biological Psychology* 80, no. 2 (2009): 203–11.

21. B. Vogelstein and others, "The Consensus Coding Sequences of Human Breast and Colorectal Cancers," *Science* 314, no. 5797 (2006): 268–74.

22. Yurii S. Aulchenko and others, "Predicting Human Height by Victorian and Genomic Methods," *European Journal of Human Genetics* 17, no. 8 (2009): 1070–75.

23. Andy Coghlan, "'Intelligence Genes' Reveal Their Complexity," *New Scientist* no. 2632 (2007): 16.

24. Peter Galison, *How Experiments End* (Chicago: University of Chicago Press, 1987), 43–70.

25. Peter Galison, "Author of Error," *Social Research* 72, no. 1 (2005): 63–76.

26. Chris E. Forest and Richard W. Reynolds, "Climate Change: Hot Questions of Temperature Bias," *Nature* 453, no. 7195 (2008): 601–02.

27. D. Wingfield and others, "Terminal Digit Preference and Single-Number Preference in the Syst-Eur Trial: Influence of Quality Control," *Blood Pressure Monitoring* 7, no. 3 (2002): 169–77.

28. Sheryl L. Rifas-Shiman and others, "Misdiagnosis of Overweight and Underweight Children Younger Than 2 Years of Age Due to Length Measurement Bias," *Medscape General Medicine* 7, no. 4 (2005): 56.

29. "Overdiagnosis of Long QT Heart Syndrome Discovered by Mayo Researchers," Medical News Today, June 7, 2007, http://www.medicalnewstoday.com/articles/72803.php.

30. P. A. Zandbergen and J. W. Green, "Error and Bias in Determining Exposure Potential of Children at School Locations Using Proximity-Based GIS Techniques," *Environmental Health Perspectives* 115, no. 9 (2007): 1363–70.

31. Barbara K. Redman and others, "Research Misconduct Among Clinical Trial Staff," *Science and Engineering Ethics* 12, no. 3 (2006): 481–89.

32. Carl Elliott, "Guinea-pigging," *The New Yorker*, January 7, 2008, 36–41.

33. Anthony Komaroff, "Public Understanding and Trust of Biomedical Research," presentation at first World Conference on Research Integrity, September 17, 2007.

34. T. Hanke, "Lessons from TGN1412," *The Lancet* 368, no. 9547 (2006): 1569–70.

35. Ismail Kola and John Landis, "Can the Pharmaceutical Industry Reduce Attrition Rates?" *Nature Reviews Drug Discovery* 3, no. 8 (2004): 711–16.

36. Pablo Perel and others, "Comparison of Treatment Effects Between Animal Experiments and Clinical Trials: Systematic Review," *British Medical Journal* 334, no. 7586 (2007): 197.

37. Daniel G. Hackam and Donald A. Redelmeier, "Translation of Research Evidence from Animals to Humans," *Journal of the American Medical Association* 296, no. 14 (2006): 1731–32.

38. J. Horn and others, "Nimodipine in Animal Model Experiments of Focal Cerebral Ischemia: A Systematic Review," *Stroke* 32, no. 10 (2001): 2433–38.

39. Mark Henderson, "Cloned Cells Bring Hope of Therapy for Parkinson's Disease," *Times* (London), March 24, 2008.

40. Rick Weiss, "Scientists Cure Mice of Sickle Cell Using Stem Cell Technique," *Washington Post*, December 7, 2007.

41. David Biello, "Cancer Resistance Found to Be Transferable in Mice," *Scientific American*, May 9, 2006.

42. Prashant Nair, "Cancer Destroyed by Antibody 'Triple Whammy,'" *New Scientist*, May 10, 2006.

43. Gaia Vince, "Exercise Protects Against Skin and Bowel Cancers," *New Scientist*, May 13, 2006.

44. Charlotte C. Burn and Georgia J. Mason, "Effects of Cage-Cleaning Frequency on Laboratory Rat Reproduction, Cannibalism, and Welfare," *Applied Animal Behaviour Science* 114, no. 1–2 (2008): 235–47.

45. Paul Greengard and others, "Alterations in 5-HT1B Receptor Function by p11 in Depression-like States," *Science* 311, no. 5757 (2006): 77–80.

46. Isabel C. Burckhardt and others, "Green Tea Catechin Polyphenols Attenuate Behavioral and Oxidative Responses to Intermittent Hypoxia," *American Journal of Respiratory and Critical Care Medicine* 177, no. 10 (2008): 1135–41.

47. Allan H. Conney and others, "Tumorigenic Effect of Some Commonly Used Moisturizing Creams When Applied Topically to UVB-Pretreated High-Risk Mice," *Journal of Investigative Dermatology* 129, no. 2 (2009): 468–75.

48. J. L. Barger and others, "A Low Dose of Dietary Resveratrol Partially Mimics Caloric Restriction and Retards Aging Parameters in Mice," *PLoS ONE* 3, no. 6 (2008): e2264.

49. Daniel L. Morgan and others, "Respiratory Toxicity of Diacetyl in C57-Bl/6 Mice," *Toxicological Sciences* 103, no. 1 (2008): 169–80.

50. Iain F. H. Purchase, "Fraud, Errors and Gamesmanship in Experimental Toxicology," *Toxicology* 202, no. 1–2 (2004): 1–20.

51. J. P. Webster and others, "Parasites as Causative Agents of Human Affective Disorders? The Impact of Anti-Psychotic, Mood-Stabilizer and Anti-Parasite Medication on *Toxoplasma gondii*'s Ability to Alter Host Behaviour," *Proceedings of the Royal Society B* 273, no. 1589 (2006): 1023–30.

52. Kenneth Walsh and others, "Fast/Glycolytic Muscle Fiber Growth Reduces Fat Mass and Improves Metabolic Parameters in Obese Mice," *Cell Metabolism* 7, no. 2 (2008): 159–72.

53. Gleb P. Shumyatsky and others, "*Stathmin*, a Gene Enriched in the Amygdala, Controls Both Learned and Innate Fear," *Cell* 123, no. 4 (2005): 697–709.

54. C. B. Saper, "Differential Rescue of Light- and Food-Entrainable Circadian Rhythms," *Science* 320, no. 5879 (2008): 1074–77.

55. Robert Greene and others, "The Role of CA3 Hippocampal NMDA Receptors in Paired Associate Learning," *Journal of Neuroscience* 26, no. 3 (2006): 908–15.

56. Leslie A. Leinwand and others, "Soy Diet Worsens Heart Disease in Mice," *Journal of Clinical Investigation* 116, no. 1 (2006): 209–16.

57. Michael R. Hayden and others, "Cleavage at the Caspase-6 Site Is Required for Neuronal Dysfunction and Degeneration Due to Mutant Huntingtin," *Cell* 125, no. 6 (2006) 1179–91.

58. Giuseppe Matarese and others, "Leptin Neutralization Interferes with Pathogenic T Cell Autoreactivity in Autoimmune Encephalomyelitis," *Journal of Clinical Investigation* 116, no. 2 (2006): 447–55.

59. Irving Langmuir, "Langmuir's Talk on Pathological Science (December 18, 1953)," http://www.cs.princeton.edu/~ken/Langmuir/langmuir.htm.

60. Erick H. Turner and others, "Selective Publication of Antidepressant Trials and Its Influence on Apparent Efficacy," *New England Journal of Medicine* 358, no. 3 (2008): 252–60.

61. Mike Stobbe, "Too Much, Too Little Sleep Tied to Ill Health in CDC Study," *Seattle Times* (online), May 9, 2008.

62. Geoffrey Lean, "Mobile Phone Radiation Wrecks Your Sleep," *Independent* (U.K.), January 20, 2008.

63. Alison Motluk, "Suicide Risks from Drugs May Be Exaggerated," *New Scientist* no. 2652 (2008): 11.

64. Jennifer A. Nettleton and others, "Diet Soda Intake and Risk of Incident Metabolic Syndrome and Type 2 Diabetes in the Multi-Ethnic Study of Atherosclerosis (MESA)," *Diabetes Care* 32, no. 4 (2009): 688–94.

65. "Study: Artificial Sweeteners Increase Weight Gain Odds," *Good Morning America* "On Call," February 11, 2008, http://www.abcnews.go.com/GMA/OnCall/story?id=4271246&page=1.

66. Adam Drewnowski and others, "Sugars and Satiety: Does the Type of Sweetener Make a Difference?" *American Journal of Clinical Nutrition* 86, no. 1 (2007): 116–23.

67. Marjolein E. J. Oerlemans and others, "A Meta-analysis on Depression and Subsequent Cancer Risk," *Clinical Practice and Epidemiology in Mental Health* 3, no. 29 (2007).

68. K. Linde and S. N. Willich, "How Objective Are Systematic Reviews? Differences Between Reviews on Complementary Medicine," *Journal of the Royal Society of Medicine* 96, no. 1 (2003): 17–22.

69. Ben D. McCallister and others, "A Randomized, Controlled Trial of the Effects of Remote, Intercessory Prayer on Outcomes in Patients Admitted to the Coronary Care Unit," *Archives of Internal Medicine* 159, no. 19 (1999): 2273–78.

70. H. Benson and others, "Study of the Therapeutic Effects of Intercessory Prayer (STEP) in Cardiac Bypass Patients: A Multicentre Randomised Trial of Uncertainty and Certainty of Receiving Intercessory Prayer," *American Heart Journal* 151, no. 4 (2006): 934–42.

71. John P. A. Ioannidis, "Why Most Published Research Findings Are False," *PLoS Medicine* 2, no. 8 (2005): e124.

72. Grant R. Wilkinson, "Drug Metabolism and Variability Among Patients in Drug Response," *New England Journal of Medicine* 352, no. 21 (2005): 2211–21.

73. Daniel Carr, "When Bad Evidence Happens to Good Treatments," *Regional Anesthesia and Pain Medicine* 33, no. 3 (2008): 229–40.

74. Rob Capriccioso, "SAT Failures Renew Suspicions," Inside Higher Ed, March 16, 2006, http://www.insidehighered.com/news/2006/03/16/sat.

75. J. E. Bekelman, "Meta-analysis of 37 COI Studies (1,000s of Trials)," *Journal of the American Medical Association* 289, no. 4 (2003): 454–65.

76. Joseph S. Ross and others, "Guest Authorship and Ghostwriting in Publications Related to Rofecoxib," *Journal of the American Medical Association* 299, no. 15 (2008): 1800–12.

77. Teddy D. Warner and John P. Gluck, "What Do We Really Know About Conflicts of Interest in Biomedical Research?" *Psychopharmacologia* 171, no. 1 (2003): 119.

78. Ibid.
79. Douglas G. Altman and others, "Ghost Authorship in Industry-Initiated Randomised Trials," *PLoS Medicine* 4, no. 1 (2007): e19.
80. Shankar Vedantam, "Psychiatric Experts Found to Have Financial Links to Drugmakers," *Washington Post*, April 20, 2006.
81. Solicitation to potential sponsors for an upcoming "Focus on MBA Programs" section, appearing in the "NatureJobs" section of *Nature*, June 14, 2007.

3. THE CERTAINTY PRINCIPLE
1. The United Kingdom Office of Science and Technology and the Wellcome Trust, "Science and the Public: A Review of Science Communication and Public Attitudes to Science in Britain," October 2000, http://www .wellcome.ac.uk/stellent/groups/corporatesite/@msh_peda/documents /web_document/wtd003419.pdf.
2. Mary Woolley and Stacie M. Propst, "Public Attitudes and Perceptions About Health-Related Research," *Journal of the American Medical Association* 294, no. 11 (2005): 1380–84.
3. Ernst Fehr and others, "Oxytocin Increases Trust in Humans," *Nature* 435, no. 7042 (2005): 673–76.
4. Richard Kluger, *Ashes to Ashes: America's Hundred-Year Cigarette War, the Public Health, and the Unabashed Triumph of Philip Morris* (New York: Alfred A. Knopf, 1996), 325.
5. Janet Rosenbaum, "Patient Teenagers? A Comparison of the Sexual Behavior of Virginity Pledgers and Matched Nonpledgers," *Pediatrics* 123, no. 1 (2009): e110–20.
6. David H. Freedman, "When Is a Planet Not a Planet?" *The Atlantic*, February 1998.
7. *Judgment Under Uncertainty: Heuristics and Biases*, ed. Daniel Kahneman and others (Cambridge: Cambridge University Press, 1982).
8. Alexander Renkl and others, "Is Underestimation Less Detrimental Than Overestimation? The Impact of Experts' Beliefs About a Layperson's Knowledge on Learning and Question Asking," *Instructional Science* 36, no. 1 (2008): 27–52.

4. THE IDIOCY OF CROWDS
1. Daeyeol Lee, "Game Theory and Neural Basis of Social Decision Making," *Nature Neuroscience* 11, no. 4 (2008): 404–09.
2. Amanda M. Seed and others, "Cooperative Problem Solving in Rooks (*Corvus frugilegus*)," *Proceedings of the Royal Society B* 275, no. 1641 (2008): 1421–29.
3. Stefan Thurner and others, "To How Many Politicians Should Government Be Left?" *arXiv:0804.2202* (2008).

4. P. R. Laughlin and others, "Groups Perform Better Than the Best Individuals on Letters-to-Numbers Problems: Effects of Group Size," *Journal of Personality and Social Psychology* 90, no. 4 (2006): 644–51.

5. Patrick Walter, "Group Size Marrs Research," *Chemistry & Industry*, March 26, 2007.

6. Christine Boesz and Nigel Lloyd, "Collaborations: Investigating International Misconduct," *Nature* 452, no. 7188 (2008): 686–87.

5. THE TROUBLE WITH SCIENTISTS, PART 2

1. William Broad and Nicholas Wade, *Betrayers of the Truth* (New York: Simon & Schuster, 1982).

2. "Leading by Example," *Nature* 445, no. 7125 (2007): 229.

3. Brian C. Martinson and others, "Scientists Behaving Badly," *Nature* 435, no. 7043 (2005): 737–38.

4. J. Ranstam and others, "Fraud in Medical Research: An International Survey of Biostatisticians," *Controlled Clinical Trials* 21, no. 5 (2000): 415–27.

5. D. Geggie, "A Survey of Newly Appointed Consultants' Attitudes Towards Research Fraud," *Journal of Medical Ethics* 27, no. 5 (2001): 344–46.

6. William Gardner and others, "Authors' Reports About Research Integrity Problems in Clinical Trials," *Contemporary Clinical Trials* 26, no. 2 (2005): 244–51.

7. Joe Hamilton and others, "Report of Ethics Task Force to APS Council," November 2, 2003, http://www.phys.utk.edu/colloquium_blume_spring2004_ethics.pdf.

8. D. G. Altman and others, "Empirical Evidence for Selective Reporting of Outcomes in Randomized Trials: Comparison of Protocols to Published Articles," *Journal of the American Medical Association* 291, no. 20 (2004): 2457–65.

9. D. G. Altman and others, "Outcome Reporting Bias in Randomized Trials Funded by the Canadian Institutes of Health Research," *Canadian Medical Association Journal* 171, no. 7 (2004): 735–40.

10. A. W. Chan and D. G. Altman, "Identifying Outcome Reporting Bias in Randomised Trials on PubMed: Review of Publications and Survey of Authors," *British Medical Journal* 330, no. 7494 (2005): 753.

11. Brian Martinson and others, "Normal Misbehavior: Scientists Talk About the Ethics of Research," *Journal of Empirical Research on Human Research Ethics* 1, no. 1 (2006): 43–50.

12. Alison McCook, "Losing Your Lab," *The Scientist* 22, no. 5 (2008): 32.

13. Martinson, "Normal Misbehavior."

14. Chris R. Triggle and David J. Triggle, "What Is the Future of Peer Review? Why Is There Fraud in Science? Is Plagiarism Out of Control? Why Do Scientists Do Bad Things? Is It All a Case of: 'All That Is Necessary for the Triumph of Evil Is That Good Men Do Nothing?'"

Vascular Health and Risk Management 3, no. 1 (2007): 39–53.

15. J. Bradford DeLong and Kevin Lang, "Are All Economic Hypotheses False?" *Journal of Political Economy* 100, no. 6 (1992): 1257–72.

16. Richard Monastersky, "The Number That's Devouring Science," *Chronicle of Higher Education*, October 14, 2005.

17. Guosheng Wu, "Misconduct: Forum Should Not Be Used to Settle Scores," *Nature* 442, no. 7099 (2006): 132.

18. Jon Cartwright, "Chinese Law to Promote Honest Research," *Physics World*, August 31, 2007.

19. Kenneth M. Weiss and others, "Dissecting Complex Disease: The Quest for the Philosopher's Stone?" *International Journal of Epidemiology* 35, no. 3 (2006): 562–71.

20. Judith Swazey and others, "Ethical Problems in Academic Research," *American Scientist*, November–December 1993.

21. Jim Giles, "Breeding Cheats," *Nature* 445, no. 7125 (2007): 242–43.

22. Barbara K. Redman and others, "Research Misconduct Among Clinical Trial Staff," *Science and Engineering Ethics* 12, no. 3 (2006): 481–89.

23. Debora MacKenzie, "New Rules Proposed to Catch Science Fraud," *New Scientist*, November 29, 2006.

24. Christopher N. Martyn and others, "Effect on the Quality of Peer Review of Blinding Reviewers and Asking Them to Sign Their Reports: A Randomized Controlled Trial," *Journal of the American Medical Association* 280, no. 3 (1998): 237–40.

25. Stefan Hornbostel and Meike Siekermann, "Peer Review: Healthy in the Core or Chronically Ill?" presentation at Prague Peer Review 2006 Conference, October 12, 2006, http://www.forschungsinfo.de/Publikationen/Download/Peer%20Review%20Conference_Hornbostel.pdf.

26. Jim Giles, "The Trouble with Replication," *Nature* 442, no. 7101 (2006): 344–47

27. Benjamin G. Druss and others, "Retractions in the Research Literature: Misconduct or Mistakes?" *Medical Journal of Australia* 185, no. 3 (2006): 152–54.

28. Murat Çokol and others, "How Many Scientific Papers Should Be Retracted?" *EMBO Reports* 8, no. 5 (2007): 422–23.

29. John P. A. Ioannidis and others, "Persistence of Contradicted Claims in the Literature," *Journal of the American Medical Association* 298, no. 21 (2007): 2517–26.

6. EXPERTS AND ORGANIZATIONS

1. George Taninecz, "Faster but Not Better: Improved Manufacturing Times Don't Always Result in Comparable Cost Reductions," *Industry Week*, April 1, 2004.

2. D. Miller and J. Hartwick, "Spotting Management Fads," *Harvard Business Review* 80, no. 10 (2002): 26–27.

3. Eric Abrahamson and Micki Eisenman, "Employee-Management Techniques: Transient Fads or Trending Fashions?" *Administrative Science Quarterly* 53, no. 4 (2008): 719–44.

4. R. J. Goeke and O. F. Offodile, "Forecasting Management Philosophy Life Cycles: A Comparative Study of Six Sigma and TQM," *Quality Management Journal* 12, no. 2 (2005): 34–46.

5. Eric Abrahamson, *Change Without Pain: How Managers Can Overcome Initiative Overload, Organizational Chaos, and Employee Burnout* (Boston: Harvard Business Press, 2003).

6. Pankaj Ghemawat, "Why the World Isn't Flat," *Foreign Policy*, March–April 2007.

7. Tom Arnold and others, "Are Cover Stories Effective Contrarian Indicators?" *Financial Analysts Journal* 63, no. 2 (2007): 70–75.

7. Experts and the Media

1. Yanxia Sun and Tong J. Gan, "Acupuncture for the Management of Chronic Headache: A Systematic Review," *Anesthesia & Analgesia* 107, no. 6 (2008): 2038–47.

2. Will Dunham, "Many Americans Turning to Unconventional Medicine," Reuters, December 10, 2008.

3. Jennifer A. Nettleton and others, "Diet Soda Intake and Risk of Incident Metabolic Syndrome and Type 2 Diabetes in the Multi-Ethnic Study of Atherosclerosis (MESA)," *Diabetes Care* 32, no. 4 (2009): 688–94.

4. Hasse Walum and others, "Genetic Variation in the Vasopressin Receptor 1a Gene (AVPR1A) Associates with Pair-Bonding Behavior in Humans," *Proceedings of the National Academy of Sciences* 105, no. 37 (2008): 14153–56.

5. Gerald Heckel and others, "Mammalian Monogamy Is Not Controlled by a Single Gene," *Proceedings of the National Academy of Sciences* 103, no. 29 (2006): 10956–60.

6. Esra Tasali and others, "Slow-Wave Sleep and the Risk of Type 2 Diabetes in Humans," *Proceedings of the National Academy of Sciences* 105, no. 3 (2008): 1044–49.

7. Philip A. Wolf and others, "Association of Alcohol Consumption with Brain Volume in the Framingham Study," *Archives of Neurology* 65, no. 10 (2008): 1363–67.

8. Richard Kluger, *Ashes to Ashes: America's Hundred-Year Cigarette War, the Public Health, and the Unabashed Triumph of Philip Morris* (New York: Alfred A. Knopf, 1996), 154.

9. Frank M. Sacks and others, "Comparison of Weight-Loss Diets with

Different Compositions of Fat, Protein, and Carbohydrates," *New England Journal of Medicine* 360, no. 9 (2009): 859–73.

8. The Internet and the Technology of Expertise

1. *The Harris Poll* no. 76, July 31, 2007, http://www.harrisinteractive.com/harris_poll/index.asp?PID=792.

2. Microsoft NHS Resource Centre, "Better Search: A Cure for Cyberchondria?" December 3, 2008, http://www.microsoft.com/uk/nhs/content/articles/better-search-a-cure-for-cyberchondria.aspx.

3. Nicholas Carr, "Is Google Making Us Stupid?" *The Atlantic*, July–August 2008.

4. University College London's CIBER research group, "Information Behaviour of the Researcher of the Future," briefing paper, January 11, 2008, http://www.bl.uk/news/pdf/googlegen.pdf.

5. Timme Bisgaard Munk and Kristian Mørk, "Folksonomy, the Power Law and the Significance of the Least Effort," *Knowledge Organization* 34, no. 1 (2007): 16–33.

6. Helga Nowotny, "Transgressive Competence: The Narrative of Expertise," *European Journal of Social Theory* 3, no. 1 (2000): 5–21.

7. Ernst Fehr and others, "Strong Reciprocity, Human Cooperation and the Enforcement of Social Norms," *Human Nature* 13, no. 1 (2002): 1–25.

8. Shay David and Trevor John Pinch, "Six Degrees of Reputation: The Use and Abuse of Online Review and Recommendation Systems," Social Science Research Network Working Paper Series, November 25, 2005, http://papers.ssrn.com/sol3/papers.cfm?abstract_id=857505.

9. Zakary L. Tormala and others, "Thought Confidence as a Determinant of Persuasion: The Self-Validation Hypothesis," *Journal of Personality and Social Psychology* 82, no. 5 (2002): 722–41.

10. Mark Reynoso, "Letter from the President," press statement from Belkin's president on Belkin's website, 2009, http://www.belkin.com/pressroom/letter.html.

11. James Felton and others, "Attractiveness, Easiness and Other Issues: Student Evaluations of Professors on Ratemyprofessors.com," *Assessment & Evaluation in Higher Education* 33, no. 1 (2008): 45–61.

12. Santo Fortunato and Claudio Castellano, "Scaling and Universality in Proportional Elections," *Physical Review Letters* 99, no. 138701 (2007): 1–4.

13. Jennifer Chayes and others, "Trust-Based Recommendation Systems: An Axiomatic Approach," Proceeding of the 17th International Conference on the World Wide Web, April 23, 2008, 199–208.

14. Sheldon Krimsky, "Risk Communication in the Internet Age: The Rise of Disorganized Skepticism," *Environmental Hazards* 7, no. 2 (2007): 157–64.

9. ELEVEN SIMPLE NEVER-FAIL RULES FOR NOT BEING MISLED BY EXPERTS

1. John Hardwig, "Epistemic Dependence," *Journal of Philosophy* 82, no. 7 (1985): 335–49.
2. David Newton and others, "Mayfield's Side Planning Counter Motion," ESPN.com News Services, June 16, 2009, http://sports.espn.go.com/rpm/nascar/cup/news/story?id=4262494.
3. Jonah Berger and Gaël Le Mens, "How Adoption Speed Affects the Abandonment of Cultural Tastes," *Proceedings of the National Academy of Sciences* 106, no. 20 (2009): 8146–50.
4. S. Joslyn and others, "Probability of Precipitation: Assessment and Enhancement of End-User Understanding," *Bulletin of the American Meteorological Society* 90, no. 2 (2009): 185–93.
5. G. S. Berns and others, "Expert Financial Advice Neurobiologically 'Offloads' Financial Decision-Making Under Risk," *PLoS ONE* 4, no. 3 (2009): e4957.
6. David M. Dosa, "A Day in the Life of Oscar the Cat," *New England Journal of Medicine* 357, no. 4 (2007): 328–29.

APPENDIX 2. THE EVOLUTION OF EXPERTISE

1. Robert P. Crease, "Gravitation," Physicsworld.com, October 1, 2007, http://physicsworld.com/cws/article/print/31251.

INDEX

ABOUT THE AUTHOR

David H. Freedman is a science and business journalist. He is a contributing editor at *Inc.* magazine and has written for *The Atlantic*, *Newsweek*, the *New York Times*, *Science*, the *Harvard Business Review*, *Fast Company*, *Wired*, *Self*, and many other publications. He is the coauthor of *A Perfect Mess*, about the useful role of disorder in daily life, business, and science, and the author of books about the U.S. Marines, computer crime, and artificial intelligence. He lives near Boston.